Freedom of Information

Free 21/12/15		tten
to ir		ities
offer 16/3/16		Act
is, h		s to
acco		best
prac		1 of
Info		
T		the
Free		e of
help		
•		
•		
•		
•		king
Sup		*n of*
Info		r all
thos		igat-
ing,		
Ma		; for
all t		riety
of t		been
base		He is
the		l for

researchers, academics, journalists and anyone involved or passionate about the Freedom of Information Act in the United Kingdom and beyond. Matt is also a frequent speaker on the Act and advises individuals on the best way to make use of it.

Freedom of Information

A Practical Guide for
UK Journalists

Matt Burgess

Routledge
Taylor & Francis Group

LONDON AND NEW YORK

First published 2015
by Routledge
2 Park Square, Milton Park, Abingdon, Oxon OX14 4RN

Simultaneously published in the USA and Canada
by Routledge
711 Third Avenue, New York, NY 10017

Routledge is an imprint of the Taylor & Francis Group, an informa business

© 2015 Matt Burgess

British Library Cataloguing in Publication Data
A catalogue record for this book is available from the British Library

Library of Congress Cataloging in Publication Data
Burgess, Matt (Journalist) author.
Freedom of information : a practical guide for UK journalists / Matt Burgess.
pages cm
1. Freedom of information--Great Britain. 2. Journalists--Great Britain--
Handbooks, manuals, etc. I. Title.
KD3756.B87 2015
342.41'0662--dc23
2014046804

ISBN: 978-1-138-79320-0 (hbk)
ISBN: 978-1-138-79321-7 (pbk)
ISBN: 978-1-315-76144-2 (ebk)

Typeset in Sabon
by GreenGate Publishing Services, Tonbridge, Kent
Printed and bound in Great Britain by Ashford Colour Press Ltd, Gosport, Hampshire

Contents

Preface

1 January 2005 was a significant, but scarcely remembered, day for the rights of those living in the United Kingdom. As midnight struck, the Freedom of Information (FOI) Act, a law that campaigners had doggedly fought for and politicians had done their utmost to derail, came into force. Its introduction gave everyone in the country, and around the world, regardless of political, social or financial status, the right to ask for information and be given it, by law – unless an exemption applies. From the highest echelons of government to those in charge of lighthouses in Scotland, information can be given to those who do no more than ask for it.

For ten years, the Act has been used to pry information from the hands of those in power and give it to the people who pay for it to be created. Although the Act allows anyone to ask for information, it has played strongly into the hands of journalists, who want to hold to account those who are responsible for making decisions that can affect tens of people, or tens of millions of people. An Act of this nature was always going to generate controversy. It provoked high-level disagreements before it made its journey through Parliament to become officially enacted and has caused political turbulence ever since.

This book aims to serve as a guide to the Act and provide as much digestible information as possible, while equipping you with the tools to successfully make requests, challenge their outcome and get the most out of the Act by using the rights that are conveyed to individuals. I draw from legislation, guidance from the regulator and decisions by tribunals and the courts, in addition to reflecting on international FOI laws and the outlines of how they operate. The book also covers the history of the Act, the media coverage of its issues and how journalists have used it.

Anecdotes and observations are given from journalists across different branches of the media, FOI professionals and officials who are involved in the Act. There are also sections on the background to the Act, political viewpoints, examples of requests and more, which put making requests into context and can be used to generate ideas for stories. The views and opinions expressed relate to utilising the Act for the purpose of creating coverage in the media, so may not be the same reflections as those whose focus is on transparency and openness. All job titles of those interviewed were correct at the time of writing and the views expressed are those of the individuals, not their employers.

Chapters are split into small, digestible sections, which will allow you to easily find the information you need to make requests and challenge responses. It is not intended to be read from start to finish but be visited when advice and guidance on making requests is needed.

Acknowledgements

This book would not have been possible without those who have offered support, kind words and occasionally the more terse line of encouragement.

I must thank all the incredibly talented journalists, FOI practitioners, academics and Information Commissioners who offered their time and expertise to be interviewed. There would not be a book without you all and the generosity that you have afforded to me.

In particular I would like to thank Paul Gibbons, Mikey Smith and my much-tortured flat mate Hannah Frost, who between them helped with interview transcription and the editing of the entire book. Thanks go to Jon Baines, Bilal Ghafoor and Tim Turner for directing me down the right FOI paths; and to Paul Bradshaw who provided the foundations for the book and everyone at Routledge who made it happen.

For their persistence in listening to me talk through ideas, structures and the shape of the book, I would like to thank my parents Arthur and Lyn, and my sister Jayne, also Fay Guest, Lizzi Sykes and everyone else who offered guidance when it was needed.

Last, but not least, Rowan Ramsden for his consistently unparalleled moral support.

All mistakes are my own, and do not reflect the quality of those above.

Abbreviations

ACPO	Association of Chief Police Officers
DN	Decision Notice
DPA	Data Protection Act
ECHR	European Convention of Human Rights
EIR	Environmental Information Regulations
EN	Enforcement Notice
FOI	Freedom of Information
HMRC	Her Majesty's Revenue & Customs
IC	Information Commissioner
ICO	Information Commissioner's Office
IN	Information Notice
IPSA	Independent Parliamentary Standards Authority
LGA	Local Government Association
NCND	neither confirm nor deny
OAIC	Office of the Australian Information Commissioner
PECR	Privacy and Electronic Communications Regulations
PIT	Public Interest Test
RIPA	Regulation of Investigatory Powers Act
SAR	Subject Access Request
SICO	Scottish Information Commissioner's Office

Chapter 1

The Act

What is the FOI Act?

The Freedom of Information Act 2000 is a piece of legislation that gives people the 'right to know'. It places two distinct responsibilities upon the public authorities to which it applies. The first is to confirm whether they hold information, and, if they do, disclose it to the person who has asked for it, unless one of the Act's exemptions applies. The second requires the authority to make information available routinely, as part of a publication scheme.

Requesting information

Anyone, anywhere, is given the right to know by the Freedom of Information Act. People are given the right to be told whether a public authority holds information they ask for, under the duty to confirm or deny (FOI, s.1(1)(a)). If the public authority does have the information requested and it is not exempt, they have to give it to the person who has asked for it (s.1(1)(b)). As well as information that is exempt, authorities can refuse requests if the request costs too much to answer; the request is vexatious; or, quite simply, the authority does not hold the information. However, by law, the public authority has to reply to a request within 20 working days and explain its decision.

Publication schemes

When the Act was created, it also committed public authorities to publishing routine information on a regular basis. This was to be achieved in the form of publication schemes. These now are considered, by some, to be largely redundant due to the growth of the internet and the ease with which it allows information to be published.

However, the requirement for a publication scheme to comply with the Act has encouraged authorities to publish more information proactively. The Information Commissioner's Office (ICO) publishes a 'model publication scheme' for all authorities, which details what should be published. Definition documents are then published by the ICO, which itemise the information that should be published to reflect the requirements of different public sectors. The model scheme can be 'adopted without modification' by an authority (ICO, 2013a, p.1). An authority can charge for the information it provides through its publication scheme. It can also charge for the photo-copying, postage and other costs directly incurred as a result of providing information (ICO, 2013a, pp.2–3).

Model publication scheme

- Who and what: this includes organisation information, contacts and governance information.
- Spending: including details on budgets, contracts issued and more.
- Priorities: plans, assessments, inspections and more.
- Decisions: policy decisions and procedures.
- Policies and procedures: this includes the protocols for providing functions and responsibilities.
- Lists and registers: information held in registers required by the law and relating to functions of the authority.
- Services: advice, guidance, booklets and more that relate to the services that are offered by the public authority.

(ICO, 2013a, p.2)

How the Act came to be

The Freedom of Information Act emerged from a long battle to bring it to fruition. The Labour Party, which eventually introduced the Act in 2000, had the basis of a Freedom of Information Act within its election manifestos since 1974. The manifesto says the party would 'put the burden on the public authorities to justify withholding information' (Labour Party, 1974).

At the front of the pack demanding that politicians have the right to request and receive information was the Campaign for Freedom of Information, who were crucial in lobbying officials for more openness. The Campaign was launched in January 1984 (Campaign for Freedom of Information, 2009).

As the Act was proposed and developed, the latter during the late 1990s, it received backing from *The Guardian*, which ran its own media campaign to get it passed into law (*Guardian*, 1999a).

Yet, despite the growing calls, and some political support for an Act to be introduced, it took until 2005 for the first requests for information to be made under the law. This chapter looks at how the Act, as we know it today, came to be. There is not enough space in these pages to give a detailed history of the political swings and roundabouts encountered throughout the journey of the Act so it focuses on the final steps along the path to a new right to know, and how the right looks ten years later.

A brief history

- 1974: Labour's manifesto included a commitment to a future Freedom of Information Act, which appeared in the manifesto until the Act was implemented (UCL Constitution Unit, 2011).
- 1979–1997: the Conservative Governments of Margaret Thatcher and John Major increased the openness and transparency that officials were subject to, which, arguably, helped to build the pressure on a desire for a Freedom of Information Act. They introduced the Data Protection Act, allowed access to environmental information and expanded local government access (UCL Constitution Unit, 2011).
- 1993–1994: the Open Government White Paper introduced a Code of Practice on Access to Government Information, which allowed people to get information and says information should be 'readily available' (Chancellor of the Duchy of Lancaster, 1993). *Guardian* journalist Rob Evans (2014) says it 'wasn't that strong' but it was still 'useable'. The Campaign for Freedom of Information (1993, p.1) says it was a 'foot in the door' but 'stops a long way short of delivering freedom of information'.
- 1997: The White Paper Your Right to Know (Cabinet Office, 1997), which led to the shape of the Act that we see today, was published. It was a strong look at what FOI should be and the Campaign for Freedom of Information (1997) says it went 'further than we had thought any British government would be willing to go'. It was subsequently watered down.
- December 1999: The draft Freedom of Information Bill was introduced to the House of Commons (UCL Constitution Unit, 2011).
- 2000: campaigners fought the government back on the draft bill's scope reducing the 40 working day time to 20 working days, gave the ICO power to enforce compliance, and forced authorities to say why they were refusing information. These were all opposed by Jack Straw, who oversaw the bill's passage through parliament (*Guardian*, 1999b).
- 1 December 2000: the bill completed its journey through parliament (UCL Constitution Unit, 2011).
- 2002: the Freedom of Information Act Scotland was passed.
- January 2005: the Freedom of Information Act became law in Britain.

The ICO

Defending and upholding the rights of an individual's ability to access information from public authorities is down to the ICO. The regulator has responsibility for overseeing a number of different information and privacy regulations. These are:

- Freedom of Information Act 2000.
- Data Protection Act 1998 (DPA).
- Privacy and Electronic Communications Regulations 2003 (PECR).
- Environmental Information Regulations 2004 (EIR).
- INSPIRE Regulations 2009.

(ICO, nd)

The ICO has jurisdiction over FOI and EIR in England, Wales, Northern Ireland and non-devolved authorities in Scotland. Otherwise, Scotland has its own FOI laws and ICO (nd), which are generally regarded as being more liberal and progressive.

The ICO (nd) was originally created in 1984 as the Data Protection Registrar. It went through a number of name and role changes until 2000, when the Office was given the responsibility of overseeing the Freedom of Information Act and formally became the ICO in 2001. The Office is headed up by the Information Commissioner (IC).

Since the inception of the Act in the UK, three Commissioners have served in the role. The first was Elizabeth France, who occupied the previous role before the creation of the ICO, retiring in 2002. Her successor was Richard Thomas, who oversaw the implementation of the Act during its early years, followed by Christopher Graham, who was appointed in 2009. Graham is due to serve in the role until June 2016, after he was re-appointed in early 2014 (ICO, 2014a).

In 2012, in an attempt to strengthen the independence of the Information Commissioner, the Protection of Freedoms Act changed these rules so that a future Commissioner will only be able to serve one seven-year term.

FOI responsibilities

The ICO employs around 400 people and currently has five locations around the UK. Its head office, where the majority of its staff are based, is in Wilmslow, in the North of England (ICO, 2014b, p.41).

The duties of the Information Commissioner, which are carried out by the Office's staff, are listed in the Freedom of Information Act (2000) legislation:

- Promote good practice and ensure authorities comply with the Act and its codes of practice (s.47(1)).

- Give information and advice to the public about the Act, good practice and the Commissioner's powers (s.47(2)).
- Assess whether an authority is following good practice (s.47(3)).
- Recommend good practice to authorities (s.48) that the Commissioner believes are failing to comply with any of the codes of practice.
- Lay reports before Parliament, including the annual report of the Office (s.49).

The most relevant of the Commissioner's responsibilities for journalists and requesters is the duty to investigate complaints made to the Office about FOI requests. Section 50 of the Act requires the Commissioner to issue a Decision Notice (DN) about a complaint made by a requester. DNs tell authorities if they handled requests properly. The ICO has the ability to issue Information Notices (INs) under the Act (s.51) and Enforcement Notices (ENs) (s.52) to make resistant authorities fulfill their responsibilities under the law. Lawyers will represent the Commissioner if complaints are escalated to the tribunal stage and beyond.

Financial pressure

The ICO is a non-departmental public body that is funded by the Ministry of Justice (Justice Committee, 2009, p.4). Information Commissioner, Chris Graham (2014), says the funding that the Office receives is not adequate as it comes under an increasing strain.

The ICO submitted evidence to the Justice Committee in 2012, which says that the number of complaints, compared with the levels of funding, pose a 'significant challenge'. Its evidence showed that the grant provided from the Ministry of Justice was £5.1 million in the first year (2005/6) for FOI (ICO, 2012). The annual budget for 2013/14 showed the grant-in-aid received from the Ministry of Justice was £4 million (ICO, 2014b). This means the authority struggles to properly enforce FOI.

If funding continues to be cut for the ICO, then there could be serious implications for citizens' access and right to information. Graham (2014) says: 'I do think I need to speak out more loudly because over the past five years we've put in place some changes that have made us infinitely more productive and infinitely more efficient but that can't go on forever.'

Who do requests apply to?

The Freedom of Information Act has a wide jurisdiction that includes more than 100,000 public authorities across the UK. These include everything from schools, hospitals, councils, government departments, police forces and fire authorities to libraries, museums, the BBC, Channel 4, the Coal Authority and other smaller public bodies that are in receipt of public money.

The legislation of the Act states that for the purposes of FOI a public authority is anybody or person that is listed in Schedule 1 of the Act (s.3(1)(a)(i)), or that has been designated under Section 5 of the Act (s.3(1)(a)(ii)), or is a publically owned company (s.3(1)(b)). Schedule 1 of the Act breaks down different organisations and public bodies that are subject to the Act and should be consulted as a first step if it is not clear whether an organisation is subject to the Act. But, as Brooke (2006, p.30) says: 'Its scope is broad in terms of who it covers, but it is not nearly as strong as it could and should have been.'

Publicly owned companies

The Act (s.6) defines what a 'publicly owned company' is. In short, it says that any company that is wholly owned by the Crown, any public authority or a combination of public authorities, is subject to the Act. The ICO (2013b, p.7) points out that a company can be owned between government departments and other authorities and still be classed as a publicly owned company, athough this was added by the introduction of the Protection of Freedom's Act in 2012 (s.103).

For example, Transport for London, which is responsible for all of the capital's public transport, is a public company that is subject to the Act. It also has three subsidiaries that are all publicly owned, including London Underground Limited, and are therefore subject to FOI laws.

Derogation

Not all public authorities are equal under FOI. There are authorities that have some types of information not covered by the Act. These include the BBC and the Houses of Parliament. Section 7 states that some authorities will only be covered in a limited way by the Act. If a Secretary of State wishes to add a public body to the Act but only where it has specific public duties, it is possible for them to do so. It is also possible for him or her to alter what information is covered by FOI for specific bodies (s.7(3)). Other authorities that are not fully covered by the legislation include the Bank of England, Channel 4, Traffic Commissioners and the Royal College of Veterinary Surgeons (sch.1).

The BBC and FOI

Anything the BBC holds for the purpose of 'journalism, art or literature' cannot be accessed through FOI (sch.1). In a seven-year FOI battle by solicitor Steven Sugar, who died before the case reached its conclusion, the Supreme Court set down a judgment that stated what the nature of journalism is. The decision Sugar v British Broadcasting Corporation and Anor (2012) UKSC 4 (par 70) says that '"journalism, art or literature" seems to be intended to cover the whole of the BBC's output in its mission, [and] this would include anything that is meant to inform, educate or entertain the public'.

The purpose of the FOI ruling on journalistic material is to, rightly, protect the journalists' sources from being disclosed. Other information such a board minutes, redundancies, hotel spend, etc., is available via FOI requests from the BBC.

Missing from the Act

Despite the range of authorities covered by the Act, there are some notable, publicly funded bodies and groups that are beyond the reach of the Act, including the following:

1   The Royal Family. In 2011, the Freedom of Information Act was modified to protect the Royal Family from being embarrassed by releases of information. The exemption, which already covered the royals, was made almost completely into an absolute exemption, meaning no Public Interest Test (PIT) is required if information is requested that relates to correspondence with the Queen or her two closest heirs (*Independent*, 2011). Other information relating to the Royal Household remains subject to a PIT.
2   Security bodies. The incredibly secretive security services are not covered by the Act in any way. This includes GCHQ, MI5, the National Crime Agency and more. Requests for information, held by other bodies, relating to their work can be refused under the absolute exemption of Section 23. This causes a distrust in their actions, and as said by Brooke (2006, p.98): 'Without public scrutiny of the intelligence and security services we are unable to judge their competence until a catastrophe occurs as happened in the London tube and bus bombings of 2005.'
3   Housing associations. The Campaign for Freedom of Information (2008, p.10) says that including the associations under the Act would help to increase their transparency as a large amount of local authority housing stock is now in their control. Housing Minister Grant Shapps (2011) says that including them in the Act would help people to find out more about how landlords work. He also says the government will consult on including housing associations in the Act. At the time of writing this consultation has not materialised.

4   The Local Government Association. This body, funded completely by councils and taxpayers' money, is not subject to the Act. But it does often issue press releases to the media about unusual requests for information that councils receive (Local Government Association, 2014). It says that some FOI requests can 'distract' councils from their other businesses, while being entirely paid for by the public and not being held accountable via FOI.

Adding new authorities

As stated above, Schedule 1 contains a general list of authorities and types of authorities that are caught under the radar of the Act. To add, or remove, an authority from the Schedule, the Secretary of State may by order amend Schedule 1 (s.4) if the body is established by a royal prerogative, legislation or by a government department or minister and that the body or office is made up of, or appointed, by the Crown or a minister. If a body ceases to exist, the Secretary of State can order it to be removed under section 4(5).

Under the Freedom of Information Act 2000, Section 5, the Secretary of State's power to change the bodies that are subject to the Act is strengthened. It gives the ability to include an authority that does not fall under the Schedule but appears to exercise functions of a public authority, or is providing a public service under a contract (s.5(1)(a–b)).

What is information?

When making a request under the Act, the person asking is entitled to information rather than documents. The ICO (2014c, pp.19–20) says that asking about a specific topic will trigger the Freedom of Information Act and the authority will have to gather the information it holds, even if it is included in multiple documents.

Information is defined in Section 84 of the Freedom of Information Act 2000 as being 'information recorded in any form'. Information that is recorded by a public authority can range from drafts of documents, emails, metadata, recordings of telephone conversations, CCTV and much more (ICO, 2014c, p.6).

However, it can also cover more specific details, as demonstrated by the Information Tribunal when it ruled on the case of invoices submitted by MPs for their expenses. Journalist Ben Leapman requested receipts submitted with expense claims by MPs and was given a summary of them by the Independent Parliamentary Standards Authority (IPSA). He then claimed that the information of the original document was not given to him as only a summary was provided, and the tribunal agreed with him.

It was decided, by the tribunal of IPSA v Information Commissioner and Ben Leapman (2013) EA/2012/0242, that logos and letterheads, handwriting, and the layout and style/design of the documents all constituted information. The IPSA tribunal says that a badly presented invoice might hold information that shows a company may not be legitimate or that a changing logo could also call into question its legitimacy.

What is an FOI request?

Making an FOI request can be simple. The difficulties often lie within what has been asked for, how the information is held, and if the authority wants to withhold what has been asked for. However, there are some stipulations to what actually makes a request. These are set out in Section 8. To be legitimate any request has to:

- be in writing;
- say the name of the requester and address (email is acceptable) for correspondence;
- describe what is being asked for.

The Freedom of Information Act goes on to say, at Section 8(2), that a request will count as being in writing if it is transmitted by electronic means, received in a legible form and is capable for being used for subsequent reference. A valid request does not have to mention the Freedom of Information Act.

The Act is not limited to UK residents: anyone, from anywhere in the world, can make a request. A company or organisation can make a request as long as a name is included. If a request is from a company, the public authority should accept its registered name or name that exists for legal purposes (ICO, 2014d, p.9). If a request is made using a pseudonym then it will be invalid. However, if it is not an obvious pseudonym (i.e. John Smith) and there is no reason to question it, the public authorities are told to take it at face value (ICO, 2014d, p.8).

At the very least, the Commissioner expects authorities to advise the requester to provide a real name rather than just ignoring the request. It is in the requester's interests to provide their real name in most circumstances, as neither the Commissioner nor the tribunals will consider a case unless the identity of the requester is clear.

Not knowing information

When making a request, there is a higher chance of a successful outcome if you know what the information you are asking for is (this is further discussed in Chapter 5). However, it is not essential to know the name of the files or documents that are being requested. As long as the authority can identify what is being asked for, this will be enough.

Different public authorities store information in different ways, even when they are authorities of the same type. For example, police forces use different information storage systems to hold the same information. Mark Wise (2014) from the Association of Chief Police Officers' central FOI team, which helps all of the UK forces coordinate answers to requests, says that an effective request from a journalist can be 'for a schedule of documents, so they are trying initially to understand what it is that the police service are likely to hold'.

The ICO (2014a, p.12) says that a requester cannot 'reasonably be expected' to be specific about the titles, details and location of what is being asked for, and so, at times, will not be able to provide enough detail to identify the information, by name, that is being asked for. Requests are valid as long as the authority can work out the relevant information to provide (ICO, 2014d, p.18).

Business as usual

In some cases, authorities will treat requests for information as a normal part of their work, rather than under the Freedom of Information Act. The ICO (2014d, p.5) says if information can be 'quickly and easily' sent to the requester then it may be sensible to treat it as normal business. This can be beneficial for journalists who have built up relationships with FOI officers, or with press officers they frequently deal with.

It will often be possible, with a strong relationship, to bypass the FOI process and get the information within hours, rather than weeks. Although, even if a request is handled as 'business as usual', it is still strictly subject to FOI requirements as long as it meets the definition of a request as is set out in Section 8 of the Act.

Social media requests

The ability to make a request by electronic purposes means they can be made on social media, something that barely existed at the time the Act was being discussed. The ICO (2012) has gone as far as to issue guidance following the rapid expansion of social media platforms.

The ability of public authorities to directly, and quickly, respond to requesters gives new opportunities to comment on their activities. In guidance for public authorities on recognising what a genuine FOI request is, the ICO (2014d, p.5) says 'social networking sites' are valid for making requests.

The ICO (2012) states the real name of the requester must be shown if it is not the Twitter handle for it to be a valid request. The authority may ask for a correspondence address or post the response online and link to it. The regulator also decided that an @ mention is 'received' by an authority as it can check the mentions it has.

Chapter 1 top tips

- Under the Act, authorities are obliged, in most circumstances, to confirm whether they have the information you have asked for.
- If no exemptions apply, they should give you the information, and in any circumstance do not have to withhold the information just because an exemption applies.
- Authorities have to reply to requests within 20 working days, and also promptly.
- If they are going to refuse to give you information, the authority must explain why.
- There are more than 100,000 public authorities covered by the Act and they range from schools to government departments.
- Information is classed as everything from documents, emails and photos to CCTV and the style of documents.
- Publication schemes that authorities are required to have will be where basic information is routinely published.
- The ICO oversees the implementation and regulation of the Freedom of Information Act, as well as the Data Protection Act.

References

Brooke, H., 2006. *Your Right to Know: A Citizen's Guide to the Freedom of Information Act*. London: Pluto Press.

Cabinet Office, 1997. *Your Right to Know* (Cm 3818). London: HMSO.

Campaign for Freedom of Information, 1993. *Secrets Number 26*. Available at: www.cfoi.org.uk/pdf/SecretsNewspaperNo26.pdf [Accessed 24 September 2014].

Campaign for Freedom of Information, 1997. *Campaign Welcomes 'Impressive' Freedom of Information Proposals*. Available at: www.cfoi.org.uk/wp111297pr.html [Accessed 24th September 2014].

Campaign for Freedom of Information, 2008. *Freedom of Information Act 2000: Designation of Additional Public Authorities*. Information Commissioner's Office. Available at: www.cfoi.org.uk/pdf/CFOI_s5response.pdf [Accessed 3 September 2014].

Campaign for Freedom of Information, 2009. *Secrets Newspaper 1984–1993*. Available at: www.cfoi.org.uk/2009/12/secrets-newspaper-1984-1993 [Accessed 24 September 2014].

Chancellor of the Duchy of Lancaster, 1993. *Open Government* (Cm 2290). London: HMSO.

Evans, R., 2014. *Interview*. Interviewed by Matt Burgess [Telephone] 29 July 2014.

Freedom of Information Act 2000 (c.36). London: HSMO.

Gibbons, P., 2014. *Interview*. Interviewed by Matt Burgess [In person] London: 22 May 2014.

Graham, C., 2014. *Interview*. Interviewed by Matt Burgess *[In person]* Wilmslow: 20 May 2014.

Guardian, 1999a. Culture of openness preferable to one of leaks and rumours, 23 June. Available at: www.theguardian.com/politics/1999/jun/23/freedomofinformation. uk3 [Accessed 30 July 2014].

Guardian, 1999b. Straw unveils freedom of information concessions, 22 October. Available at: www.theguardian.com/politics/1999/oct/22/freedomofinformation. uk [Accessed 20 September 2014].

Independent, 2011. Royal Family granted new right of secrecy, 8 January. Available at: www.independent.co.uk/news/uk/home-news/royal-family-granted-new-right-of-secrecy-2179148.html [Accessed 1 September 2014].

Independent Parliamentary Standards Authority (IPSA) v Information Commissioner (IC) and Ben Leapman, 2013. EA/2012/0242.

Information Commissioner, 2012. *Written Evidence from the Information Commissioner*. Available at: www.publications.parliament.uk/pa/cm201213/cmselect/cmjust/96/96we12.htm [Accessed 12 July 2014].

Information Commissioner's Office (ICO), 2012. *Can Freedom of Information Requests be Submitted using Twitter?* Available at: http://web.archive. org/web/20140121121439/http://ico.org.uk/~/media/documents/library/Freedom_of_Information/Practical_application/can_foi_requests_be_submitted_using_twitter.ashx [Accessed 8 March 2014].

Information Commissioner's Office (ICO), 2013a. *Model Publication Scheme*. Available at: http://ico.org.uk/for_organisations/freedom_of_information/guide/~/media/documents/library/Freedom_of_Information/Detailed_specialist_guides/model-publication-scheme.pdf [Accessed 16 June 2014].

Information Commissioner's Office (ICO), 2013b. *Public Authorities Under the Freedom of Information Act*. Available at: http://ico.org.uk/for_organisations/guidance_index/~/media/documents/library/Freedom_of_Information/Detailed_specialist_guides/public_authorities_under_the_foia.ashx [Accessed 16 June 2014].

Information Commissioner's Office (ICO), 2014a. *Information Commissioner Reappointment*, 18 February. Available at: https://ico.org.uk/about-the-ico/news-and-events/news-and-blogs/2014/02/information-commissioner-reappointment [Accessed 8 March 2014].

Information Commissioner's Office (ICO), 2014b. *Information Commissioner's Annual Report and Financial Statements 2013/14*. Available at: https://ico. org.uk/media/about-the-ico/documents/1042191/annual-report-2013-14.pdf [Accessed 8 March 2014].

Information Commissioner's Office (ICO), 2014c. *The Guide to Freedom of Information*. Available at: http://ico.org.uk/for_organisations/freedom_of_information/~/media/documents/library/Freedom_of_Information/Detailed_specialist_guides/guide_to_freedom_of_information.pdf [Accessed 27 July 2014].

Information Commissioner's Office (ICO), 2014d. *Recognising a Request Made Under the Freedom of Information Act (section 8)*. Available at: http://ico.org. uk/~/media/documents/library/Freedom_of_Information/Research_and_reports/recognising-a-request-made-under-the-foia.pdf [Accessed 17 July 2014].

Information Commissioner's Office (ICO), nd. *Introduction to the ICO*. Available at: http://ico.org.uk/about_us/our_organisation/introduction [Accessed 14 September 2014].

Justice Committee, 2009. *The Work of the Information Commissioner: Appointment of a New Commissioner* (HC 146, 2008–09). London: HMSO.

Labour Party, 1974. *October 1974 Labour Party Manifesto Britain Will Win With Labour*. Available at: www.labour-party.org.uk/manifestos/1974/Oct/1974-oct-labour-manifesto.shtml [Accessed 24 September 2014].

Local Government Association, 2014. *Councils Quizzed on Dragon Attacks, Asteroid Crashes and Possessed Pets in Wacky FoI Requests*, 16 August. Available at: www.local.gov.uk/media-releases/-/journal_content/56/10180/6445913/NEWS [Accessed 1 September 2014].

Protection of Freedoms Act 2012 (c.9). London: HMSO.

Shapps, G., 2011. *Grant Shapps Calls for More Transparency in Social Housing*, 23 June. Available at: www.gov.uk/government/news/grant-shapps-calls-for-more-transparency-in-social-housing [Accessed 8 March 2014].

Sugar v British Broadcasting Corporation and Anor, 2012. UKSC 4 (15 February 2012).

UCL Constitution Unit, 2011. *What is Freedom of Information and Data Protection? History and Links*. Available at: www.ucl.ac.uk/constitution-unit/research/foi/what-is-foi2 [Accessed 24th September 2014].

Wise, M., 2014. *Interview*. Interviewed by Matt Burgess *[Telephone]* 31 July 2014.

FOI in the media's view

Positive press

Although there have been – and continue to be – major concerns regarding how effective the Act can be for the media, how journalists are treated and wider issues with what the Act does and does not allow to be released, the media does speak positively about the Act. The Society of Editors (2012) says the Act has been an 'essential journalistic tool' that has helped to create more openness. *The Telegraph* (2012a) says it allows information that a public authority has decided not to proactively publish to be extracted.

The Kent Messenger Group (2012) says it has allowed 'greater openness about how public money is being spent'. In a similar vein, Perry Austin-Clarke (2012), editor of the *Bradford Telegraph* and *Argus*, says it has helped to expose 'public spending excesses' as well as to 'highlight health issues and provide a deeper insight for our readers'.

The *Financial Times* (2012) argued that it makes it harder for officials to try to 'cut out journalists who write things that they would rather not have reported', while *The Guardian* (2012) says it has proven to be a vital part of freedom of expression. While Hayes (2009, p.59) says that the stories may not provide 'banner headlines' all the time, 'but stories about botched operations, children taken into care because of obesity, or clumsy use of firearms by police officers do make interesting reading'.

Of course, these opinions are from the perspectives of the journalists making requests, not from the point of view of the public authorities, or the officials the information concerns. These are discussed in the section on political attitudes below.

Negative noise

The biggest complaint from journalists, and most requesters, is the amount of time that it takes for authorities to respond to requests, particularly regarding the delays that can be caused by authorities not complying with the 20 working day deadline, which is imposed by law. This can scupper any chance a journalist has of producing a timely story.

In order to anticipate these delays, Cynthia O'Murchu (2014) from the *Financial Times* advises that it is best to send requests early in a project as 'it is going to take a long time'. Carey and Turle (2008, p.220) say 'that the FOIA may be of limited use to news journalists working against daily or weekly news pressures. Its effectiveness may be restricted to specialist or investigative reporters working to much longer timescales or on specific projects or investigations.'

Rob Evans (2014), from *The Guardian*, says: 'You can win but it is sort of several years down the line and no one is really interested in the story anymore.' Doug Wills, managing editor of the *Evening Standard*, *The Independent* and *The Independent on Sunday* (2012), says that, although some authorities perform well, others do the bare minimum that they can get away with; he says authorities can 'grudgingly observe the letter [of the law] only'. This, in some cases, leads to political and press office interference in the handling of requests, which was said to be against the spirit of the Act by *Trinity Mirror*'s David Higgerson (2012).

The Times investigations editor Dominic Kennedy (2014) says, when asked how much of a tool the Act has been for investigative journalists, 'I think it is really disappointing. The balancing act tends to rule so much information out of being put into the public domain.' Kennedy (2014) continued, based upon the MPs' expenses case in which details were eventually leaked to *The Telegraph*, to say that the most effective way to get sensitive information is via leaks: 'The only way to find out something that happens in this country is to actually get someone to leak something to you. The Freedom of Information Act won't find it out.'

The Campaign for Freedom of Information (2014) says that its biggest issues with the Act, as it currently is, are the lack of a time limit to complete internal reviews and Public Interest Tests, and the delays in responding to requests. These are some of the major issues that journalists using the Act have faced within the first ten years of its enactment. Nevertheless, the volume of media-generated FOI stories produced from them show there is a value to using the Act; a dearth of requests would support views that the Act is not worth having.

Prominent media use

The Freedom of Information Act covers almost all of the corridors of power in the UK, giving journalists an unprecedented level of access to information regarding all areas of public life and public expenditure – provided the authorities agree to give it up. The fundamental principles of the Act give the media the ability to access more official information than ever before.

Journalists are able to prise open files, e-mails and official data, which would otherwise never see the light of day.

There have been the incredibly high-profile cases of the MPs' expenses scandal, Iraq War Cabinet minutes and the 'dodgy dossier' (see Chapter 7), and many other cases in which FOI requests forced authorities to reveal information they did not want the public to know. Other issues that have been revealed include:

- Footage of the London 7/7 bombers on their way to killing 52 people (*Daily Mirror*, 2009).
- Police leaving 2 million crimes uninvestigated (*Telegraph*, 2007).
- Councils paying for prostitutes for the disabled (*Telegraph*, 2010).
- UK military forces' attacks on Afghanistan civilians (*Guardian*, 2011).
- Temporary staff being paid £1,250 a day by a council cutting jobs (*Daily Mail*, 2011).
- 600 convicted killer drivers allowed back onto the roads (*Daily Mirror*, 2012).
- Roald Dahl, and many others, turning down honours from the Queen (*Telegraph*, 2012a).

These are just the tip of the iceberg. Every type of media, encompassing print, radio, television and online, has used requests at some point to help uncover information and stories. From Radio 4 to *BuzzFeed*, the media has utilised the Freedom of Information Act regardless of their audience or content type.

Effect of the Act

Almost all of the journalists interviewed for this book say that the Act has had some positive effects on how they work and that they are able to write stories in greater detail than before it was in place.

Scottish journalist Paul Hutcheon (2014) says the Act has been like 'having another club in the bag', while investigative journalist David Hencke (2014) says it can be crucial and allows journalists to create 'a much more accurate, detailed and hard hitting story that people can't challenge very easily because it is all based on documents'. Additionally, Dave West (2014), from the *Health Service Journal*, says it has allowed access to a 'vast' quantity of information that journalists 'wouldn't have been able to have got, which is generally very significantly in the public interest'.

Worthy (2010, p.564), who worked for the Constitution Unit at University College London, researching FOI, highlighted six key themes of the Freedom of information Act, as follows:

1   Increasing transparency and openness.
2   Increasing accountability.

3   Improving the quality of government decision-making.
4   Improving public understanding of decision-making.
5   Increasing public participation.
6   Increasing public trust.

The government says it believes the core objectives of the Act have been achieved. It believes the Act's impact on increased openness, transparency and accountability has led to 'significant enhancements' of democracy, although it has not had a 'significant positive impact' on the public's trust in government (Ministry of Justice, 2012, p.6).

Broadly, the media's use of the Act can be seen to relate to all of these aims as use of the Act raises awareness of it, and its purpose. Specifically, the media's use of FOI requests will mostly relate to increased accountability and scrutiny. Reports revealing that rape allegations are being left off official crime records (*BBC News*, 2009), Manchester council not spending money allocated to improve the high street for the public (*Manchester Evening News*, 2013) and criminals in Sussex still owing £14 million in fines (*Argus*, 2013) show how FOI can increase accountability while also leading to greater levels of public knowledge.

Political discrepancies

Politicians' publicly expressed attitudes towards FOI are best described as 'faltering'. Any law that allows people to uncover almost every decision, speech, e-mail, expenditure and action of elected officials and those that are responsible for public services will always cause tension, as it forces authorities to give information that could cause embarrassment or ruffle feathers and raise heckles.

Labour Prime Minister Tony Blair, who introduced the Freedom of Information Act in 2000, says in his autobiography that making the Act a reality was the worst thing he did while in charge of the country. He wrote:

> Freedom of Information. Three harmless words. I look at those words as I write them, and feel like shaking my head till it drops off my shoulders. You idiot. You naive, foolish, irresponsible nincompoop. There is really no description of stupidity, no matter how vivid, that is adequate. I quake at the imbecility of it. Once I appreciated the full enormity of the blunder, I used to say – more than a little unfairly – to any civil servant who would listen: Where was Sir Humphrey when I needed him? We had legislated in the first throes of power. How could you, knowing what you know, have allowed us to do such a thing so utterly undermining of sensible government?

(Blair, 2011, p.516)

This is despite Blair pledging to introduce the Act in his manifesto, as it was during six previous Labour general election campaigns (Campaign for Freedom of Information, 2000).

It appears that coming to power acts as a catalyst for politicians' changeable attitudes towards the Act – while they are in opposition, they are often in favour of the Freedom of Information Act, but this changes when their party is in power. Academic Ben Worthy (2014) says:

> The classic problem is that politicians go off FOI. More interestingly, what we found in local authorities is that people had different views within the authority itself, people who work with FOI support it, find it troublesome, people higher up support the idea of openness and then some, and only some, politicians at the top don't like it at all, so even within one local authority you get a whole range of views.

This can be seen even from the more recent example of Prime Minister David Cameron saying that the Act would be extended but making no obvious move to bring about this change once in power. The Conservative Party (c2009) set out a plan before being elected in 2010, called 'Big Ideas to Give Britain Real Change', which included a specific section on extending the Act's reach. The plan says:

> We will expand the scope of the Freedom of Information Act to include taxpayer funded bodies such as Northern Rock or Network Rail, together with bodies such as the Local Government Association. This will give the public access to huge amount of government information currently only available to ministers.
>
> (Conservative Party, c2009, p.5)

However, by summer 2015, six years after Cameron's pledge, only one of these changes had occurred, as following the re-categorisation of Network Rail to a public body it would be subject to FOI (Department of Transport, 2014, p.9).

Are they scared of the Act?

The most prominent arguments against the FOI Act, from politicians at the highest levels, are that it does not give them a safe space in which to think, and it creates a chilling effect, resulting in officials becoming less likely to record and keep information discussed in a frank manner because they believe it will be accessible by FOI requests.

When retiring in 2011, Cabinet Secretary Sir Gus O'Donnell says that FOI needed to give Cabinet Ministers room to have discussions. He says: 'Freedom of information that allows the public to ask questions about things is fine, but the bit that I'm really against in freedom of information is that bit where it reduces the quality of our governance' (*BBC News*, 2011a). Professor Robert Hazell (2012) wrote to provide evidence for the purpose of a government review to say that his research showed 'that there is very little hard, first hand evidence of a chilling effect caused by FOI'. He went on to say that officials' fears that FOI takes away the safe space they need to make decisions may not be 'wholly rational'.

Information Commissioner Christopher Graham agreed with this view (2012, Q206, Q198), and told the government's review that the fears of politicians' discussions being disclosed was 'greatly overdone' and a 'self-fulfilling prophecy'. This was also supported by Deputy Information Commissioner Graham Smith (2012, Q200), who says that the ICO had not seen any evidence of full and frank discussions not happening because of the Act. He also says the only evidence of a chilling effect they have seen amounted to 'anecdotal stories from people in government departments'.

Ministerial veto

Under the FOI Act, government ministers are able to veto the disclosure of information. In the ten years the Act has been in force, the veto has been used seven times. It gives ministers the power to block disclosure of information, although they in theory should have a good reason for doing so.

The majority of these have came in recent years, the first being issued in 2009 for the contents of legal advice on military action in Iraq. The remaining six vetoes, to date, have been used: twice on devolution issues; the NHS Transitional Risk Register; a second time for the Iraq minutes; Prince Charles' letters to ministers; and the final one was issued over the High Speed 2 train plans (House of Commons Library, 2014, p.1).

At the time of writing, the veto is under a huge level of scrutiny as the government is appealing the Court of Appeals' overruling of Dominic Grieve's use of the veto in the Supreme Court. Previously the Court of Appeal ruled that the Attorney General's use of the veto in the case of Prince Charles' letters was unlawful (*BBC News*, 2014). See Chapter 7 for more on this case.

Public bodies' disdain towards the Act

It is not just leading politicians who scaremonger about the Act – public bodies often raise issues about how much it costs them to respond to requests. Although many civil servants and public authorities hold the FOI laws in high regard and will often go the extra mile to help requesters, the increasing cost is a common complaint. *Trinity Mirror*'s David Higgerson (2012) says:

No politician or senior officer should be afraid of FOI. They should welcome the public's use of the system. However, a growing number of politicians, particularly at local council level, seem determined to raise the rising cost of FOI as a reason to curtail it.

Press reports seem to be in agreement, showing local authorities bemoaning the cost of informing people. Birmingham City Council estimated its annual spend on FOI requests to be approximately £800,000 in 2010 (*Local Government Chronicle*, 2010), out of its 2010/11 gross expenditure budget of £3.5 billion (Birmingham City Council, 2010, p.3). However, the council (2012) has also taken a more progressive approach by calling for authorities to receive more resources to equip them to deal with the rising number of requests.

Similarly, Lincolnshire County Council complained in 2012 that it cost them up to £500,000 a year to respond to requests (*BBC News*, 2012a). In the financial year of 2012/13, the council's revenue spending on public services totalled £929.9 million. This, it says, equated to £1,295 per person in Lincolnshire (Moore, 2013, p.2).

In the same year, Broadland District Council complained about having to spend almost £15,000 a year on answering FOI requests (*Norwich Evening News 24*, 2012). Its estimated revenue expenditure for the year was more than £45 million (Broadland District Council, nd, p.5). These examples highlight the comparatively low spend on responding to FOI requests compared to a public authority's budget.

For the smallest authorities, the financial burden of answering FOI requests may have a bigger impact. For example, the Parish Council of Goring says it would have to pay an extra £5,000 to answer FOI requests (*Henley Standard*, 2014).

Staffordshire County Council also publishes a list of those who had cost the council money by making requests on their website. Local paper the *Express and Star* reported the council as saying some requests were a 'wrongful use of the Act' (*Express and Star*, 2014). The council's website says that requests from press and commercial organisations cost it £22,050 to answer between January 2012 and September 2014. At the top of their list sits the *Express and Star* newspaper, followed by the BBC and the *Daily Mail*. The council says 'we believe it is right to publish more information on the cost to council taxpayers' (Staffordshire County Council, nd).

Although the councils above argue against the cost of FOI, Jim Amos, Honorary Senior Research Associate at the UCL Constitution Unit, says that generally the costs for responding to requests are decreasing as time goes on. He says: 'In summary, my view is that FOIA costs are reasonable, are on a downward trend and there is scope for that trend to go much further with positive leadership, good management and with intelligent use of web publication' (Amos, 2012).

The Act can also be useful for authorities, as it can help them identify areas where they may be overspending or operating inefficiently. FOI consultant Paul Gibbons says it is equally important despite times of austerity (*Telegraph*, 2012b), as people have a right to know how money is being spent and how decisions are being made.

Despite some authorities' negativity towards their lawful obligations to respond to requests for information, the case of Walberswick Parish Council must be the most extreme reaction from a public authority: five members of the tiny council stepped down, in November 2012, in protest at the number of FOI requests the authority had received. The authority received more than 100 requests from angry residents who were not happy with the decisions being made (*BBC News*, 2012b). The requests prompted the council to get rid of the parish's Christmas tree as it could not afford it (*BBC News*, 2011b).

Stemming the flow

The attitudes of politicians and officials towards FOI, as demonstrated above, can often be disparaging and negative. It is therefore not surprising that there have been attempts to curtail, limit and restrict the Act's permitted rights. Each time the government has intended to make changes that would reduce the level of accessible information, campaigners and FOI enthusiasts have defended against the proposed changes.

At the end of 2006, less than two years after the Act came into force, the first moves to try to limit its reach were launched. Lord Falconer proposed attempts to speedily push measures through Parliament without any consultation period open to the public (*Guardian*, 2006a). These proposals included plans to restrict the Act's reach and include the time of those answering FOI requests in the cost estimates they can use for not complying with a request. It was claimed that in including this time authorities would be able to save £5 million per year (*BBC News*, 2006). Falconer also suggested (*Guardian*, 2006b) that the time spent working out the cost of a request should also include the official's reading time, as well as any time needed to consult with lawyers or other officials. Press and campaign groups strongly opposed this. Newspaper editors met with government minister Baroness Ashton and asked if journalists would be excluded from the proposed changes (*Guardian*, 2007a). This sort of treatment can be seen in the US, where requests to federal government agencies can be expedited so they are looked at before other requests. Although this only occurs if the requester can show there is an urgency to inform the public about an actual or alleged federal government activity (US Customs and Border Protection, 2014).

Falconer says that the Act was for the people, not the media: 'People, not the press, must be the priority. There is a right to know, not a right to tell'

(*Metro*, 2007). However, the Select Committee on Constitutional Affairs (2007) published a report stating there was not enough evidence to show the need for change and that the Ministry of Justice should focus on improving compliance with the Act.

It was the first of a raft of attacks upon the Freedom of Information Act. Conservative MP David Maclean (2007) also tabled a Bill to exempt the House of Commons and the House of Lords from the Act. It included provisions to ensure that MPs' correspondence to public authorities was classed as exempt. The Bill managed to pass through the entire House of Commons but fell at the first hurdle in the House of Lords, with no one from the Lords willing to sponsor the Bill. Jack Straw (*Guardian*, 2007b) says that guidance would be introduced to help with the disclosure of MPs' correspondence instead.

Royals locked in the palace

One of the biggest, if not *the* biggest, change to the Act since it became law was limiting access to information about the Royal Family and their affairs. It was decided that information relating to the monarch and heirs to the throne was to fall under an absolute exemption rather than a qualified one (*Independent*, 2011).

This means that the information would not be accessible even if it was in the public interest. The Royal Household was already not classed as a public authority. Information on the communications of the senior royals can only be obtained five years after their death, or after 20 years of it being created (*Telegraph*, 2012c).

The Constitution Reform and Governance Act 2010 brought in the changes at the start of 2011. In announcing the alterations, Lord Chancellor and Secretary of State for Justice Ken Clarke says: 'The changes provide an absolute instead of a qualified exemption for information relating to communications with the sovereign, heir to the throne or second in line to the throne or those acting on their behalf' (HC Deb, 2010–11, col. 35WS).

Thirty-year rule

It becomes easier to access information as it becomes older, fades from memories and is unlikely to influence ongoing political and policy decisions. To aid the publication of ageing information, concessions have been introduced to allow for the relaxing of information being revealed. *Daily Mail* editor Paul Dacre led a review of the 30-year rule, in 2009, which helped to change the accessibility of historical documents and make them available for release earlier than they would have been previously.

Dacre says the rule needed updating, after it had previously been reduced from 50 years, to reflect the changes in modern society. He says:

A rule that secured a break with a more secretive past has itself been overtaken by developments such as the televising of Parliament, 24-hour news, email and web access and the unprecedented transparency of many of today's public bodies. Parliament recognised these fundamental changes by passing the Freedom of Information Act, which reversed centuries-old official attitudes.

(30 Year Rule Review, 2009, p.iii)

The time frame was reduced from 30 years to 20, which the Ministry of Justice says would cost £52 million to implement (*BBC News*, 2012c).

Plans afoot

The coalition government appeared to be intent on changing the Freedom of Information Act, having announced it would consult on the issues the Justice Select Committee's Post Legislative Scrutiny of Act touched upon in 2012. Following the publication of the report, the government's response hinted at changes in the following areas:

- Disproportionate burdens caused by 'industrial' use of the Act.
- Considering and redacting time could be included in the cost limits estimate.
- Reducing the overall cost limits of £600 and £450.
- Where a person or group use the Act to make frequent unrelated requests to an authority and causes a burden.
- The potential for users to contribute more towards the cost of tribunals.
- Review the Section 45 Code of Practice, in respect of time lengths for internal reviews and Public Interest Tests, and the position of contractors in relation to FOI.
- Extend provisions that allow the prosecution of those who try to deliberately stop information from being disclosed.

(Ministry of Justice, 2012)

While these, at the time of writing, have not been formally announced, it is likely the Conservative majority government will return to examine these issues before 2020. The issues raise the same complaints that local authorities have raised about the Act.

Use it or lose it

The number of FOI requests made per year has increased significantly since the Act's inception. In 2005, when enacted, there was a barrage of requests from all areas of public life, particularly to central government. After this, the use of the Act fell to a level that more accurately reflected public awareness and interest.

Worthy (2014) says the number of requests may eventually stop rising.

> We may hit a plateau but it may be a very high plateau compared with international regimes. One of the things is that Freedom of Information never settles down. It never settles down bureaucratically but it never settles down politically. There's always controversy and problems.

However, Worthy continued to say that fewer than one in 1,000 people make use of the Act.

Figures collected by the Ministry of Justice, for requests made to central government, show that there has been a steady climb for each year. In 2013, 51,696 FOI requests were made to central government bodies (Ministry of Justice, 2014, p.2). The department says its statistics show an average 6 per cent increase each year, following the 2005 spike.

WhatDoTheyKnow.com, which allows anyone to make requests online and then publishes the results, has had more than 250,000 requests made through its service and told the government review that it believes 10 per cent of all requests in the UK are made through the website (WhatDoTheyKnow. com, 2012).

When events are particularly newsworthy, controversial or in the public interest, authorities usually see a spike in requests as interest rises, according to the Ministry of Justice (2014, p.8). The BBC received an 'unprecedented volume' of requests during 2012 that related to Jimmy Savile, following revelations about him committing sexual assaults. In total, that year the authority received 1,557 requests (BBC, 2013).

As non-central government authorities are not required to compile figures on their performance in answering FOI requests, there are no directly comparable figures to see how they are performing, and an authority's direct duty to respond to requests to information is not accountable, or easily traceable. However, the number has risen.

The steady rise in requests to all authorities is a sign of the Act's importance as a method to obtain statistics and reasons behind decisions that are made. The right to access information is an indirect way of giving people the power to scrutinise the officials that are elected, or forced upon them. It is clear that more people are willing to ask those in power to justify their decisions.

Chapter 2 top tips

- For a large investigative project that is supported by FOI requests it is best to send the requests as early as possible.

- You should often be prepared for long FOI request battles with public authorities and not see the requesting process as the only way to get the information.
- A story based on documents obtained under the Freedom of Information Act cannot be challenged as easily by a public authority, as they will have provided the documents.
- There is very little evidence of a 'chilling effect' that stops officials from privately sharing their candid opinions.
- By the year 2022 the government will have to release all but the most sensitive files 20 years after they were created. Up until 2022 their release is on a sliding scale from 30 years.
- Government ministers can apply a veto to a request if they feel that the information should not be disclosed.
- Public authorities will often see a spike in requests when there is an issue of a high public interest. In these circumstances it is always worth monitoring other FOI responses on the same topic from a public authority.

References

30-Year Rule Review, 2009. *Review of the 30-Year Rule.* HMSO. Available at: http://webarchive.nationalarchives.gov.uk/20090516124148/http://www2.nationalarchives.gov.uk/30yrr/30-year-rule-report.pdf [Accessed 20 April 2009].

Amos, J., 2012. *Supplementary Evidence from Jim Amos, Honorary Senior Research Associate, UCL Constitution Unit.* Available at: www.publications.parliament.uk/pa/cm201213/cmselect/cmjust/96/96we20.htm [Accessed 12 July 2014].

Argus, 2013. Sussex courts still owed £14m by criminals, 20 March. Available at: www.theargus.co.uk/news/10301198.Sussex_courts_still_owed___14m_by_criminals/ [Accessed 22 September 2014].

Austin-Clarke, P., 2012. *Written Evidence from Perry Austin-Clarke, Group Editor Newsquest Bradford and Editor of The Telegraph and Argus.* Available at: www.publications.parliament.uk/pa/cm201213/cmselect/cmjust/96/96vw53.htm [Accessed 10 July 2014].

BBC, 2013. *Freedom of Information Act 2000 – RFI20130989.* WhatDoTheyKnow.com. Available at: www.whatdotheyknow.com/request/168151/response/416783/attach/2/RFI20130989%20final%20response.pdf [Accessed 22 September 2014].

BBC News, 2006. Ministers to limit openness law, 14 December. Available at: http://news.bbc.co.uk/1/hi/uk_politics/6179617.stm [Accessed 10 July 2014].

BBC News, 2009. Records of rape crime 'distorted', 21 September. Available at: http://news.bbc.co.uk/1/hi/uk/8266014.stm [Accessed 22 September 2014].

BBC News, 2011a. Cabinet debates should be private – Cabinet Secretary, 17 December. Available at: www.bbc.co.uk/news/uk-politics-16229867 [Accessed 22 September 2014].

BBC News, 2011b. Walberswick council axes Christmas tree in information row, 7 December. Available at: www.bbc.co.uk/news/uk-england-suffolk-16074603 [Accessed 23 September 2014].

BBC News, 2012a. Zombie FOI request costs Lincolnshire County Council, 14 August. Available at: www.bbc.co.uk/news/uk-england-lincolnshire-19254046 [Accessed 22 September 2014].

BBC News, 2012b. Walberswick parish councillors quit over FOI requests, 3 October. Available at: www.bbc.co.uk/news/uk-england-suffolk-19804046 [Accessed 23 September 2014].

BBC News, 2012c. Move to '20-year-rule' for secret papers will cost £52m, 13 July. Available at: www.bbc.co.uk/news/uk-politics-18828219 [Accessed 22 September 2014].

BBC News, 2014. Attorney general's block on Prince Charles's letters ruled unlawful, 12 March. Available at: www.bbc.co.uk/news/uk-26544124 [Accessed 12 October 2014].

Birmingham City Council, 2010. *Budget 2010/11*. Available at: www.birmingham. gov.uk/cs/Satellite?blobcol=urldata&blobheader=application%2Fpdf&blobhea dername1=Content-Disposition&blobkey=id&blobtable=MungoBlobs&blobw here=1223449284472&ssbinary=true&blobheadervalue1=attachment%3B+fi lename%3D984356Budget_Book_2010-11.pdf [Accessed 22 September 2014].

Birmingham City Council, 2012. *Written Evidence from Birmingham City Council*. Available at: www.publications.parliament.uk/pa/cm201213/cmselect/ cmjust/96/96vw27.htm [Accessed 10 July 2014].

Blair, T., 2011. *A Journey*. Reading: Arrow.

Broadland District Council, nd. *Budget 2012–13*. Available at: www.broadland. gov.uk/PDF/Complete.pdf [Accessed 22 September 2014].

Campaign for Freedom of Information, 2000. *Labour Commitments to Freedom of Information*. Available at: www.cfoi.org.uk/pdf/labcmits.pdf [Accessed 23 September 2014].

Campaign for Freedom of Information, 2014. *Interview*. Interviewed by Matt Burgess *[In person]* London: 19 May 2014.

Carey, P. and Turle, M., eds, 2008. *Freedom of Information Handbook*, 2nd edn. London: The Law Society.

Conservative Party, c2009. *Big Ideas to Give Britain real Change*. Available at: www. conservatives.com/~/media/Files/Downloadable%20Files/Big%20ideas%20 to%20give%20Britain%20Real%20change.ashx?dl=true [Accessed 12 July 2014].

Constitution Reform and Governance Act, 2010 (c.25). London: HMSO.

Daily Mail, 2011. The temps paid up to £1,250 a day by council that's slashing hundreds of jobs (that's three times David Cameron's daily wage), 12 June. Available at: www.dailymail.co.uk/news/article-2006076/Six-fat-cat-temps-paid-1-250-PER-DAY-council-thats-slashing-hundreds-jobs.html [Accessed 5 July 2014].

Daily Mirror, 2009. 7/7 bombers on way to killing 52, 2 May. Available at: www. mirror.co.uk/news/uk-news/77-bombers-on-way-to-killing-52-391690#.U-dQNYBdU10 [Accessed 13 August 2014].

Daily Mirror, 2012. More than 600 convicted killer drivers allowed back on the road, 23 January. Available at: www.mirror.co.uk/news/uk-news/more-than-600-convicted-killer-drivers-165419 [Accessed 4 August 2014].

Department for Transport, 2014. *Network Rail Framework Agreement*. Available at: www.gov.uk/government/uploads/system/uploads/attachment_data/file/349439/framework-agreement.pdf [Accessed 23 September 2014].

Evans, R. 2014. *Interview*. Interviewed by Matt Burgess *[Telephone]* 29 July 2014.

Express and Star, 2014. Concerns raised over Staffordshire County Council's published names data, 7 July. Available at: www.expressandstar.com/news/2014/07/05/concerns-raised-over-staffordshire-county-councils-published-names-data [Accessed 22 September 2014].

Financial Times, 2012. Written evidence from the *Financial Times*. Available at: www.publications.parliament.uk/pa/cm201213/cmselect/cmjust/96/96vw39.htm [Accessed 10 July 2014].

Graham, C., 2012. *Oral Evidence taken before the Justice Committee, Post Legislative Scrutiny of the Freedom of Information Act 2000*. Available at: www.publications.parliament.uk/pa/cm201012/cmselect/cmjust/uc1849-iii/uc184901.htm [Accessed 10 July 2014].

Guardian, 2006a. Ministers plan to break pledge on freedom of information, 27 November. Available at: www.theguardian.com/politics/2006/nov/27/uk.freedomofinformation [Accessed 22 September 2014].

Guardian, 2006b. FoI curbs 'rip heart out of right to know law', 14 October. Available at: www.theguardian.com/politics/2006/oct/17/uk.freedomofinformation [Accessed 10 July 2014].

Guardian, 2007a. Editors unite over FoI changes, 28 February. Available at: www.theguardian.com/media/2007/feb/28/pressandpublishing.uknews [Accessed 22 September 2014].

Guardian, 2007b. Straw sounds death knell for FoI curbs, 14 June. Available at: www.theguardian.com/politics/2007/jun/14/freedomofinformation.uk1 [Accessed 22 September 2014].

Guardian, 2011. UK forces' attacks on Afghan civilians investigated by military police, 4 October. Available at: www.guardian.co.uk/uk/2011/oct/04/uk-forces-afghan-civilians-deaths [Accessed 1 August 2014].

Guardian, 2012. Written evidence from *The Guardian*. Available at: www.publications.parliament.uk/pa/cm201213/cmselect/cmjust/96/96vw97.htm [Accessed 10 July 2014].

Hayes, J., 2009. The FOI: Whitehall strikes back. *British Journalism Review*, vol. 20, no. 3.

Hazell, R., 2012. *Supplementary Submission to the Commons Justice Committee by Prof Robert Hazell, the Constitution Unit, School of Public Policy, UCL June 2012*. Available at: www.publications.parliament.uk/pa/cm201213/cmselect/cmjust/96/96we26.htm [Accessed 11 July 2014].

HC Deb (2010–11) col. 35WS. Available at: www.publications.parliament.uk/pa/cm201011/cmhansrd/cm110118/wmstext/110118m0001.htm#11011870000126 [Accessed 17 August 2014].

Hencke, D., 2014. *Interview*. Interviewed by Matt Burgess *[Telephone]* 27 May 2014.

Henley Standard, 2014. Concern at the cost of answering queries, 22 September. Available at: www.henleystandard.co.uk/news/news.php?id=1525696 [Accessed 22 September 2014].

Higgerson, D., 2012. *Written Evidence from David Higgerson, Digital Publishing Director, Trinity Mirror Regionals*. Available at: www.publications.parliament. uk/pa/cm201213/cmselect/cmjust/96/96vw50.htm [Accessed 10 July 2014].

House of Commons Library, 2014. *FoI and Ministerial Vetoes*. Available at: www. parliament.uk/briefing-papers/SN05007.pdf [Accessed 20 November 2014].

Hutcheon P., 2014. *Interview*. Interviewed by Matt Burgess *[Telephone]* 4 June 2014.

Independent, 2011. Royal Family granted new right of secrecy, 8 January. Available at: www.independent.co.uk/news/uk/home-news/royal-family-granted-new-right-of-secrecy-2179148.html [Accessed 17 August 2014].

Kennedy, D., 2014. *Interview*. Interviewed by Matt Burgess *[Telephone]* 28 May 2014.

Kent Messenger Group, 2012. *Written Evidence from the Kent Messenger Group*. Available at: www.publications.parliament.uk/pa/cm201213/cmselect/ cmjust/96/96vw60.htm [Accessed 10 July 2014].

Local Government Chronicle, 2010. Cost of FOI requests rises to £34m, 16 September. Available at: www.lgcplus.com/briefings/corporate-core/legal/ cost-of-foi-requests-rises-to-34m/5019109.article [Accessed 22 September 2014].

Maclean, D., 2007. *Freedom of Information (Amendment) Bill 2006–07*. Available at: www.publications.parliament.uk/pa/pabills/200607/freedom_of_ information_amendment.htm [Accessed 22 September 2014].

Managing editor, *Evening Standard, The Independent* and *The Independent on Sunday*, 2012. *Written Evidence from the Managing Editor, Evening Standard, The Independent and The Independent on Sunday*. Available at: www. publications.parliament.uk/pa/cm201213/cmselect/cmjust/96/96we16.htm [Accessed 11 July 2014].

Manchester Evening News, 2013. Greater Manchester councils spend just £11k of £800k fund to save high street, 21 March. Available at: www. manchestereveningnews.co.uk/news/greater-manchester-news/greater-manchester-councils-spend-just-1805579 [Accessed 22 September 2014].

Metro, 2007. Openness is 'for public, not press', 20 March. Available at: http:// metro.co.uk/2007/03/20/openness-is-for-public-not-press-181898 [Accessed 22 September 2014].

Ministry of Justice (MoJ), 2012. *Government Response to the Justice Committee's Report: Post-legislative scrutiny of the Freedom of Information Act* (Cm 8505). London: HMSO.

Ministry of Justice (MoJ), 2014. *Freedom of Information Statistics: Implementation in Central Government*. Available at: www.gov.uk/government/uploads/system/ uploads/attachment_data/file/305525/foi-act-2000-statistics-implementation-in-central-government-2013-q4-annual.pdf [Accessed 18 September 2014].

Moore, P., 2013. Open report on behalf of Pete Moore, Executive Director Resources and Community Safety. *Lincolnshire County Council*. Available at: http://uk.sitestat.com/lincolnshire/lincolnshire/s?Home.local-democracy. how-the-council-works.finances.budgets-and-financial-strategy. Download.51511&ns_type=pdf&ns_url=www.lincolnshire.gov.uk// Download/51511 [Accessed 22 September 2014].

Norwich Evening News 24, 2012. Companies accused of wasting Broadland taxpayers' cash on Freedom of Information requests, 9 October. Available at:

www.eveningnews24.co.uk/news/companies_accused_of_wasting_broadland_
taxpayers_cash_on_freedom_of_information_requests_1_1650526   [Accessed
22 September 2014].

O'Murchu, C., 2014. *Interview*. Interviewed by Matt Burgess *[Telephone]* 13 May
2014.

Select Committee on Constitutional Affairs, 2007. *Summary*. Available at: www.
publications.parliament.uk/pa/cm200607/cmselect/cmconst/415/41503.htm
[Accessed 23 September 2014].

Smith, G., 2012. *Oral Evidence taken before the Justice Committee, Post Legislative
Scrutiny of the Freedom of Information Act 2000*. Available at: www.
publications.parliament.uk/pa/cm201012/cmselect/cmjust/uc1849-iii/uc184901.
htm [Accessed 10 July 2014].

Society of Editors, 2012. *Written Evidence from the Society of Editors*. Available at:
www.publications.parliament.uk/pa/cm201213/cmselect/cmjust/96/96vw74.htm
[Accessed 11 July 2014].

Staffordshire County Council, nd. *The Cost of FOI Requests*. Available at: www.
staffordshire.gov.uk/yourcouncil/dataprotectionandfreedomofinformation/
HowMuchFOIsCost/home.aspx [Accessed 22 September 2014].

Telegraph, 2007. Official: Police leave 2m crimes uninvestigated, 11 November.
Available at: www.telegraph.co.uk/news/uknews/1568991/Official-Police-leave-
2m-crimes-uninvestigated.html [Accessed 29 July 2014].

Telegraph, 2010. Councils pay for prostitutes for the disabled, 14 August. Available
at: www.telegraph.co.uk/health/7945785/Councils-pay-for-prostitutes-for-the-
disabled.html [Accessed 29 July 2014].

Telegraph, 2012a. Written evidence from The Telegraph Media Group. Available
at: www.publications.parliament.uk/pa/cm201213/cmselect/cmjust/96/96vw63.
htm [Accessed 10 July 2014].

Telegraph, 2012b. What price freedom (of information)? 22 March. Available at:
www.telegraph.co.uk/news/politics/9149322/What-price-freedom-of-information.
html [Accessed 22 September 2014].

Telegraph, 2012c. Prince of Wales letters: How the Freedom of Information Act has
protected the Royal family, 16 October. Available at: www.telegraph.co.uk/news/
uknews/prince-charles/9613159/Prince-of-Wales-letters-how-the-Freedom-of-
Information-Act-has-protected-the-Royal-family.html [Accessed 22 September
2014].

US Customs and Border Protection, 2014. *Expediting a FOIA Request*. Available
at: https://help.cbp.gov/app/answers/detail/a_id/1552/~/expediting-a-foia-request
[Accessed 22 September 2014].

West, D., 2014. *Interview*. Interviewed by Matt Burgess *[Telephone]* 10 June 2014.

WhatDoTheyKnow.com, 2012. *Written Evidence from WhatDoTheyKnow.com*.
Available at: www.publications.parliament.uk/pa/cm201213/cmselect/cmjust/96/
96we10.htm [Accessed 12 July 2014].

Worthy, B., 2010. More open but not more trusted? The effect of the Freedom
of Information Act 2000 on the United Kingdom Central. *Governance*, 23(4),
561–82.

Worthy, B., 2014. *Interview*. Interviewed by Matt Burgess *[In person]* London:
21 May 2014.

Accessing other information

Environmental Information Regulations

The Environmental Information Regulations 2004 (EIR) are a progressive set of information access regulations, which allow people to get their hands on environmental information. The UK was obliged to implement these as part of its membership of the European Union and they are widely accepted as being easier to access information from than under the provisions of the Freedom of Information Act.

The EIR legislation (reg 5) makes it possible for anyone to ask for environmental information and an authority covered by the regulations must give it to them unless it is covered by an exemption. As with the Freedom of Information Act, authorities must respond, with the information or a rejection, within 20 working days of receipt of the request.

However, an authority may be granted more time (reg 7) if a request is made that involves complex information or requires that a difficult decision is made as to whether to release it. The regulations allow the 20 working day period to be extended up to 40 working days if the authority 'reasonably believes that the complexity and volume' would mean it is not possible to answer in the initial period. The ICO (2013a, p.13) says the authority is still obliged to tell the requester that it is extending the time period within the first 20 working days.

A request to an authority that asks for environmental information has to be considered under the EIR. Section 39 of the Freedom of Information Act 2000 automatically exempts any environmental information from FOI disclosure, and there are no additional rights under FOI if an EIR exemption prevents disclosure.

The BBC's FOI expert Martin Rosenbaum (2014) says that he thinks there is an argument that journalists have not asked for as much environmental information as they could have done. He also says there are ways to get more under the EIR: 'One example is the security services being subject to the Environmental Information Regulations but not being subject to the

FOI Act.' FOI consultant Paul Gibbons (2014) agreed, saying that there is 'more of an expectation' to disclose information coming from EIR tribunals and court cases than there is under FOI.

As pointed out by Rosenbaum (2014), the authorities that are covered by the environmental regulations are not entirely the same as those under the Freedom of Information Act. The regulations (reg 2) say that authorities that carry out 'functions' of a public authority are included. The ICO (2014a, p.5) says this can include 'private companies or public private partnerships' as well as those that are under the control of public authorities, if they carry out functions that relate to the environment.

Like the Freedom of Information Act, public authorities are expected to publish some information even if they are not asked for it under EIR (reg 4), which requires proactive publication; however, unlike FOI there is no publication scheme that details what has to be published.

What is environmental information?

Environmental information covers a wide range of material that is captured by an authority. The encompassing nature of the regulations is summed up by the ICO (2014a, p.8) which says that even financial information can be classed as being environmental if, for example, it relates to the costs of redeveloping land or building a new leisure facility.

Regulation 2 describes what is classified as environmental information; and is derived from the European Council's Directive on access to environmental information:

- State of the elements of the environment: everything from the air, water, soil to costal, genetically modified organisms and biological diversity.
- Factors such as energy, noise, radiation, waste, emissions or other things released into the environment that are likely to affect the state of elements.
- Measures: this includes policies, legislations, plans and activities which that affect the factors and state of the environment, and those measures to protect them.
- Reports on the implementation of environmental information.
- Cost: the value for money and economic analysis of the environmental measures.
- Health and safety: including contamination of the food chain, conditions of human life (where relevant), cultural sites and built structures that may be affected by the elements, or any of the factors or measures.

(Environmental Information Regulations, 2004, reg 2)

Differences from FOI

Adverse effect

Some FOI exemptions refer to the 'prejudice' that could be caused if particular information were to be disclosed. Many of the equivalent exemptions in the EIR (i.e. those set out at Regulation 12(5)) use the alternative phrasing of causing an 'adverse effect'. It is intended to be the equivalent of prejudice, in that it will mean harm caused by disclosure. However, the EIR require a higher bar to block disclosure than FOI does.

The stipulations for this were set out in the tribunal case of Benjamin Archer v IC and Salisbury District Council (2007) EA/2006/0037. The tribunal says the disclosure must cause an adverse effect, that it *would* happen – not may happen or would be likely to – and the PIT must also find that maintaining the exemption would outweigh the reasons for disclosure. The tribunal concluded (par 51) that in EIR cases the 'threshold to justify non-disclosure is a high one'.

Public Interest Test

Most, but not all, exemptions under FOI are subject to a PIT. Several exemptions though, for example information provided in confidence, are absolute, meaning that as long as the information meets the definition set out in the Act, the information can be withheld.

However, all of the exemptions included in the EIR are subject to a PIT, due to the effect of Regulation 12(1)(b), with the exception being personal information. This means that if a public authority wants to use any exemption then the public interest in withholding the information has to outweigh that of disclosing it. The principle can lead to much more information being disclosed under the EIR than under FOI.

If non-disclosure is to be challenged, the ICO says the following public interest factors will be in favour of disclosure. It should be noted that the more specific an argument can be made, the higher the chance of disclosure.

*   Creating and keeping a sustainable environment.
*   Transparency and accountability.
*   Promoting public understanding.
*   Safeguarding democratic processes.
*   Securing the best use of public and environmental resources.
*   Right to live in an adequate environment.
*   Suspicion of wrongdoing.
*   Age of the information.

(ICO, 2013b, p.11)

Exemptions to the regulations

Many of the exemptions in the regulations are similar in scope to the Freedom of Information Act. All of the exemptions are listed in Regulation 12, other than the one for personal information, as follows. There are two classes of exemption, class exemptions (under reg 12(4)) and 'adverse effect' exemptions (under reg 12(5)).

The EIR refers to exemptions as exceptions, however for clarity the former has been used throughout these pages. It will instantly become clear from the number of exemptions as to why the regime is considered to allow more access than the Freedom of Information Act.

- Information not held (EIR reg 12(4)(a)): when the authority does not have the information at the time the request is received.
- Manifestly unreasonable requests (EIR reg 12(4)(b)): if the request is manifestly unreasonable. The exemption can be used when the request is considered to be vexatious, or when the cost of complying with the request will be too great. Therefore this is broadly the equivalent of Sections 12 and 14 in the Freedom of Information Act. There are, though, two significant differences. If the authority applies the exemption due to cost, the Freedom of Information Act's fees regulations do not apply to environmental information, and it will often be appropriate for public authorities to provide more information than under the Freedom of Information Act. The second difference is that there is a PIT. So whether refusing on grounds of cost, or arguing that a request is vexatious, the authority will have to carefully consider whether there is a public interest in disclosing the information nevertheless (ICO, 2013c).
- Requests formulated in too general a manner (EIR reg 12(4)(c)): where what is asked for is from too wide a scope and the authority has tried to clarify and narrow the request. This allows for requests that are unclear or not specific, too large or would contain too much information to be refused. When refusing a request, the ICO (2012a, p.2) states that under the exemption the authority should issue a refusal notice and ask for the request to be clarified, while providing reasonable advice.
- Material in the course of completion, unfinished documents and incomplete data (EIR reg 12(4)(d)): the exemption can include information created in the process of formulating and developing policy, including draft documents, which are, by their very nature, always unfinished even if a report has been published.
- Internal communications (EIR reg 12(4)(e): if internal discussions will be given out. What can be classed as internal communications is very wide ranging but the PIT limits the exemption's bite, the ICO (2013d, p.2) says.

- International relations, defence, national security or public safety (EIR reg 12(5)(a): broadly covering requests for information which, if disclosed, may put the public at risk. Areas include fighting terrorism, protecting the UK islands and the safety of individuals (mental and physical health). An authority can choose to neither confirm nor deny the information is held if, in doing so, it would reveal any of the information that the exemption covers (ICO, 2012b, pp.2–3).

- The course of justice and inquiries (EIR reg 12(5)(b)): where a request may stop a fair trial from taking place or stop an inquiry by a public authority. Covered in the exemption are matters that would adversely affect the course of justice, and the correct and fair application of the law. Despite this, the ICO (2014b, p.2) says there is always a presumption in favour of disclosure, as specified by reg 12(2).

- Intellectual property rights (EIR reg12(5)(c)): the exemption applies when the authority can show that material is covered by intellectual property rights, the rights holder would suffer harm, the harm would be because of a loss of control or use of the information and the harm could not be prevented by enforcing the rights (ICO, 2013e, p.2).

- Confidentiality of proceedings (EIR reg 12(5)(d)): where disclosure may break a legally confidential agreement between two or more parties. The exemption can only be used when it is more probable than not that confidentiality would be breached. There is always an assumption of disclosure of the information over that of withholding it. A key factor in determining the public interest is how far publishing the information would add to public understanding of issues, says the ICO (2014c, p.2).

- Confidentiality of commercial or industrial information (EIR reg 12(5) (e)): where releasing the information may damage the confidentiality of an economic interest. The information that is being withheld cannot be about emissions, it has to be commercial or industrial, there has to be confidentiality under law or contract. Also, the confidentiality must protect a legitimate economic interest that would be damaged by disclosure (ICO, 2012c, p.10).

- Interests of the person who provided the information to the public authority (EIR reg 12(5)(f)): where a person who has given information to a public authority was not obliged to do so by law, if it is not given in a way that would allow a public authority to disclose it, and they have not consented to its disclosure. Also the information cannot be exempt if it is about emissions (ICO, 2013f, p.2).

- Protection of the environment (EIR reg 12(5)(g)): for information to be correctly exempt it must relate to the aspect of the environment that is being protected, and how and to what extent it would be affected. It cannot be about emissions. The ICO (2012d, p.2) says that there is a public interest in avoiding harm to the environment but this will depend on the nature of the harm.

- Information on emissions (EIR reg 12(9)): the exemptions for confidentiality of proceedings through to the protection of the environment described above cannot apply where the information relates to emissions. The exemption will not apply to information that is only indirectly on emissions.

Additionally, Regulation 13 provides an exemption for personal information where it would breach the Data Protection Act 1998. It is an absolute exemption when the personal data of the requester and authorities should handle it under the Data Protection Act as a Subject Access Request. For a more detailed overview, consult the regulations or seek guidance from the Commissioner.

Data Protection Act

What is the Act?

The Data Protection Act 1998 exists to safeguard personal data. The ICO (2009, p.2) says that the Act balances the needs of organisations to collect and use personal data against the right to privacy. At the heart of the Act are eight principles that were designed to be easy to understand and accessible to those who do not have any expertise in the Act. The Act applies to the activity of 'processing personal data', rather than to any set bodies.

The ICO (2009, p.3) says, broadly, if you collect or hold information about 'an identifiable living individual, or if you use, disclose, retain or destroy that information' then it will be highly likely that you will be processing personal data – whether this is as an individual or part of an organisation. The Data Protection Act 1998 legislation (s.1) defines data as information that:

- is processed by means of equipment operating automatically in response to instructions given for that purpose;
- is recorded with the intention that it should be processed by such equipment;
- is recorded as part of a relevant filing system or is intended to be;
- is part of a record as defined by the Data Protection Act (effectively medical records, education records, social service records or housing records);
- can also be recorded data that is held by a public authority but does not fall into any of the above sections. This final area was added by the Freedom of Information Act.

Data can also be classed as 'sensitive' personal data under the Act. The Act stipulates that sensitive personal data will be only disclosed on rare occasions where it is justified. The Data Protection Act 1998 (s.2) says that the following is sensitive personal data: racial or ethnic origin; political opinions; religious beliefs; membership of a trade union; physical or mental health conditions; details relating to sexual life; commission of an offence; proceedings for any committed (or alleged) offence; and the sentence of a court in any such proceedings. Schedule 1, Part 1, of the Data Protection Act lists the eight principles of data protection.

The eight data protection principles

1   Personal data shall be processed fairly and lawfully and, in particular, shall not be processed unless:
    (a) at least one of the conditions in Schedule 2 is met; and
    (b) in the case of sensitive personal data, at least one of the conditions in Schedule 3 is also met.
2   Personal data shall be obtained only for one or more specified and lawful purposes, and shall not be further processed in any manner incompatible with that purpose or those purposes.
3   Personal data shall be adequate, relevant and not excessive in relation to the purpose or purposes for which they are processed.
4   Personal data shall be accurate and, where necessary, kept up to date.
5   Personal data processed for any purpose or purposes shall not be kept for longer than is necessary for that purpose or those purposes.
6   Personal data shall be processed in accordance with the rights of data subjects under this Act.
7   Appropriate technical and organisational measures shall be taken against unauthorised or unlawful processing of personal data and against accidental loss or destruction of, or damage to, personal data.
8   Personal data shall not be transferred to a country or territory outside the European Economic Area unless that country or territory ensures an adequate level of protection for the rights and freedoms of data subjects in relation to the processing of personal data.

(Data Protection Act, 1998)

Exemptions

As well as the data protection principles that underpin the Act, there are a series of exemptions. These are very different from the exemptions in the

Freedom of Information Act. Some do allow organisations to refuse access to data to the individual who has made a subject access request. But exemptions apply to other aspects of the Data Protection Act, such as allowing organisations to share personal data in certain circumstances or to legitimately breach particular data protection principles.

The exemptions are set out in the legislation in Part IV of the Data Protection Act and further reading on them and the principles can be found in the ICO's *Guide to Data Protection* (2009).

How it relates to journalists

Within the Data Protection Act lies an exemption for the media, which allows journalists greater freedoms to process/use an individual's personal data. It is not an absolute exemption but the allowance gives credence to the media's role in defending the public interest and the ability to investigate matters without fear of breaching the Data Protection Act.

Section 32 of the Data Protection Act provides an exemption to the processing of personal data when it is for the purposes of journalism, literature or art. In this section personal data is exempt from the data provision principles (except the seventh) if:

- it is undertaken with a view to publication by any person of journalistic, literary or artistic material (s.32(1)(a));
- the data controller reasonably believes that the public interest in publishing the information, for any of the previous purposes, as part of freedom of expression, would be in the public interest (s.32(1)(b));
- the data controller believes that compliance with the data protection principles is not compatible with the journalistic, literary or artistic material.

(Data Protection Act, 1998, Section 32)

The key phrase here is with a 'view to publication' as it means the information that has been collected does not have to be used in a story. It only has to be be collected for the consideration of publication. The Data Protection Act says that publishing information consists as making the information available to the general public or any section of the public (s.32(1)(6)).

Jon Baines (2014), who is the Chairman of the National Association of Data Protection Officers, says:

It is a very tricky exemption, it is almost absolute but it is not quite. With my pro-journalism hat on it's great, with my hat on from under which I have observed some poor journalistic practices I think it possibly gives too much leeway to those poor practices.

The ICO's (2014d, p.9) guide for the media says that journalists should only collect personal information about an individual's health, sex life or criminal behaviour if they are confident it is in the public interest and doing so justifies the intrusion into their privacy. The guidance goes on to say: 'For instance, if a story would be highly intrusive or harmful then it is less likely to be fair to publish personal data' (ICO, 2014d, p.12).

Subject Access Requests

Under the Freedom of Information Act 2000 (s.40(1)), personal information about the requester is exempt from disclosure. This exemption is discussed in detail in Chapter 4. An individual's right to access information about themselves is covered under the Data Protection Act. This right is conferred by the ability to make a Subject Access Request (SAR), Section 7 of the Data Protection Act allows the right of access to personal data.

If there is information on the individual then they are to be given a summary of their personal data, details of the purposes for which the data controller has the information and details of any recipients that may receive the information (Data Protection Act, s.7(1)(b)). The organisation must then communicate the requested personal information along with any information about the source of the data (s.7(1)(c)). The legislation also says that where decisions are being taken by automated means (e.g. using algorithms) using the individual's personal data, such as personal evaluations at work, then they have to be told the logic involved in the decisions that were made (s.7(1)(d)).

It is possible for bodies to charge for SARs, up to £10 per request (ICO 2014e, p.6) unless the information requested includes health or education records in which case a fee of up to £50 can be charged. The Data Protection Act (s.7(10)) says the bodies have a maximum of 40 calendar days after receiving a request to respond.

Exemptions to SARs

As with all information access laws, there are some exemptions to the ability to access what is held, even if it is about you. These are all outlined in the ICO's Code of Practice for authorities and include:

* confidential references;
* publicly available information;
* crime and taxation;
* management information;
* negotiations with the requester;
* regulatory activity;

- legal advice and proceedings;
- social work records;
- health and education.

(ICO, 2014e, pp.43–50)

INSPIRE

INSPIRE (2009) allows access to map data by giving people the ability to view and discover spatial datasets. The INSPIRE regulations are not request based. Authorities are obliged to publish certain types of information under the regulations (ICO, 2012e). Documentation by the Department for Environment Food & Rural Affairs (nd, p.1) says that the purpose of the regulations is to help join up geographic information that can allow us to 'manage the environment better'. The regulations in the UK are overseen by DEFRA, but the ICO also has some responsibilities that relate to them.

The regulations apply to public authorities, as with the Freedom of Information Act, and more broadly any other organisation or person that carries out functions of public administration. In particular, it covers those people or bodies that have responsibilities relating to the environment and that exercise functions of a public nature that relate to the environment (INSPIRE, reg 3).

In the regulations (reg 2), spatial data is defined as having a direct, or indirect, reference to a specific location or geographic area. It is fundamentally based around the aim to create a better level of environmental policy across the EU. The UK government says the regulations will achieve this by:

- improving the joining up and access to existing special data in the EU;
- improving data sharing between public authorities;
- allowing the public access to spatial data.

(data.gov.uk, 2013)

Those holding spatial data must make it possible to search for spatial datasets and services based on their metadata, and must have viewing services making it possible to display, navigate, zoom in and out, pan or overlay other spatial datasets. The authorities also have to allow the spatial datasets to be downloaded and must also enable spatial datasets to be transformed, so they could be combined with others (INSPIRE, reg 7(2)).

As ever there are some exemptions to what spatial data is required to be published by authorities, set out by INSPIRE (reg 9). Public access must not be provided to spatial data if it would breach Data Protection Act principles (reg 9(2)). If prejudice could be caused to national security, intellectual property rights, the course of justice and more, the authority does not have to publish the spatial data (reg 9(5)).

Reuse of public sector information

The European Union updated its directive on the reuse, without a fee, of public sector information by members of the public to promote more reuse of information created by public authorities. It is intended to make it easier for members of the public to reuse information published by public bodies.

The ICO (2013g) summed up the key features of the revised directive as including a mandatory obligation on authorities to consider reuse of information; broadening the scope to consider libraries and museums; and ensuring only marginal cost charges can be made for information.

In practice, this has few repercussions for public authorities, as the National Archives (2013, p.3) say many authorities already make their information reusable under the open government licence. But some authorities will be required to justify any charges 'in excess of marginal cost pricing'.

Access and reporting from meetings

Journalists and members of the public have had the right to access to the meetings of public bodies since the Public Bodies (Admission to Meetings) Act 1960. The powers to attend meetings and communicate information from them were boosted in 2012 after the government passed the Local Authorities (Executive Arrangements) (Access to Information) (England) Regulations 2012. These regulations (reg 4(6)) made sure that meetings are open to all and those wanting to report from them should be allowed to have reasonable facilities from which to do so.

A government press release (Department for Communities and Local Government, 2012) at the time says the changes would 'make it easier for new "social media" reporting of council executive meetings thereby opening proceedings up to internet bloggers, tweeting and hyperlocal news forums'. However, not all councils took the regulations on board, leading to a spate of cases where journalists and citizen journalists were removed from council meetings for trying to use Twitter or record proceedings.

Journalist Ted Jeory was ordered to be removed from a Tower Hamlets council meeting after complaining that the space for journalists had been intentionally given to members of the public (London Evening Standard, 2014). In Wales, where the regulations do not apply, a journalist from the Daily Post (2013) was banned from Tweeting proceedings of a council meeting as it constituted a form of broadcast.

Eventually, the government introduced more regulations to curb such occurrences. The Openness of Local Government Bodies Regulations 2014 specifically addresses the recording of decisions. The regulations say that reporting on a meeting, defined as filming, photographing, recording audio and any other means, is allowed (reg 3(6)). This can be published by any communication method, including the internet (reg 7).

Guidelines called 'Open and accountable local government' were also produced for the press and public about reporting on the meetings of public bodies. They explicitly state that all public bodies should 'adopt maximum openness and transparency' (Department for Communities and Local Government, 2014, p.7).

The Local Government Act 1972 ensures that councillors declare their interests and councils publish agendas, documents and reports, while the Local Government (Access to Information) Act 1985 allows the access to local authority meetings, reports and the documents.

Contracts Finder

The government's online Contracts Finder allows you to find and search for information about contracts the government and other agencies have made that are worth more than £10,000. It also allows searching for contracts which are scheduled to be put out to tender in the coming months.[1]

Health records

Specific provisions also allow access to medical records about an individual. These may be used to access information about yourself, or getting a source to access data to find out background. Health records are often difficult to obtain as they incorporate sensitive personal data that due to the limitations of the Data Protection Act is not able to be disclosed (this type of information is limited from disclosure under the Freedom of Information Act (s.40)). There are also confidentiality issues as there will be an inherent duty of confidence given to the documents. Personal records can generally be accessed through the use of SARs, as outlined above.

Health records can contain a large amount of detail about the individual they concern and about the organisation they are produced by. Typical details include treatments that have been received; allergies; medication; results of health tests; and personal information. Health records can also give indications about how well a hospital is performing, track the spread or risks of a disease and provide details on how well treatments are working (NHS choices, 2013a).

The Access to Health Records Act 1990 gives limited access, to some individuals, to health records of those who have died. NHS Choices (2013b) says that the health records of someone who has died will be accessible if you are a personal representative, or someone who has a claim resulting from the death. Applications can be made for GP records to the NHS area where the person died.

Court records

Court records and related documents are included in the absolute exemption of Section 32 of the Freedom of Information Act. This exemption is discussed in detail in Chapter 4. However, this does not mean that it is impossible to get information about court cases through other access regimes.

There are two main rules that give people the ability to access court information that is not about them: the Criminal Procedure Rules and the Civil Procedure Rules. Access to personal information contained within court records should be accessed by making a SAR. The rules for accessing these types of files are complex, particularly so for civil cases, and the details outlined below are only a basic guide. When making requests for information from the courts, further details should be sought.

Criminal Procedure Rules

The Criminal Procedure Rules 2014 provide a right of access for journalists and members of the public to be able to access information about court cases. The specific right is laid out in rule 5.8. It says that when the desired information about a case is accessible to the court officer, the request can be made orally. This will relate to information where trials have not yet finished, or if the verdict was less than six months ago and will often be given out over the phone. If it is more than six months ago then the request must be made in writing and also explain why the details are being requested. When appropriate to do so, under the rules, the office should give out the date of the hearing, the alleged offence and any pleas, the court's decision about bail, committal, sending or transfer of the case, whether there is an appeal, the outcome of a trial or appeal.

Applications can also be made for the identity of the prosecutor, defendant, the representatives of the parties, and the judge or magistrates. Any reporting restrictions that were in place must also be supplied to the person asking for information. The court can allow access to inspect or copy a document, or a permitted part of it, that contains information about the case.

Civil Procedure Rules

Civil Procedure Rules allow a person who is not involved in a case to have some access to details about a civil case. Rule 5.4C (Ministry of Justice, 2014) allows some access to the documents. These say that a person who was not party to proceedings can receive a statement of the case, and a judgment, where it has been made in public.

However, this only applies to cases that were filed after 2006 – separate rules apply for applying for documents that were filed prior to this date. It also says that a non-party may, with permission from the court, obtain a copy of any other documents filed by a party or communications that have happened.

Common law rights of access

Outside of the Freedom of Information Act there is an evolving right to information under common law. A judgment of the Supreme Court on an FOI request made by Dominic Kennedy, the investigations editor at *The Times*, says he may be able to access some information, exempt from FOI, under common law principles. The request concerned details of three inquiries conducted by the Charity Commission into the 'Mariam Appeal' which was launched by on-and-off MP George Galloway and related to the sanctions imposed upon Iraq following the first Gulf War.

The case passed its way through the two tribunal stages, allowed by the Act, followed by the Court of Appeal and finally reached the Supreme Court in 2014. The questions that the Supreme Court had to answer, summed up by the Panopticon (2014) blog of information law practice 11KBW, were whether the absolute FOI exemption, which covers inquiries, continued to do so after the inquiry was over, and whether Article 10 of the European Convention of Human Rights (ECHR) (Council of Europe, 1950, p.5), would infringe his rights under the Act if information was refused under the exemption. The Supreme Court ruled that the absolute exemption did in fact apply after the inquiry ended.

The ECHR, given effect in the UK through the Human Rights Act 1998, says that everyone has a right to freedom of expression as well as to receive and impart information and ideas without interference by public authority. The Supreme Court in Kennedy (Appellant) v Charity Commission (2014) UKSC 20 says, if necessary, it would have ruled that Article 10 'did not contain a freestanding right to receive information from public authorities'.

The Supreme Court says that Section 32, an absolute exemption, was not made so that information should not be disclosed, but rather its intention was to take the information away from disclosure under the Freedom of Information Act. It says that disclosure would fall within the jurisdiction of other schemes and Acts, in this case the Charities Act 2011. This meant that human rights under the Freedom of Information Act were not infringed as there may be another way to obtain the information. Although the court did not allow the disclosure and refused the appeal, it did consider common law rights to information.

The Charities Act 2011 (s.15) says that the Charity Commission has functions that include 'disseminating information' in line with the Commission's functions and objectives. This was outlined by the Kennedy case and it was decided that it would be in the public interest to disclose information about the inquiries and would be under a common law duty of openness (*Press Gazette*, 2014).

The court says that the Charity Commission had never been asked to consider disclosing the information under its general powers. They say it had only been asked under FOI, which carried no obligation to disclose the information. But if it was asked for the information in relation to its public functions then it may be a different case.

In the Kennedy appeal (p.60), the Supreme Court says:

> If the Commission had been asked to disclose under its general powers, it would have had to consider the public interest considerations for and against disclosure which were relevant to the performance of its statutory functions under the Charities Act. Its assessment of these matters would in principle have been reviewable by the court.

Lord Mance says that the Charity Commission has the power to disclose information to the public under its statutory objectives. The information could potentially be disclosed by a judicial review (Kennedy tribunal, p.28).

Kennedy (2014) says that when he is requesting information he explicitly states that he is making it under the Freedom of Information Act but also mentions common law rights to the information in the public interest. He says:

> It has affirmed that there is a common law right to information in the public interest as well as the Freedom of Information Act. The Freedom of Information Act is obviously limited so what the Supreme Court seem to be saying and what we would now say is the thing I have asked for it's not in the Freedom of Information Act, if you say it's not then that's fine, but just give it to me anyway because you're a public authority and it's in the public interest to release it.
>
> (Kennedy, 2014)

Audit documents

There is a limited right of access to documents that relate to the auditing of accounts of public bodies. The Audit Commission Act 1998 requires that public authorities make their financial accounts complete by the end of each financial year, before they are audited. Section 15 of the Audit Act allows anybody to visit the authority and inspect the documents, while the authority is being audited, although this does not apply for the accounts of a health service body. The Act says that any person interested may inspect and make copies of books, deeds, contracts, bills, vouchers and receipts.

The rights that are given by the Audit Act are backed up by the Accounts and Audit Regulations 2003. These say that the public authority shall make the accounts and documents available for public inspection for 20 working days before the date of the audit. Under the regulations (reg 16), the authority is required to declare that the documents will be available for inspection by members of the public. It has to do this at least 14 days before they are going to be available for viewing, and must state when and where they can be viewed, and the names of the auditor(s).

Chapter 3 top tips

- When requesting environmental information the authority is required to answer it under the EIR as it is exempt under the Section 39 of the Freedom of Information Act.
- All exceptions under the EIR contain a PIT that the body holding the information has to conduct if it wants to withhold what has been asked for.
- EIR requests do not have to be made in writing, they can be made verbally.
- Journalists have greater freedom to process personal data under Section 32 of the Data Protection Act 1998, as long as the personal data is collected with a view to publication.
- A public authority is required to make its accounts available to members of the public for 20 days before they are audited. During this time it will be possible to access them.
- Journalists can obtain information about themselves that a body holds by making a SAR, in writing, under the Data Protection Act.
- SARs cost up to £10 per time, although this may be up to £50 if it is for contain health- or education-related records.
- Government contracts that have been tendered out to companies can be found via the Contract Finder website.

Note

1 The Contracts Finder for England can be found at https://online.contractsfinder.businesslink.gov.uk. Welsh procurement details, Sell2Wales, can be found at www.sell2wales.gov.uk. For Public Contracts Scotland visit www.publiccontractsscotland.gov.uk and Northern Irelands' eSourcing NI can be found at https://e-sourcingni.bravosolution.co.uk (Gov.uk, 2014).

References

Access to Health Records Act 1990 (c.23). London: HMSO.
Accounts and Audit Regulations 2003 (SI 2003/53). London: HMSO.
Audit Commission Act 1998 (c.18). London: HMSO.

Baines, J., 2014. *Interview*. Interviewed by Matt Burgess *[Telephone]* 22 May 2014.

Benjamin Archer v IC and Salisbury District Council, 2007. EA/2006/0037.

Charities Act 2011 (c.25). London: HMSO.

Council of Europe, 1950. *Convention for the Protection of Human Rights and Fundamental Freedoms and Protocol*. Available at: www.echr.coe.int/Documents/Collection_Convention_1950_ENG.pdf [Accessed 10 October 2014].

Criminal Procedure Rules 2014 (SI 2014/1610 (L. 26)). London: HMSO.

Daily Post, 2013. Journalist banned from tweeting from public council meeting, 8 January. Available at: www.dailymail.co.uk/news/article-2006076/Six-fat-cat-temps-paid-1-250-PER-DAY-council-thats-slashing-hundreds-jobs.html [Accessed 17 September 2014].

Data.gov.uk, 2013. *INSPIRE*. Available at: http://data.gov.uk/location/inspire [Accessed 11 September 2014].

Data Protection Act 1998 (c.29). London: HMSO.

Department for Communities and Local Government, 2012. *Town Hall Doors Unlocked to Social Media and Bloggers*, 23 August. Available at: www.gov.uk/government/news/town-hall-doors-unlocked-to-social-media-and-bloggers [Accessed 16 September 2014].

Department for Communities and Local Government, 2014. *Open and Accountable Local Government*. Available at: www.gov.uk/government/publications/open-and-accountable-local-government-plain-english-guide [Accessed 24 September 2014].

Department for Environment Food & Rural Affairs, nd. *The INSPIRE Directive*. Available at: http://data.gov.uk/sites/default/files/Factsheet%20-%20INSPIRE%20%20Directivepdf_10.pdf [Accessed 11 September 2014].

Environmental Information Regulations 2004 (SI 2004/3391). London: HMSO.

Freedom of Information Act 2000 (c.36). London: HMSO.

Gibbons, P., 2014. *Interview*. Interviewed by Matt Burgess *[In person]* London: 22 May 2014.

Gov.uk, 2014. *Contracts Finder*. Available at: www.gov.uk/contracts-finder [Accessed 24 September 2014].

Human Rights Act 1998 (c.42). London: HMSO.

Information Commissioner's Office (ICO), 2009. *Guide to Data Protection*. Available at: http://ico.org.uk/for_organisations/data_protection/~/media/documents/library/Data_Protection/Practical_application/the_guide_to_data_protection.pdf [Accessed 16 September 2014].

Information Commissioner's Office (ICO), 2012a. *Requests Formulated in too General a Manner (Regulation 12(4)(c))*. Available at: http://ico.org.uk/for_organisations/guidance_index/~/media/documents/library/Environmental_info_reg/Detailed_specialist_guides/requests_formulated_in_too_general_a_manner_eir_guidance.ashx [Accessed 10 September 2014].

Information Commissioner's Office (ICO), 2012b. *International Relations, Defence, National Security or Public Safety (Regulation 12(5)(a))*. Available at: http://ico.org.uk/for_organisations/guidance_index/~/media/documents/library/Environmental_info_reg/Detailed_specialist_guides/eir_international_relations_defence_national_security_public_safety.ashx [Accessed 10 September 2014].

Information Commissioner's Office (ICO), 2012c. *Confidentiality of Commercial or Industrial Information (Regulation 12(5)(e))*. Available at: http://ico.

org.uk/for_organisations/guidance_index/~/media/documents/library/
Environmental_info_reg/Practical_application/eir_confidentiality_of_
commercial_or_industrial_information.ashx [Accessed 10 September 2014].

Information Commissioner's Office (ICO), 2012d. *Protection of the Environment
(Regulation 12(5)(g))*. Available at: http://ico.org.uk/for_organisations/
guidance_index/~/media/documents/library/Environmental_info_reg/Practical_
application/eir_guidance_protection_of_the_environment_regulation.ashx
[Accessed 10 September 2014].

Information Commissioner's Office (ICO), 2012e. *The INSPIRE Regulations
2009*. Available at: https://ico.org.uk/media/about-the-ico/policies-and-
procedures/2782/inspire_regulations_2009_and_the_role_of_the_ico.pdf
[Accessed 8 March 2014].

Information Commissioner's Office (ICO), 2013a. *Time Limits for Compliance
Environmental Information Regulations*. Available at: http://ico.org.uk/~/media/
documents/library/Environmental_info_reg/Detailed_specialist_guides/time-for-
compliance-eir-guidance.pdf [Accessed 8 September 2014].

Information Commissioner's Office (ICO), 2013b. *How Exceptions and the Public
Interest Test Work in the Environmental Information Regulations*. Available at:
https://ico.org.uk/media/for-organisations/documents/1629/eir_effect_of_
exceptions_and_the_public_interest_test.pdf [Accessed 8 March 2014].

Information Commissioner's Office (ICO), 2013c. *Manifestly Unreasonable Requests
(Regulation 12(4)(b))*. Available at: https://ico.org.uk/media/for-organisations/
documents/1615/manifestly-unreasonable-requests.pdf [Accessed 8 March 2014].

Information Commissioner's Office (ICO), 2013d. *Internal Communications
(Regulation 12(4)(e))*. Available at: http://ico.org.uk/for_organisations/
guidance_index/~/media/documents/library/Environmental_info_reg/Detailed_
specialist_guides/eir_internal_communications.ashx [Accessed 10 September
2014].

Information Commissioner's Office (ICO), 2013e. *Intellectual Property Rights
(Regulation 12(5)(c))*. Available at: http://ico.org.uk/for_organisations/
guidance_index/~/media/documents/library/Environmental_info_reg/Detailed_
specialist_guides/eir_intellectual_property_rights.ashx [Accessed 10 September
2014].

Information Commissioner's Office (ICO), 2013f. *Interests of the Person who
Provided the Information to the Public Authority (Regulation 12(5)(f))*. Available
at: http://ico.org.uk/for_organisations/guidance_index/~/media/documents/
library/Environmental_info_reg/Practical_application/eir_guidance_protection_
of_the_environment_regulation.ashx [Accessed 10 September 2014].

Information Commissioner's Office (ICO), 2013g. *ICO e-newsletter July 2013*.
Available at: http://web.archive.org/web/20140704043407/http://ico.org.uk/
news/e-newsletter/~/media/documents/e-newsletter-html/e-newsletter-072013.
html [Accessed 8 March 2014].

Information Commissioner's Office (ICO), 2014a. *The Guide to the
Environmental Information Regulations*. Available at: http://ico.org.uk/
for_organisations/environmental_information/~/media/documents/library/
Environmental_info_reg/Detailed_specialist_guides/guide_to_environmental_
information_regulations.pdf [Accessed 8 September 2014].

Information Commissioner's Office (ICO), 2014b. *The Course of Justice and Inquiries Exception (Regulation 12(5)(b))*. Available at: http://ico.org.uk/for_organisations/ guidance_index/~/media/documents/library/Environmental_info_reg/Detailed_ specialist_guides/course_of_justice_and_inquiries_exception_eir_guidance.pdf [Accessed 10 September 2014].

Information Commissioner's Office (ICO), 2014c. *Confidentiality of Proceedings (Regulation 12(5)(d))*. Available at: http://ico.org.uk/for_organisations/ guidance_index/~/media/documents/library/Environmental_info_reg/Detailed_ specialist_guides/eir_confidentiality_of_proceedings.pdf [Accessed 10 September 2014].

Information Commissioner's Office (ICO), 2014d. *Data Protection and Journalism: A Guide for the Media*. Available at: http://ico.org.uk/~/media/documents/library/ Data_Protection/Detailed_specialist_guides/data-protection-and-journalism- media-guidance.pdf [Accessed 18 September 2014].

Information Commissioner's Office (ICO), 2014e. *Subject Access Code of Practice*. Available at: http://ico.org.uk/for_organisations/data_protection/~/media/ documents/library/Data_Protection/Detailed_specialist_guides/subject-access- code-of-practice.PDF [Accessed 10 September 2014].

INSPIRE Regulations 2009 (SI 2009/3157). London: HMSO.

Kennedy (Appellant) v Charity Commission, 2014. UKSC 20.

Kennedy, D., 2014. *Interview*. Interviewed by Matt Burgess *[Telephone]* 28 May 2014.

Local Authorities (Executive Arrangements) (Access to Information) (England) Regulations 2012 (SI 2012/2089). London: HMSO.

Local Government Act 1972 (c.70). London: HMSO.

Local Government (Access to Information) Act 1985 (c.43). London: HMSO.

London Evening Standard, 2014. Transparency fears raised in Tower Hamlets after journalist evicted from council meeting, 11 June. Available at: www.standard. co.uk/news/london/transparency-fears-raised-in-tower-hamlets-after-journalist- evicted-from-council-meeting-9530604.html?origin=internalSearch [Accessed 15 September 2014].

Ministry of Justice (MoJ), 2014. *Part 5: Court Documents*. Available at: www.justice. gov.uk/courts/procedure-rules/civil/rules/part05#5.4C [Accessed 24 September 2014].

National Archives, 2013. *Introductory Guide to the Amended PSI Directive*. Available at: www.nationalarchives.gov.uk/documents/information-management/psi- directive-transposition-intro-guide.pdf [Accessed 18 September 2014].

NHS choices, 2013a. *Your Records*. Available at: www.nhs.uk/NHSEngland/thenhs/ records/healthrecords/Pages/overview.aspx [Accessed 24 September 2014].

NHS choices, 2013b. *Can I Access the Medical Records (Health Records) of Someone who has Died*? Available at: www.nhs.uk/chq/Pages/access-to-medical-or-health- records-of-someone-who-has-died.aspx [Accessed 24 September 2014].

Openness of Local Government Bodies Regulations 2014 (SI 2014/2095). London: HMSO.

Panopticon, 2014. FOIA's not all that: Kennedy v The Charity Commission [2014] UKSC 20, 28 March. Available at: www.panopticonblog.com/2014/03/28/ foias-not-all-that-kennedy-v-the-charity-commission-2014-uksc-20 [Accessed 17 September 2014].

Press Gazette, 2014. Times Supreme Court victory in fight to see Galloway Iraq appeal files could 'blow open' Freedom of Information Act, 26 March. Available at: www.pressgazette.co.uk/times-supreme-court-victory-fight-see-galloway-iraq-appeal-files-could-blow-open-freedom-information [Accessed 17 September 2014].

Public Bodies (Admission to Meetings) Act 1960 (c. 67). London: HMSO.

Rosenbaum, M., 2014. *Interview.* Interviewed by Matt Burgess *[In person]* London: 30 May 2014.

Chapter 4

FOI exemptions

A public authority can refuse a request on grounds that range from protecting commercial interests of companies and an individual's personal information to the need to protect national security and legal professional privilege. In total, there are 23 exemptions that can be applied to reject a request for information under the Freedom of Information Act. However, public authorities are not prevented from voluntarily giving out any information outside the provisions of the Act. If doing so, public authorities must be wary of breaching any of laws that releasing the information may infringe, such as the Data Protection Act (ICO, 2014a, p.35).

Every decision to withhold information can be challenged and done so through internal systems and later by the ICO. The exemptions are classified as 'absolute' and 'qualified' exemptions. All of the exemptions are listed below – some contain both absolute and qualified subsections.

Absolute exemptions

Section 21: information accessible by other means.
Section 23: national security.
Section 32: court records.
Section 34: parliamentary privilege.
Section 37: communications with Her Majesty, the Royal Family.
Section 40: personal information.
Section 41: information provided 'in confidence'.
Section 44: prohibitions on disclosure.

Qualified exemptions

Section 22: information intended for future publication exemption.

Section 24: national security (other than information supplied by or relating to named security organisations, where the duty to consider disclosure in the public interest does not apply).

Section 26: defence.

Section 27: international relations.

Section 28: relations within the United Kingdom.

Section 29: UK economic interests.

Section 30: investigations and proceedings conducted by public authorities.

Section 31: law enforcement.

Section 33: audit functions.

Section 35: formulation of government policy and ministerial communications.

Section 36: prejudice to effective conduct of public affairs (except information held by the House of Commons or the House of Lords).

Section 38: health and safety.

Section 39: environmental information.

Section 40: personal information relating to a third party access request.

Section 42: legal professional privilege.

Section 43: commercial interests.

Qualified and absolute exemptions

A qualified exemption requires a public authority to conduct a PIT to consider whether the public interest in not disclosing information outweighs the interest in disclosure. The Freedom of Information Act has an assumption in favour of giving out information. This was confirmed by the tribunal ruling Guardian Newspapers Ltd and Heather Brooke v IC and BBC (2007) EA/2006/0011; EA 2006/0013 (par 82) in which the minutes from a BBC governors' meeting on the day the Chairman and the Director General of the BBC resigned over the Hutton Report, were requested.

The Freedom of Information Act 2000 (s.17(3)) says the public authority must explain why 'the public interest in maintaining the exemption

outweighs the public interest in disclosing the information'. If, in a qualified exemption response, it does not provide reasons, the response should
be challenged and the authority asked to provide a response in line with
the Act.

However, when a PIT is required the authority can extend the time it has
to respond, with no maximum extension time stipulated. For more on the
PIT, see Chapter 8.

Class and prejudice-based exemptions

It is likely that many officials answering requests will think of exemptions
in two further classes: prejudice and class-based exemptions. Guidance from
the ICO (2014a, p.37) says, for the purposes of the Act, prejudice means if
that if the information was disclosed it would 'harm the interests covered
by the exemption'.

A prejudice-based exemption is likely to say the information is exempt if
it 'would, or would be likely to' cause harm to the subject of the exemption.
Section 24, Section 36(2)(b) and Section 38 use the terminology 'inhibit'
but also count as prejudice-based exemptions. The ICO's interpretation
and guidelines on the prejudice test come from the tribunal case of Oxford
City Council and Christopher Martin Hogan v IC (2006) EA/2005/0026;
EA/2005/0030. The ICO (2013a, p.5) summarises Hogan as requiring the
authority to:

* identify the 'applicable interests' within the relevant exemption;
* identify the 'nature of the prejudice';
* show that the prejudice claimed is 'real, actual or of substance';
* show that there is a 'causal link' between the disclosure and the prejudice claimed;
* decide on the 'likelihood of the occurrence of prejudice'.

The key area for challenging a PIT for a prejudice-based exemption is how
real and likely the prejudice could be. The prejudice must relate to the specific prejudice of an exemption's subsection and not the whole exemption
(ICO, 2013a, p.5). If the consequences of disclosure would be trivial or
insignificant there is no prejudice. The authority must also consider the
range of circumstances in which prejudice could occur, how often they are
likely to occur and how certain it is that the prejudice results in those circumstances (ICO, 2013a, p.6).

The prejudice test makes the authority decide whether the information
'would' or 'would be likely' to cause harm if released. In its most simple
sense, the ICO (2013a, p.8) says that 'would' equates to 'more probable
than not', a greater than 50 per cent chance of causing the prejudice.

In the Data Protection Act case of Mr Justice Munby in R (on the application of Lord) v Secretary of State for the Home Office (2003) EWHC 2073 (Admin) (cited in ICO, 2013a, p.9), it was said that the inclusion of the word 'likely' 'connotes a degree of probability that there is a very significant and weighty chance of prejudice to the identified public interests'.

An authority should, according to the ICO (2013a, p.14), see if the prejudice exists before a PIT is completed. If the exemption is not engaged by the prejudice then it cannot be relied upon. If an authority does not indicate a level of prejudice, the request should be challenged as it is not possible to conduct a proper PIT without stating the level of prejudice.

Notable decisions

The Information Tribunal case of Pauline Reith v IC and London Borough of Hammersmith and Fulham (2007) EA/2006/0058 concerned the council saying prejudice would be likely to occur despite having no evidence of its likelihood. In London Borough of Bexley and Mr Colin P. England v IC (2007) EA/2006/0060; 0066, it was decided that it was necessary to extrapolate from the evidence available to come to a conclusion about what could happen.

What comes with a refusal?

The public authority, in almost all cases, must respond to your request for information. Even if it is not going to give you the requested information, it is obliged to disclose the reasons for withholding it. The legislation places the following obligations upon authorities, under Section 17, when they refuse requests:

- Issue a refusal notice that says they are refusing the request, what the exemption is, including the subsection, and why the exemption applies to what has been asked for.
- When applying a qualified exemption and using the PIT it must give the reasons why the public interest is outweighed by the information.
- Tell you that you have a right to complain through any Internal Review procedure they have, and that you are able to complain to the IC.

However, occasionally the public authority does not need to provide all this information. This applies when it is relying on cost limits (s.12), or when saying a request is vexatious (s.14) and it isn't the first time the information has been requested.

The authorities do have to reply if they do not hold the information. FOI officer Bilal Ghafoor (2014) says it is 'unbelievably common' to receive requests from journalists for which the information is not held, which emphasises the need for requests to be properly researched before they are made.

Neither confirm nor deny

Section 1(1)(a) of the Act obligates a public body to say whether it holds the information, even if it is planning on not releasing it. When a public body wishes to use an exemption, but confirming or denying whether information is held would reveal information, the authority may be able to 'neither confirm nor deny' (NCND). This is applicable to the majority of exemptions.

The ICO (2013b, p.8) says 'it is sufficient to demonstrate that either a hypothetical confirmation or denial would engage the exemption'. This means the authority does not have to show that both confirming and denying information would engage the exemption. Those wishing to NCND that they hold information where the exemption is a qualified exemption must also conduct a PIT.

Section 12: cost compliance exceeds appropriate limit

When it applies

The cost limits section of the Act allows authorities not to comply with a request when the 'cost of compliance is estimated to exceed the appropriate limit'. The appropriate limit differs for central government bodies, legislative bodies and the armed forces, compared with other authorities such as local councils or police forces.

For central government it is £600 and for other authorities it is £450. In estimating the cost of staff time it should be calculated at £25 per hour regardless of whether the staff member dealing with the request is paid more or less than this. The fees are laid out in the Freedom of Information and Data Protection (Appropriate Limit and Fees) Regulations 2004. This means that if the request will exceed 24 hours of work for central government, and 18 hours for others, the authority does not have to comply with the request.

Working out the costs

When estimating the cost of answering a request the body cannot include every step of the process. In fact, according to the Fees Regulations (reg 4(3)), an authority is broadly only able to include four actions into its estimate:

1   Determining whether the information is held.
2   Locating the information, or a document containing it.
3   Retrieving the information, or a document containing it.
4   Extracting the information from a document containing it.

Where a request may include information that is exempt from disclosure under an exemption of the Act – for example a person's personal data – the authority can remove this information by redacting it. It cannot, however, include the time taken to do this, whether it is by hand using a black marker or digitally, in its cost estimate. The High Court appeal of South Yorkshire Police v Information Commissioner (2011) EWHC 44 (Admin) confirmed this viewpoint.

Aggregation

A public authority can claim that the estimate is exceeded is when they receive requests for which they can aggregate the costs. This is to ensure that individuals, or groups, do not bombard the authority with requests over a narrow period of time.

The Fees Regulations (reg 5) state that if requests are made by an individual or a group that appears to be acting in a pursuance of a campaign and they request the same or similar information within a period of 60 days, they can be aggregated. Each question is technically a separate request, so where there are multiple questions in a 'request' the authority can only refuse by aggregating the cost of some or all of the questions.

Calculating the cost

When a public authority is working out a cost estimate, it does not have to search for, or collect, any of the information before it can use Section 12 to not provide the information asked for. The case of Randall v Information Commissioner and Medicines and Healthcare Products Regulatory Agency (2007) EA/2006/0004, quoted in the ICO guidance (2012b, p.7), made it clear that a reasonable estimate of the costs is one that is 'sensible, realistic and supported by cogent evidence'.

The ICO (2012b, p.8) states it is good practice to give the requester arguments or evidence to help them understand the application of the exemption. A good refusal notice will usually have a breakdown of the costs in meeting the request and what could be provided under the limit (ICO, 2012a, p.8). This will also help to fulfil an authority's obligations under Section 16 of the Act, which says they have a duty to provide advice and assistance to requesters. The ICO says it is useful if a public authority goes as far in its estimate as detailing its search strategy. If a public official wishes to they can search up to the cost limit, or over it, on a voluntarily basis (ICO, 2012b, p.9).

FOI officer Bilal Ghafoor (2014) says requesters should consider whether the public body can give a 'good coherent story' when using the exemption and part of this should be an 'explanation of how they arrived at the cost limit'.

Similarly, Paul Gibbons (2013a), FOI officer, trainer and blogger, says on his FOIMan website that it could be worth a requester challenging a response if the estimate and justifications do not seem reasonable or there is no estimate given.

Section 14: vexatious or repeated requests

When it applies

A public authority does not have to comply with a request for information if the request is considered to be vexatious. By dictionary definition, to be vexatious means: 'Causing or tending to cause annoyance, frustration, or worry' (Oxford Dictionaries, nd).

This is not the case with the Freedom of Information Act. The main test case that decided what the nature of a vexatious request is was the Upper Tribunal ruling of Information Commissioner v Devon CC and Dransfield (2012) UKUT 440 (AAC). However, at the point of writing, Dransfield is being appealed to the Supreme Court.

In this case, for the definition of what constituted vexatious behaviour, the judge agreed with the previous decision in the case of Lee v Information Commissioner and King's College Cambridge (2012) EA/2012/0015; 0049; 0085, which says that 'vexatious', for the purpose of the Freedom of Information Act could be judged to mean 'manifestly unjustified, inappropriate or improper use of a formal procedure'.

The provision can only be applied to a particular request, and not the individual requester (ICO, 2013c, p.5). When considering vexatiouness, the authority can consider who the requester is, and what the motives behind the request may be. This is a break away from the vast majority of the Freedom of Information Act, which was created to be applicant and purpose blind.

In order for a public authority to be able to consider whether the burden, motive, value or, if any, harassment has been caused by the request, it will need to consider who has made the request, and potentially why they have made the request.

What can be considered as vexatious?

The legislation (s.14(1)) says an authority is not obliged to provide the information when the request is vexatious. It also states that where an authority has answered a specific request from a person then it does not have to comply with 'identical or substantially similar' requests from the same person unless a reasonable interval has passed since the last request (s.14(2)).

The tribunal, in the Dransfield case, outlined four possible ways that a request could be vexatious:

1   The burden (on the public authority and its staff).
2   The motive (of the requester).
3   The value or serious purpose (of the request).
4   Any harassment or distress (of and to staff).

It is unlikely that requests that only have weak arguments for multiple sections, or only touch upon one of them, may be considered to be vexatious. The Dransfield tribunal says the broad themes that it outlined are not meant to create a 'check-list' and vexatious interpretation is 'inherently flexible'.

The ICO (2013c, p.5) says that public authorities should not consider Section 14 in just the 'most extreme circumstances, or as a last resort'. The Information Commissioner Christopher Graham (2014) also says that he wanted more authorities to use the vexatious provisions when it is appropriate to do so: 'We, for example, have been giving advice to public authorities about being really tough with vexatious complaints.'

Notable decisions

Persistence for investigation: narrowing a request after a previous one, when in 'dogged' pursuit of an investigation, is not vexatious (Thackeray v ICO (2012) EA/2011/0082).

'Fishing request' not vexatious: the ICO (2014b) issued a DN (FS50522278) that says the continued requests of a journalist that the public authority considered to be part of 'fishing expedition' was not enough to make the request vexatious.

Disproportionate burden: an administrative burden was caused by 20 FOI requests, 73 letters and 17 postcards being sent to the authority in around two years (R H Coggins v ICO (2008) EA/2007/0130).

Re-opening resolved issues: when a complaints system has been exhausted, or an independent review has been taken over an issue to try to re-open the issue by the use of FOI, the request can considered to be vexatious (Vaithilingam Ahilathirunayagam v ICO and London Metropolitan University (2007) EA/2006/0070).

Volume of requests: an 11-page letter that asked 122 separate questions (93 were directed to one member of staff) was considered to be vexatious because of the harassment to the staff members, according to Dadswell v ICO (2012) EA/2012/0033.

Section 21: information accessible by other means

When it applies

The exemption is intended to stop authorities having to complete research for those who cannot find information they already publish or have access to via other means and laws. It is an absolute exemption and it is one of only two exemptions to which the duty to NCND does not apply (ICO, 2013d, p.3).

The Act states, at Section 21(1), that information that is 'reasonably accessible' can be exempt from disclosure. It may even be reasonably accessible if it has to be paid for (s.21(2)). Section 21(2)(b) says that for the information to be allowed to be inspected only on the property of the public authority, and be reasonably accessible, then it has to be stated as this in the publication scheme. But the model publication scheme, published by the ICO (2013e, p.3), does say that 'only in exceptional circumstances' should information be made available only by viewing in person.

The ICO (2013d, p.5) states that information should be regarded as already being in the public domain if it is accessible to the general public at the time of the request. The Ministry of Justice (2008a, p.3, p.8) simplifies the whole exemption down to 'whether information is reasonably accessible "to the applicant"'.

The ICO's (2013d, p.5) FOI Policy Knowledge Base says that information being in the public domain does not mean that the section automatically applies – an example of this may be if the requester does not have access to the internet.

Advice and assistance under the Act

A public authority's duties under Section 16 of the Act imply that they should explicitly highlight how an applicant might obtain the information they seek. Paul Gibbons (2013b) says that when Section 21 has been applied, if you feel the person answering the request has not given enough advice for you to be able to find the information, then it would be correct to highlight Section 16 of the Act to them. In particular, he points towards the decision of Ames v Information Commissioner and Cabinet Office (2008) EA/2007/0110.

In this case, which concerned the identity of those who had re-drafted the Iraq Weapons of Mass Destruction Dossier's executive summary, the Ames tribunal ruled that if there was a 'specific' piece of information on the Hutton Inquiry's 'large website', they could not be sure it was a 'legitimate' use of the exemption. The tribunal says: 'It may be different if the public authority were to provide a link or some other direct reference to where the requested information can actually be found.'

This highlighted that, if the authority wanted to successfully claim Section 21, it should have provided some assistance to the requester. This was reinforced by the tribunal decision of K v Information Commissioner (2014) EA/2014/0024, which stated that because a piece of information was in an 'obscure' location on a council's website and the council did not know it was there, Section 21 could not apply.

As the exemption, when applied, means the public authority should provide means to access the information, there is no provision for it to NCND it is held.

Notable decisions

Newcastle upon Tyne NHS Foundation Trust v Information Commissioner (2012) EA/2011/0236: if the public authority wants to claim Section 21 where the information is available by another access scheme, the other scheme must not place restrictions on the use of the information.

Ian Benson v Information Commissioner and Governing Body of the University of Bristol (2011) EA/2011/0120: information under the publication scheme is reasonably accessible.

Transport for London could not rely upon Section 21 when the requester wanted court records from a range of magistrates courts that were also held by the transport service. The ICO (2006a, p.10) in DN FS50075171 says this was not reasonably accessible, as the court service does not easily make records available to members of the public.

DN FS50104541: the Health and Safety Executive should disclose the names of those who had died at work, when an inquest had started, as it would not be reasonably accessible for the requester to visit 60 coroner's courts on a daily basis to find out the names of the deceased (ICO, 2008a, p.7).

Section 22: future publication

When it applies

The exemption is designed to allow authorities to block the release of information when it is planned to be published at a later date. The legislation says (s.22(1)(a)) that there has to be a 'view to its publication' at some point in the future. A timescale does not have to be set for its release. This only applies if the information was already held at the time of the request.

The ICO (2014c, p.2) says that if a decision of future publication is made after the request, the exemption cannot apply, and that 'publication' means that the information will be available to the general public.

In the same guidance (ICO, 2014c, p.7), the regulator makes clear that it considers it good practice for the public authority to provide a likely publication date for the material that the exemption applies to. However, it does go on to say that if it is decided that the information will not be published, it should inform the original requester and give them the option to resubmit their request for the information.

The Ministry of Justice (2008b, p.2) says material that may have been leaked, or only partially published, may still fall into the scope of the exemption.

PIT considerations

The major public interest balancing considerations for this exemption relate to whether or not sticking to the original timescale for disclosure would be in the public interest (Ministry of Justice, 2008b, p.5). In the case of the MPs' expenses, the ICO's DN FS50209662 says that the House of Commons should have disclosed the information as soon as possible (ICO, 2009a).

The Ministry of Justice (2008b, pp.5–6) outlines some factors that may be important in determining the public interest of releasing the documents early.

- The more drawn-out or uncertain the publication timescale, the less reasonable the delay.
- Any harm caused by the early release or longer timescale.
- Allowing everyone to view the publication at the same time. Is there an importance, or necessity, for the information to be released to everyone at once?
- Are there any procedures that need to be completed before publication, i.e. if it relates to a complaint allowing those directly involved to receive the information first?

Notable decisions

Under the ICO DN FS50121803 relating to files held on convicted murderers Myra Hindley, Fred West, Harold Shipman and Reggie Kay, it was found that Section 22 could not be applied to any of the information. The ICO (2009b) found that although the Home Office was planning to publish some information in the future, it could not identify what information it was going to publish. Therefore the exemption could not apply.

The ICO (2012c) says, in DN FS50425762, if some information is redacted in the process of preparation for publication, then Section 22 will no longer apply to the redacted information. It was said that this is because the authority no longer holds the information with a view to publication.

Section 23: security matters

When it applies

Section 23 of the Freedom of Information Act protects some of the most secretive, sensitive, and underscrutinised information in the UK. The security and intelligence agencies, such as MI5, MI6, Government Communications Headquarters and newly created bodies such as the National Crime Agency, are not subject to the Freedom of Information Act at all. This exemption covers information that relates to them and is held by other public authorities. The Act states (s.23(1)) that information is exempt, under the absolute exemption, 'if it was directly or indirectly supplied to the public authority by, or relates to' any of the security bodies mentioned in Section 23(3). This exemption is broad due to the term 'relates to'. The ICO (2013f, p.4) says that the exemption 'includes any information concerning or linked to the activities of a security body'.

In the words of the tribunal, in Dowling v Information Commissioner and Police Service for Northern Ireland (2012) EA/2011/0118, the exemption is 'quite regardless of sensitivity or importance or perceptions of the public interest'.

Under Section 23(5) the public authority can decide to NCND the information is held. If a government minister decides that the exemption should be applied, he or she can issue a certificate saying it is engaged. A certificate issued under Section 23(2) acts as conclusive proof that the information is covered by the exemption. Where a certificate has been issued under the exemption, it is possible it can be appealed at a tribunal stage.

Notable decisions

It was ruled that there should be a broad interpretation of Section 23(1) but it should be subject to a remoteness test to see whether the information requested is so remote from the security services that the exemption cannot apply. This was decided in All Party Parliamentary Group on Extraordinary Rendition v Information Commissioner and FCO (2012) EA/2011/0049–0051.

Section 24: national security

When it applies

The exemption was designed to protect the UK, or those living in the country, from a national security threat. The Act says if the information does not fall within the Section 23 exemption and it is needed for 'safeguarding national security' (s.24(1)), the exemption can apply.

However, unlike its closely related exemption, it is a qualified exemption and subject to a PIT. In the Act there is no definition of what national security is. The ICO, in the tribunal case of Norman Baker v Information Commissioner and Cabinet Office (2007) EA/2006/0045, relies on the House of Lords case, Secretary of State for the Home Department v Rehman (2001) UKHL 47. Here, the former reiterates a meaning of national security:

- The protection of democracy, legal and constitutional systems of the state.
- If security would be indirectly affected by the action of a foreign state.

- Reciprocal cooperation between the UK and other states in combating international terrorism.
- Not limited to actions of an individual, which are targeted at the UK, or systems.

The exemption can be used by any public authority. An ICO (2011a) DN says West Yorkshire Fire and Rescue Service was right to apply the exemption on the grounds that its headquarters, which is used for coordination during national incidents, could be infiltrated if its vehicles were able to be cloned.

PIT considerations

In balancing the PIT there are a number of factors that will always come into play, but ultimately each individual case will be judged on its merits. The ability to combine the information that could be dangerous to national security with other information could create a risk, which would not favour disclosure. In Peter Burt v Information Commissioner and Ministry of Defence (2011) EA/2011/0004 20, it was decided that technical information could be combined with details to create a nuclear device.

The public interest in withholding the information is significantly strengthened by the level of damage that could be caused. ICO (2012d, p.9) guidance sums potential harm arguments as follows:

> The consequences of a successful terrorist attack on a plane were so great that even if there was only a low risk that disclosing the Information would aid such an attack, there was a very strong public interest in withholding the information.

Therefore significant consequences combined with almost any level of risk will increase the likelihood of the information not being disclosed. But as the Ministry of Justice (2012a) makes clear, the public authority must be able to 'identify an undesirable effect' that could happen and may damage national security. This was also pertinent in the ICO's (2009c) DN FS50178276 which concerned a request to the Metropolitan Police for information on a terrorist plot to attack London.

Certificate

As with Section 23, a government minister is able to issue a ministerial certificate (under Section 24(3)) to say the information is conclusively covered by the national security exemption, either to disclose the information, or to confirm whether the information is held. But the Ministry of Justice (2012a, p.7) says that the ministerial certificate does not make the exemption absolute. There is still a duty to conduct a PIT before deciding whether to withhold the information. Where a certificate is issued under Section 24, it is possible for the applicant or the ICO to appeal to the tribunal.

Mutuality

Sections 24(2) and 23(5), which both give the ability to NCND, can be used together. But Section 23(1) and Section 24(1) cannot be used for the same piece of information.

Notable decisions

In DN FS50512927, the ICO (2014d) says Section 24 may be used for what seems like harmless information on its own, but when combined with more information could assist terrorist or individuals.

Transport for London was told to disclose information on the speed limits of trains on the Victoria Underground Line as Section 24 did not apply. The ICO (2012e) says, in DN FS50421919, that the speed limits would not increase in the likelihood of a terrorist attack on the line, as there was already information in the public domain that would allow them to identify the location and movements of the trains.

Section 25: certificates under Sections 23 and 24

This part of the Act allows ministerial certificates to be issued under the security exemptions.

Section 26: defence

When it applies

Information can be kept under wraps using Section 26(1) if its disclosure would, or would be likely to, prejudice the defence of the British Islands (or its colonies) or the capability, effectiveness or security of any relevant forces. The forces are defined, in Section 26(2), as the armed forces of the Crown and any forces working with them.

Guidance published by the ICO (2006b, p.1) says the exemption comes down to whether disclosure 'would assist or be likely to assist an enemy or potential enemy'. The Ministry of Justice (2008c, p.3) describes information as, potentially, falling within the exemption as being related to size, shape, readiness and training of the armed forces; the deployment of forces; weapons; future military plans; general capability; and defence policy and strategy.

The ICO (2006b, p.2) says that the exemption is for information that could cause prejudice to 'defence matters'. If a document is marked as classified, or top secret, or another security rating, this does not mean it can automatically be withheld (ICO, 2006b, p.4).

PIT considerations

In cases where a public authority wants to apply Section 26, the Ministry of Justice (2008c, p.7) says that the public interest will be strong when it comes to information which will help to 'inform debate and improve public understanding'. Examples it gives that may be in the public interest to disclose are issues relating to the safety of military personnel or loss of life, safety to civilians, the use of land or environment impact of military activity, procurement and the use of public funds (MoJ, 2008c, pp.7–8).

Other factors that may be in favour of disclosure, put forward by the ICO (2006b, p.5), can include more accountability and those related to equipment improvement. The Information Tribunal of Chris Cole v IC and Ministry of Defence (2013) EA/2013/0042; 0043 says that the public interest in withholding information under Section 26 is 'exceptionally weighty' and there would need to be 'significant' factors to disclose information.

Notable decisions

Section 26 was not applied when a ministerial direction was issued about the order of 20 Hawk jet trained aircraft. DN FS50093000 says that it did not apply as the exemption relates more to the matters of defence and physical security (ICO, 2008b, p.6).

The status of weapons in development is likely to be withheld under Section 26(3), which allows the provision to neither confirm nor deny that information is held. The Ministry of Defence withheld the development status of 'direct energy' weapons. The authority told the ICO (2013g, p.4), DN FS50498917, that although knowledge of the scheme to develop the weapons was in the public domain, it would be prejudicial to confirm its progress.

Section 27: international relations

When it applies

The UK's dealings with other countries around the world are protected by the exemption for international relations. Information can be exempt under the Freedom of Information Act (s.27(1)) if it would, or would be likely to, prejudice:

- relations between the UK and any other state (s.27(1)(a));
- relations between the UK and any international organisation or international court (s.27(1)(b));

- the interests of the UK abroad (s.27(1)(c));
- the promotion or protection by the UK of its interests abroad (s.27(1)(d)).

Requested information can also be exempt from disclosure, under Section 27(2), if it is confidential information from a non-UK state, international organisation or international court. There is also the option for the public authority to NCND that it holds the information (s.27(4)).

'Relatively innocuous' information about a state that it may not want the UK to publish will not be covered by the exemption, the ICO's (2008c) DN FS50140872 against the Cabinet Office says. The age of the information also plays a role if disclosure is likely to prejudice the relationships between the UK and others.

DN FS50134744 (ICO, 2008d, p.4) says that certain information should be disclosed when the 'information pertains to international issues which are no longer live or affecting United Kingdom relations with other states'.

PIT considerations

The Ministry of Justice (2008d, p.10) says that in many cases the public interest is likely to be strong in maintaining the exemption. The Information Tribunal made it clear that, in respect to Section 27, a 'one process fits all' approach is not appropriate to the PIT in the Freedom of Information Act. It also says a proportionate approach must be taken (All Party Parliamentary Group on Extraordinary Rendition v Information Commissioner and FCO (2013) UKUT 560 (AAC)).

When balancing the public interest, the authority may consider if disclosure would:

- be against international laws;
- undermine the UK's reputation for honouring commitments;
- have an adverse effect of information sharing in the future;
- cause a negative reaction from the other party;
- be objected to by the other party.

(ICO, 2006c)

Notable decisions

Which world leaders and heads of state the Prime Minister has on his Christmas card list was ruled not to fall under Section 27 as the level of prejudice by revealing them would not be strong enough. The ICO (2007a, p.13, 14) says the exemption was not engaged in DN FS50080115.

APG v Information Commissioner and Ministry of Defence (2011) UKUT 153 (AAC): applications of Section 27 were found to be unconvincing 'bearing in mind what the text actually says and what was already in the public domain' on allegations against US forces and the process of review that was being undertaken by the UK government.

Section 28: relations within the UK

When it applies?

As with the exemption to protect the UK's interests abroad, there is an exemption to protect internal relations. Information may be exempt when the public interest in keeping it secret outweighs the need for disclosure, and it would, or would be likely to, prejudice relations between any administration in the UK (s.28(1)). This includes the UK government and the Scottish Administration. As the exemption relates to administrations in the UK, it does not apply to local authorities.

If matters would be prejudiced by saying if the information is held, or not held, then the authorities have the right to NCND they hold the information under Section 28(3). Examples of information that may fall into the exemption's scope, according to the ICO (2008e, p.4), include:

- a critical report about an administration that had not had the chance to see it and make representations;
- comments within the UK government on a devolved administration's policy proposal or legislation;
- information on another administration's spending plans or proposed policies.

The main grounds for a public authority relying on the exemption will be if releasing the information will compromise an administration's negotiating position, or the formulation of policy towards other administrations, or that it would breach memorandums of understanding (ICO, 2008e, p.6).

PIT considerations

The ICO's guidance (2008e, p.4) says 'mere political embarrassment' should not be taken into account. The Ministry of Justice (2008e, p.9) gives these examples of cases where the information is more likely, under the PIT, to favour disclosure:

- Information that helps people understand devolution.
- Information that would explain how decisions were taken.
- Details of negotiations where enough time has passed so that they are not sensitive.
- Where the administration, which provided the information, would have disclosed it anyway.

Notable decisions

Information created 15 years prior to the particular request should be disclosed as the political climate had considerably changed and as such there would not be a prejudicial impact today, says DN FS50121252 (ICO, 2008f). The view was reinforced by DN FS50347714, which says that documents regarding devolution policy would not mean the exemption could be used as they were created 12–13 years before the request. The ICO (2011b, p.10) says the knowledge of the policy decisions were known as devolution occurred. As such if the policies are not live, they are less likely to cause prejudice.

Section 29: the economy

When it applies

This exemption is intended to protect the economy of the UK and ensure it is not damaged, or could potentially be damaged, by the release of information that may be sensitive or affect trade deals. It applies, under Section 29(1), when a disclosure of information would, or would be likely to, prejudice the economic interests of the UK or part of the UK (s.29(1)(a)), or prejudice the financial interests of any administration in the United Kingdom (s.29(1) (b)). The authority, or administration, does not need to confirm or deny that information is held when doing so would prejudice either of the above sections (s.29(2)).

Information can be withheld if it would have a prejudicial impact on an individual company, where their performance has a major impact on a local or national economy (ICO, 2008g, p.10). For example, in the case of an agreement between airline operator Ryanair and Derry City Council about flights between Derry and London, the Information Tribunal found that the exemption would be engaged, because the airport they operated from contributed significantly to the regional economy. However, the exemption could not be maintained due to an overwhelming public interest in the case (Derry City Council v IC (2006) EA/2006/0014).

PIT considerations

The Ministry of Justice says that the following general areas may have an effect on the balancing of the PIT:

- where disclosure could pre-empt pending decisions on taxation, etc.;
- where selective disclosure could undermine financial markets and their transparency requirements of financial data simultaneously to the whole market;
- where information has been obtained from confidential sources;
- when information contains assessments of the viability of an institution or the economy's viability.

(Ministry of Justice, nda, p.5)

Notable decisions

DN FS50464968 stated that the combination of an unknown high-profile individual's personal opinion and some of the information being in the public domain would not be enough for the exemption to be engaged (ICO, 2013h, p.18).

The ICO (2008h, p.5) says, in DN FS50142678, that just because data was inaccurate and may be misleading it does not mean the exemption can be engaged. It was also considered that the information was more than 20 years old, it still may re-open debate without prejudicing economic interests.

Section 30: investigations and proceedings

When it applies

The exemption, which is complicated and detailed, was designed by politicians to protect ongoing investigations and proceedings, to allow them to run their course and bring about the correct decision. Broadly the exemption is split into two different areas. Section 30(1) allows information to be exempt if it has been held, at any time, for the purpose of an investigation, while Section 30(2) covers information the authority has obtained from confidential sources, for the purpose of investigating.

As with almost all of the exemptions in the Act, Section 30(3) contains the provision to NCND that the information is held. The tribunal of Toms v Information Commissioner (2006) EA/2005/0027 says that the information must be held for a specific or particular investigation. The tribunal says it would not appear to relate to the manner or procedure that 'investigations in general are, or should be, conducted' (par 6).

Sections 30 and 31 cannot be applied to the same information and it is wrong for an authority to do so (ICO, 2013i, p.2).

PIT considerations

When an investigation is ongoing, the ICO (2013i, p.19) says that there will always be a strong public interest in maintaining the exemption. If a case has not been solved by authorities and there is a chance the case will be re-opened, there will still be a public interest in not prejudicing any investigations, the ICO (2013i, p.19) says.

The Ministry of Justice (2008f, p.12) states the following factors may contribute to the balancing test:

- If disclosure would increase, or decrease, the chances of prosecution, charges or arrests.
- Increase or decrease the chance of a fair trial.
- Be fair to those who the investigation has involved.
- Improve or decrease the gathering of intelligence from confidential sources.
- Be useful or unhelpful to ongoing or upcoming proceedings.
- Further the interests of justice with the participation of victims, information, etc. and protect or endanger them.

Notable decisions

Following revelations that undercover police used the identities of dead children in their work, a request was made for the ages of the children whose identities were used. The ICO, in DN FS50530384, found that while the exemption was engaged there was a greater public interest. The requester made the argument that revealing the age number (e.g. 4 years old) of any children whose identity was not used by the officers could be a 'significant relief' to any parents who may have had a child that age and been that suspicious their identity was used (ICO, 2014d, p.18).

Information on the overall cost of expenditure on police informants could be disclosed due to the public interest in doing so, and the accountability factors that publishing the information would bring (ICO, 2009d, p.9).

The ICO (2014f, p.6) says, in DN FS50518770 about a trading standards investigation into an Asda supermarket selling products containing horse meat, that the information should be disclosed. There would be no trial by media as the investigation was closed and no safe space for judicial proceedings was necessary.

A draft copy of the Newton Report, detailing large-scale corruption within South Yorkshire, was ordered to be disclosed by the ICO (2013j, p.7) due to the 'scale of wrongdoing exposed', despite the fact that the draft contained much of the same information as the final published report. The exemption could not apply when the information held could only be used for bringing a private prosecution (ICO, 2010a, p.12).

Section 31: law enforcement

When it applies

The exemption is closely linked to Section 30, which relates to investigations, but they cannot be used together. Authorities are told to consider Section 30 initially. Information will fall into the range of the exemption if its disclosure would, or would be likely to, prejudice any of nine wide areas.

- The prevention and detection of crime.
- Apprehension or prosecution.
- Administration of justice.
- Assessment or collection of tax (or similar impositions).
- Immigration controls.
- Maintenance of security and order in prisons (or similar institutions).
- The exercise of a public authority of duties listed in Section 31(2).
- Civil proceedings falling within Section 31(2).
- An inquiry, rising from an investigation, under the Fatal Accidents and Sudden Deaths Inquiries (Scotland) Act 1976 or another authority with the same powers.

(s.31(1))

PIT considerations

The PIT will see a strong interest in not disclosing information when it is likely to prejudice or make law enforcement less effective. However, when it makes processes more transparent to members of the public, then there will be a greater case for disclosure.

The Ministry of Justice (ndb, p.5) gives a long list of things that should be considered when an authority conducts a PIT:

- Effects of crime on a person. If an operation is compromised where the target of surveillance could be suspected of a series of violent assaults.
- Effects of crime on society. Plans to tackle crime in a particular area may encourage those who are intending to commit them to do so in a different area in a bid to avoid being caught.
- Effects of crime on the economy. It may be against the public interest to disclose strategies against those who fail to pay fines as it could encourage others to do the same.

Notable decisions

In DN FS50122063 (2007b, pp.9–10), the number of drug seizures at particular ports was refused, as responding would mean setting a precedent, and if a longer term pattern was exposed, it would allow criminals to identify where to try to smuggle drugs into the country.

Similarly, Decision Notice FS50089784 (ICO, 2006g) stated that Her Majesty's Revenue & Customs (HMRC) could withhold information into a company's tax affairs as it would prejudice current investigations and some of the information would reveal processes, which would make it harder to investigate cases in the future.

The tribunal of WS v Information Commissioner and North Lancashire PCT (2013) UKUT 181 (AAC) defines how the exemption interacts with Section 30. The authority that will be prejudiced should provide details of how this would occur.

Disclosure of Royal Mail statistics on mail thefts from private cars would not be prejudicial to the levels of crime as details of the practices were already in the public domain (ICO, 2007c).

A request for the number of authorised covert surveillances in prisons across the UK on one particular day did not warrant the information being withheld, the ICO (2014g) says. This is because it was worded as 'snapshot of a moment in time', rather than the bigger picture, or focused on one particular prison or area.

Section 32: court records

When it applies

Information relating to court records and their proceedings are heavily guarded by the Act. The exemption is absolute. If the information falls into the areas set out by the legislation it can be withheld.

Information is exempt if it is held in any document filed or placed in the custody of a court for its proceedings (s.32(1)(a)). Under Section 32(1)(b), any document served upon, or by, a public authority for the purposes of proceedings is exempt, as is any document created by the court of a member of the court administration's staff when it is for the purposes of proceedings in a particular case or matter (s.23(1)(c)).

However, it is not just courts that can apply the absolute exemption. The legislation, at Section 32(2), states that information is exempt if it is held by a public authority, if it is in a document looked after by someone, and for the purpose of conducting an inquiry or arbitration. Documents created by a person for the purposes of an inquiry or arbitration are also exempt. The authority is able to NCND (s.32(3)). For the purposes of the Freedom of Information Act, a 'court' also includes any tribunal, inquest, post-mortem examinations and more (s.30(4)).

The type of documents that can be considered to fall under the exemption are vast in their number. Witness statements, correspondence from the courts, cost schedules, court application notices, skeleton arguments and miscellaneous documents in court use were all confirmed to be included as being exempt by the tribunal in Ganesh Sittampalam v Information Commissioner and Crown Prosecution Service (2014) EA/2014/0001.

However, transcripts of court proceedings do not fall within the exemption. The following tribunal says they were not exempt 'not because the person recording proceedings is employed by an outside agency but because he is not the judge' (Alistair Mitchell v IC (2005) EA/2005/0002).

General information that may be useful for journalists, which surrounds the performance or the courts and the types of cases heard, is unlikely to fall under the exemption. Wadham *et al.* (2013, p.99) say this includes 'disclosure of a statistical analysis of conviction rates for particular offences in particular courts'.

The Civil and Criminal Procedure Rules give some right of access to court information. These and more are discussed in Chapter 3.

Notable decisions

The exemption continues to apply to documents related to proceedings after they have finished and there is no chance of an appeal (Kennedy (Appellant) v Charity Commission (2014) UKSC 20 (par 34)).

Where an inquiry has not started, the authority cannot claim that the exemption covers the information, says DN FS50103691 (ICO, 2007d).

Section 33: audit functions

When it applies

The general principle behind the exemption is to protect auditing bodies and allow their functions to be completed effectively. The Act (s.31(2)) states information held is exempt if its disclosure would, or would be likely to, prejudice an authority's audit functions.

It applies to authorities that have functions in relation to the audit of accounts of public authorities (s.33(1)(a)) or those that have functions relating to the examination of the economy, efficiency and effectiveness where other authorities use their resources. Wadham *et al.* (2013, p.144) say that the most obvious authorities the exemption will apply to are the National Audit Office, the Audit Commission and the Office of Central Government Commerce. Authorities have the ability, under Section 33(3), to NCND.

PIT considerations

General public interest arguments for disclosure, the ICO (2013k, p.9) says, include:

- furthering public understanding in decisions made by public bodies;
- improving public participation in debates;
- promoting accountability and transparency in relation to decision-making;
- promoting accountability and transparency in the use of public funds by public bodies.

However, in one case, the ICO (2013k, p.7) says where a final audit report is not published, experience has shown that reports benefit from the 'frankness and candour' of the advice.

Notable decisions

Auditing does not have to be the primary function of the authority affected, the ICO (2006c) says in DN FS50070878. School inspections fall under the scope of the exemption, as decided in the tribunal case of OFSTED v Information Commissioner (2012) EA/2009/0121.

Section 34: parliamentary privilege

When it applies

The concept of Parliamentary Privilege grants legal immunity to members of the House of Commons and House of Lords, which allows elected officials to speak freely without the fear of defamation action occurring from their appearances in the Houses (HM Government, 2012). Information is exempt if it is needed for the purposes of avoiding an infringement of the privileges of Parliament (s.34(1)). It is an absolute exemption and the authorities can NCND, under (s.34(2)).

The Ministry of Justice (2008g, p.3) points out that the House of Commons and the House of Lords are included as public authorities for the purpose of FOI but individual Members of Parliament, such as MPs and Lords, are not. The ICO (2013l, p.4) says that for the purposes of the FOI, the key part of Parliamentary Privilege is to allow it to control publication.

If some information has already been published and is in the public domain, then disclosure is less likely to infringe privilege (ICO, 2013l, p.9). The ICO (2013l, p.7) also says exemption can also be relevant to other public authorities outside of the House of Commons and the House of Lords that hold information that relates to parliamentary proceedings.

Section 35: formulation of government policy

When it applies

The exemption is designed to allow government officials the ability to air their views in private and experiment with policy decisions before they are made public. Arguments often relate to providing officials with a 'safe space' to discuss policies and also avoiding a 'chilling effect' where they will be less likely to be honest or discuss controversial options if they know their views are going to be disclosed.

The ICO (2013m) says the reasoning behind the exemption is to 'protect good government', while the Ministry of Justice (2012b) concludes that it is designed to ensure there is a 'safe space' to allow policy to be formed and developed, as well as government decision-making.

Information can be covered by four broad limbs of the exemption: if it relates to the formulation of government policy (s.35(1)(a)), ministerial communications (s.35(1)(b)), advice of the Law Officers (s.35(1)(c)) or the operation of any ministerial private office (s.35(1)(d)).

Once a decision on government policy has been taken, statistical information used to provide background to the decision cannot be exempt from the Act when it relates to the formulation (s.35(2)(a)), or ministerial communications (s.35(2)(b)). Government departments can NCND using Section 35(3).

As with other parts of the Freedom of Information Act, the term 'relates to' can be interpreted as being very broad in its scope. For Section 35, this has the impact of, depending on the circumstances, meaning a whole document may be covered if a significant element relates to the formulation of government policy (ICO, 2013m, p.6).

Under Section 35(1)(a), the development or formulation of government policy can include, but is not limited to:

- White Papers, bills and the legislative process;
- initiatives to review and improve existing policies;
- ministerial speeches;
- press releases;
- responding to unexpected events;
- responding to questions put to ministers;
- unusually sensitive or high-profile operational decisions.

(ICO, 2013m, p.6)

If someone who is not a minister takes the final decision on a policy, it means the decision itself will not be a government policy, the ICO (2013m, p.8) says.

PIT considerations

The Ministry of Justice (2012b) says the PIT for Section 35 is 'particularly complex'. However, the department does suggest some public interest considerations, which, if argued well, could help prompt disclosure:

- Increasing trust in the government by increasing transparency.
- Increasing public participation in policy-making due to a greater knowledge of the way government works.
- Allowing the assessment of the quality of advice being given to ministers and their decisions following this.
- The greater impact on the country or public spending will lead to an increased public interest in the way that policy is formed.

(Ministry of Justice, 2012b, p.14)

Safe space, chilling effect and collective responsibility

There are three main issues when it comes to the practical application of Section 35: allowing a safe space; minimising any potential chilling effect; and protecting the convention of the collective responsibility of the government. Each of these are examined below.

The ICO (2013m, pp.24, 48) accepts that the government needs to have a space where it can 'develop ideas, debate lives issues and reach decisions away from external interference and distraction'. The ICO also says the safe space may be needed for a short time after a major policy is finalised. The exemption is intended to preserve this space by not allowing ministers' communications, thoughts or thinking behind policies to be exposed. Politicians often refer to the chilling effect.

At times it has been argued that disclosure could reduce the effectiveness of government and stop officials taking accurate notes of meetings due to fears of them being disclosed. The tribunal of Department for Business, Enterprise and Regulatory Reform v Information Commissioner and Friends of the Earth (2008) EA/2007/0072 says:

> However, we consider it is unlikely that notes would cease to be taken or that they would become substantially less informative. Indeed the prospect of disclosure might have the beneficial effect of introducing a certain degree of rigour in drawing up notes.

The collective responsibility of Cabinet Ministers is a convention that they all publicly support the decisions of the government. The principle developed through a growing level of national politics during the eighteenth and nineteenth centuries so that a 'united' government could be presented to the country (House of Commons Library, 2004, p.5).

The ICO (2013m, p.30) says that there is a 'substantial' public interest in keeping collective responsibility, while the government has significant issues with releasing the minutes from Cabinet meetings. For example, even when the ICO and an Information Tribunal says it was in the public interest to release minutes from the Cabinet over the UK going to war in Iraq, these were blocked by the use of the ministerial veto (*BBC News*, 2009).

Notable decisions

Cabinet Office v Information Commissioner (2010) EA/2010/0031, which concerned Cabinet minutes from 1986, established the general principles that disclosure within 30 years will rarely be ordered (although the decrease in the 30-year rule, to 20, will have an impact). In Department of Education and Skills v Information Commissioner and the *Evening Standard* (2007) EA/2006/0006, the tribunal decided that the whole document was covered if the meeting or discussion of the topic was covered, as a whole, with the formulation and development of policy. The Education and Skills tribunal also says that a statement from Parliament announcing the policy will usually end the process of formulation.

The ICO (2013n, p.13) DN FS50451254 says emails about a press release on PIP breast implants were exempt under the Act as they related to a response that constituted the formulation or development of government policy. When the Act is interpreted literally, 'it covers information that cannot possible be confidential' as the scope of Section 35 is 'very wide' (Office of Government Commerce v Information Commissioner (Rev 1) (2008) EWHC 737 (Admin)).

The tribunal in O'Brien v Information Commissioner and Department for Business, Enterprise and Regulatory Reform (2008) EA/2008/0011 says that information created after a policy was finalised can still be covered if it refers to formulation or development. Scotland Office v Information Commissioner (2008) EA/2007/0070 ruled that communications from a private secretary on behalf of a minister, to another minister, are covered by the exemption. Department for Culture, Media and Sport v Information Commissioner (2010) EA/2009/0038 says that drafts of ministerial communications, even if they are never sent, can be exempt.

Section 36: prejudice to the effective conduct of public affairs

When it applies

FOI officer Paul Gibbons (2014) has described it as an exemption that can sometimes be used by FOI officers when they may not be sure what other exemption to apply. The exemption is closely linked to Section 35. Information is covered by the exemption if when disclosed it would, or would be likely to prejudice the concept of collective responsibility (s.36(2)(a)(i)), or the lead bodies of other administrations. It is also exempt if it would, or would be likely to, inhibit the free and frank provision of advice (s.36(2)(b)(i)), or the free and frank exchange of views for discussion (s.36(2)(b)(ii)). Additionally, this could be applied if it would, or would be likely to, prejudice the effective conduct of public affairs (s.36(2)(c)).

However, to withhold the information, the above must be in the 'reasonable opinion of a qualified person'. The exemption can apply when it is not exempt as part of Section 35 but does not apply if the information is more than 20 years old (Wadham *et al.*, 2013, p.153). The exemption has elements that fall into the scope of a qualified exemption and in part it acts as an absolute exemption. In most cases, a PIT must be considered by the authority.

For statistical information that has been requested, the opinion of the qualified person does not need to be consulted (s.35(4)). The authority has the option to NCND (s.36(3)).

Who is the qualified person?

Who the qualified person is depends on which public authority is answering the request. The Ministry of Justice (2008h, p.3) says the qualified person in a central government department must be a minister or, if the information is held by a non-ministerial organisation, the person in charge.

If a qualified person is not consulted, or the opinion is provided by the wrong person, the exemption cannot be used, as found in the tribunal decision of Salmon v Information Commissioner and King's College Cambridge (2008) EA/2007/0135, in which the university college had no authorised qualified person when the request was made (p.5). The authority cannot pick who is the qualified person themselves. A list of who would be the qualified person is included in the Act, although if the body is not listed the person will usually be nominated by a minister.

The qualified person does not have to go through all of the case's details and collect evidence of why the exemption should be applied; this can be done by an FOI officer or other member of staff. The qualified person, however, should know the details and have arrived at that opinion before signing it off (MoJ, 2008h, p.10).

Reasonable opinion

The opinion provided by the qualified person has to be 'reasonable' – this is based on the dictionary definition of the word. The ICO (2013o, p.7) says that while the opinion does not have to be the only reasonable opinion that could be held on the subject, the significance lies in whether it is reasonable, or realistic, for someone in the decision-making position.

It is important that the authority makes a record of the opinion being reached. The tribunal of University of Central Lancashire v Information Commissioner and David Colquhoun (2009) EA/2009/0034 says 'no set formula is required, just a simple clear record of the process' of the opinion making. The University of Central Lancashire tribunal also says that the reasonable opinion does not have to be one that the tribunal, and by default the requester, agrees with as long as it is 'based on sound argument and evidence'.

It also said that, in this particular case, they did not find the argument to be reasonable as it was produced without much consideration and 'far short' of the 'careful assessment and investigation' that Section 36 requires. This opinion has to be one that is restricted to prejudice alone – it cannot involve the PIT – and the person who is making the decision must be aware of all the facts, although they do not have see the information themselves (Wadham *et al.*, 2013, p.153).

PIT considerations

The general points that fall in favour of disclosure are made clear by the Ministry of Justice (2008h, p.13):

- There may be more trust of politicians if the policy-making process is open for all to see.
- A public knowledge of arguments relating to a debate will improve the quality of those arguments being made.
- Open policy-making can result in better policy formulation, as more views can be sought.
- To demonstrate to the public that ministers are adhering to the regulatory codes.
- If the information would expose government wrongdoing.
- To demonstrate if any wrongdoing had been dealt with.
- Public debate could be informed by disclosure and increase the general understanding of an issue by the public.

Notable decisions

The ICO's (2011c) DN FS50297517 stated that as information was statistical, the authority did not have to get the reasonable opinion of the qualified person. The ICO's (2010b, p.15) DN FS50209659 says releasing notes of a meeting involving politicians and the BBC would mean future discussions would be less candid.

Section 37: communications with Her Majesty, etc. and honours

When it applies

This exemption allows those who have the highest status in the United Kingdom, were not elected to their position and cost the taxpayer an increasing amount, to be completely unaccountable to the people they represent (*Independent*, 2014). The royal exemption is controversial and involves one important battle, which has been ongoing for almost the entire duration of the Act, to release information about the lobbying of those with unelected power. This has only been possible as when the original request was made, the exemption was subject to the PIT. Now the exemption is an absolute one when the information relates to the monarch and two heirs.

It allows communications with the sovereign (s.37(1)(a)), the heir (s.37(1)(aa)), someone who has acceded to the throne or become heir to or second in line to the throne (s.37(1)(ab)) and communications with members of the Royal Family (s.37(1)(ac)) or Royal Household (s.37(1)(ad)) to be covered by the exemption. Information relating to information by the Crown to any honour or dignity (s.37(1)(b)) is also exempt unless disclosure is in the public interest. Section 37(2) allows the authority to NCND.

Section 38: health and safety

When it applies

The exemption was created to protect the safety of people, in terms of both physical and mental health considerations. The latter can cause authorities to take some time to carefully consider the potential unseen implications of disclosure. To keep information under wraps, the public authority has to find that it would, or would be likely to, endanger (prejudice) the physical or mental health of any person (s.38(1)(a)), or endanger the safety of an individual (s.37(1)(b)). The authority may rely on both parts of the exemption at once.

Some examples of information that may be covered by the exemption include plans or policies relating to accommodation of individuals, negotiations with kidnappers and relating to national infrastructure. Health and safety issues can also be applied where there is an increased risk of a physical attack (Wadham *et al.*, 2013, p.159).

The ICO (2006e, p.2) says mental health issues may be more difficult for an authority to judge but an authority should not equate a danger to mental health with a risk of distress. The ICO considers that endangerment to mental health implies that if the information is released it will 'exacerbate an existing mental illness or psychological disorder'. A public authority can NCND under Section 37(2).

PIT considerations

There will never be public interest in putting a person in danger. So when a public authority is considering the PIT, the ICO says the following should be considered:

- How much of a risk is involved and if it could be reduced, or managed.
- The nature and seriousness of any danger, or risk, caused by disclosure.
- If disclosure would help to protect the health and safety of others.
- If disclosure could be avoided, or managed.
- If disclosure would reduce the potential danger to people by making them more informed.
- If keeping the information a secret could give the impression that there is something to hide from the public.
- If disclosing may increase the trust in information supplied by departments with health responsibilities.
- If the release of incomplete information could mislead people and lead them to act against their own interests.

(ICO, 2006e, pp.4–5)

Notable decisions

Geographical telephone number information could not be given out by NHS Direct, a tribunal ruled, as it would have the potential for individuals to be left 'hanging' on the phone and not receive health advice that they could be put at risk without (Derrick Lawton v IC and NHS Direct (2008) EA/2007/0081).

As TV licensing officials have a duty to identify themselves, senior officials could not remain anonymous under FOI due to a fear for their safety, says DN FS50296349 (ICO, 2011d). The naming approach was reinforced in Decision Notice FS50207235, where names of parliamentary pass holders were requested. The ICO (2011e) says because some names were already published, there could not be a health and safety argument for those who did not have their details published.

Section 39: environmental information

When it applies

This exemption is designed to exclude all environmental information from the scope of the Freedom of Information Act. Instead of making it unattainable for the requester, it is available under the EIR 2004. Wadham *et al.* (2013, p.161) say that the exemption is not designed to prevent individuals from accessing environmental information, but is merely a 'gateway' to allow members of the public to access the EIR regime. EIR is discussed further in Chapter 3.

Section 40: personal information

When it applies

This is one of the most complicated exemptions due to its heavy entwine-ment with the Data Protection Act 1998. It is a qualified exemption in part but mostly an absolute exemption (ICO, 2013p, p.5). The legislation says that any request where you ask for your own personal information can be refused (s.40(1)), although your own information can be accessed using a SAR (see Chapter 3). The exemption for personal data can be complex and tricky to apply. The Ministry of Justice (2008i, p.3) says that what can con-stitute personal data is 'very wide'.

It is possible that in many cases authorities are cautious about releas-ing information, most likely because if they get it wrong then they may breach data protection laws and may be liable for a fine from the ICO. The Ministry of Justice (2008i, p.3) says: 'Even where accidental, if the breach causes damage or distress and damage to the individual data subject they may be entitled to compensation.'

The Data Protection Act 1998 Section 1(1) defines personal data as being data from which a living individual can be identified or data that when com-bined with other information provides the identity of a living individual. The personal data of others can be refused under Section 40(2)(a) if it fulfils one of two conditions.

First, if it is listed under the definition of data in the Data Protection Act and that disclosing it would contravene any of the data protection princi-ples (s.40(3)(a)(i)) or be likely to cause damage or distress (s.40(3)(a)(i)). Second, it can be refused if it is personal data and it is, according to the Data Protection Act, included in the Act's exemption for a data subject's right of access to personal data (s.40(4)).

Jon Baines (2014), chairperson of the National Association of Data Protection Officers says:

> If the information requested under FOI can identify a living individual and if disclosing that information would be unfair to that individual then it is likely to be exempt from disclosing that information under FOI. Obviously what fairness means is not a straight forward thing, it is going to depend on the context, it will depend on the individual and it will depend on what the personal data is and whether it is sensitive personal data, as it is a higher category.

The ICO in a submission to the tribunal of Evans v Information Commissioner (2012) UKUT 313 (AAC) that looked at Prince Charles' let-ters to ministers, accepted that the 'question of fairness involves a balance of competing interests, taking account of the interests both of Prince Charles and of other persons (and including the public's interest in disclosure of the requested information)'. But it does not mean that we cannot access any personal information.

FOI officer Bilal Ghafoor (2014), who has worked for the NHS, which, by its very nature, deals with a lot of personal data, says:

> I mean there is no point in pretending that you can't have any personal data because there's some that you self-evidently can. Personal data about members of the public, you just can't have it, no matter what you do you're not going to get it.

He went on to say that authorities, in most circumstances, when using the Section 40 exemption should have considered fairness, lawfulness and Schedules 2 and 3 of the Data Protection Act. There are data protection allowances for journalists, which allow the processing of personal data in ways that others cannot. It does not mean that personal data should be released under the Freedom of Information Act to a journalist.

The tribunal of APG v Information Commissioner and Ministry of Defence (2011) UKUT 153 (AAC) (par 114) says 'the test is whether disclosure to a member of the public otherwise than under FOIA would contravene the data protection principles'.

Notable decisions

Whether personal information is fair to disclose will depend on the individual facts and circumstances of each request. When these issues are being considered by the ICO, it says: 'It['s] useful to balance the reasonable expectations of the individual and the potential consequences of the disclosure against the legitimate public interest in disclosing the information' (ICO, 2013q, p.3).

The ICO (2012f, p.4) DN FS50488287 says that even in the case of a low number of statistics that were spread over two, individually unidentifiable, years it would not constitute personal data as the information would not lead to identification, and that 'the fact that other professionals or friends may know all the data behind the statistics, and recognise it from the statistics, should not be classed as identification'.

An address of a property is personal data as you would be able to identify the individual by using other sources, the tribunal of the London Borough of Bexley and Mr Colin P England v IC (2007) EA/2006/0060; 0066 says.

Information Commissioner v Magherafelt District Council (2012) UKUT 263 ruled that even an anonymised summary detailing a disciplinary offence and the action taken by the council against an employee constitutes personal data, as the organisation was small, with small teams of employees, the local community may know the employees and, in many cases, the court says, people may be able to identify the disciplined staff member to a journalist.

The tribunal of Edem v Information Commissioner and Anor (2014) EWCA Civ 92 confirmed that names of individuals constitute personal data, as they could be identified from them. Anonymised data is not personal data. 'If it was impossible for the recipient of the barnardised [altered] data to identify those individuals, the information would not constitute "personal data" in his hands', says the tribunal of Common Services Agency v Scottish Information Commissioner (Scotland) (2008) UKHL 47.

Section 41: information provided in confidence

When it applies

The exemption is based on the legal concept of confidence. It is intended to protect confidential information and is, as such, an absolute exemption. The legislation of the Freedom of Information Act says that information is exempt, under this section, if it was obtained by an authority from another person (s.41(1)(a)). This means it cannot be applied to information the authority has created itself. As well as being provided by another party, for the exemption to correctly apply, disclosure would have to cause a breach of confidence actionable by that or any other person (s.41(1)(b)). The authority can NCND under Section 41(2).

The Ministry of Justice (2008j, p.6) simplifies what information requires to be confidential. It says it needs to have some worth to someone: 'For example, even if a commercial contract states that everything in the contract is "confidential", any useless or trivial information cannot be confidential and no duty of confidence will arise in relation to that information.'

A duty of confidence does not have to be defined in writing. The ICO (2008i, p.2) says that it can be inherent in some situations, such as a doctor not needing to be told to avoid passing on a patient's medical records to the press. Generally there are four areas that the ICO will look at, and public authorities should look at, to establish confidence:

- Whether the information has the necessary quality of confidence.
- Whether it was imparted in circumstances importing an obligation of confidence.
- Whether an unauthorised use of the information would result in detriment to the confider.
- Whether there would be a public interest defence to an action complaining of disclosure.

> (James and Lynn Case v IC and Colehill Parish Council (2013) EA/2013/0045)

The ICO (2008j, p.2) also says there will be a duty of confidence between employers and their staff, but this is unlikely to stretch as far as job titles, or names of staff, although other parts of the Act may prohibit this information from being published.

Public interest considerations

As Section 41 of the Freedom of Information Act is an absolute exemption, a PIT is not required. However, the common law duty of confidence has an inbuilt PIT which presumes that information should only be disclosed if the public interest outweighs the need to keep the exemption, says the ICO (2008i, p.1).

In the following circumstances the public interest may be strong and help to lead towards disclosure when an authority conducts a PIT:

- Misconduct or the mismanagement of public funds.
- Details that a public contract is bad value.
- Where it would correct untrue statements or misleading behaviour on the part of public authorities or high-profile individuals.
- The time that has passed since the information was created has minimised the harm disclosure would cause.

(MoJ, 2008j, pp.13–14)

Notable decisions

The mere fact that someone has communicated information to a public authority can be deemed as being confidential, as well as the general subject matter, as decided by the tribunal of Evans v Information Commissioner (2012) UKUT 313 (AAC).

The process of creating a contract does not mean that the information in it is protected by the exemption as it has not been obtained by a public authority, therefore cannot be confidential. This is because it is an agreed set of obligations and not information provided from one party to the other, says the tribunal of Derry City Council v IC (2006) EA/2006/0014.

Section 42: legal professional privilege

When it applies

Section 42 exists to protect confidence within the legal system between legal professionals, individuals and authorities. It is an exemption that is based in law and the legal principles of privilege, the right to a fair trial and, as such, holds a very high level of public interest in protecting these conventions.

However, as it is a qualified exemption, there will be times when it is possible the information will be disclosed, although this is very rare. The exemption (s.42(1)) excludes information from release that is in respect of a claim to legal professional privilege to confidentiality of communications could be obtained in legal proceedings.

The ICO (2012g, p.3) says that the exemption is designed to protect 'the client's ability to speak freely and frankly with his or her legal adviser in order to obtain appropriate legal advice [that] is a fundamental requirement of the English legal system'.

There are two types of legal privilege, according to the ICO (2012g, p.3): litigation privilege and advice privilege. Despite there being a 'very substantial public interest in maintaining the confidentiality' (MoJ, 2008k, p.4) of legally privileged information, this does not mean that it cannot be disclosed. The authority has the ability to NCND under Section 42(2).

Public Interest Test

As stated above there is a very strong public interest in upholding the principle of legal professional privilege, but an authority wanting to do so is still obligated by the Act to conduct a PIT. It does not matter whether the legal advice received is correct or not, say Wadham *et al.* (2013, p.163). Arguments in favour of disclosing information are:

- Public authorities being accountable for the quality of their decision-making, including that decisions have been made on the basis of good quality legal advice.
- Knowing whether or not legal advice has been followed. However, 'instances of departments overriding unequivocal legal advice will be very rare'.

(MoJ, 2008k, p.9)

Notable decisions

As cited by the ICO, the tribunal of Calland v Information Commissioner and Financial Services Authority (EA/2007/0136, 8 August 2008) says communications between in-house lawyers and external legal representation is subject to legal professional privilege. When looking at a complaint about the application of the exemption, the ICO (2013r, p.6) will look at 'whether the advice is likely to affect a significant number of people, the timing of the request and the status of the advice'.

Section 43: commercial interests

When it applies

The exemption covers information about businesses and public bodies, how they work, their information and, increasingly, contractors who have been paid with public money to run and maintain public services on behalf of an authority or government department. The exemption includes information for two difference purposes.

The first of these is if it is deemed to be a 'trade secret' (s.43(1)). In the Act, there is no definition of what a trade secret is, but the ICO (2008k, p.3) says it can 'have a fairly wide meaning'. The ICO also says that it can 'extend to such matters as names of customers and the goods they buy, or a company's pricing structure, if these are not generally known and are the source of a trading advantage'.

Second, information is also exempt if disclosing it would, or would be likely to, prejudice the commercial interests of any person. This also includes the commercial interests of the public authority that holds the information (s.43(2)). The ICO (2008k, pp.4, 6) says this boils down to the 'ability to participate competitively in a commercial activity'.

Wadham *et al.* (2013, p.165) say: 'One practical difficulty with this exemption is that a public authority may not be well-placed to judge whether information falls within its scope, nor will they have the same interest in resisting disclosure that a third party may have.'

But as the ICO (2008k, p.10) says, if a public authority is to claim the exemption on the basis that commercial damage could occur to a third party, they must have 'evidence provided by' the third party.

An authority, when deciding if they can apply the exemption, should identify the interests and how they may be prejudiced, and who the interests belong to. Commercial interests may be prejudiced where a disclosure would, or would be likely to:

- damage a business reputation or confidence people may have in it;
- have a negative effect on its commercial revenue;
- weaken its position in a competitive environment by revealing market-sensitive information.

(MoJ, 2012c, pp.5–6)

The public authority can NCND under Section 43(3).

Public Interest Test

Factors that strengthen the public interest in disclosure can include the following:

- Transparency in the accountability of public money.
- Proper scrutiny of government actions in carrying out licensing functions.
- Value for money is being achieved when purchasing using public money.
- Procurement is conducted in an open and honest way.
- Businesses can respond better to government opportunities.

(MoJ, 2012c, p.11)

- There is competition for public sector contracts.
- Increasing the available information to tendering process may encourage more companies to apply.

(ICO, 2008k, p.9)

Notable decisions

Bodies such as universities are able to have commercial interests as in some ways they are selling a course to a student, the tribunal of University of Central Lancashire v Information Commissioner and David Colquhoun (2009) EA/2009/0034 says.

A commercial interest will most likely not be prejudiced if the information asked for only combines some details from a third party, for example if information from the third party was combined with information in the public domain to create a new set of data. The ICO's (2012h) DN FS50449512 says: 'Therefore disclosure would not actually reveal information obtained from a third party but rather information that is derived in part from that information.'

For commercially sensitive information, the public authority should be as precise as possible when considering the information. The Panopticon (2012) blog on Information Law, from 11KBW says: 'For example, a clause in a contract might appear commercially sensitive at first glance, but upon closer scrutiny all that really warrants withholding might be the numbers.' This was based on the tribunal of UK Coal Mining v IC, Nottinghamshire County Council and Veolia (2012) UKUT 212 AAC.

Section 44: prohibitions on disclosure

When it applies

Other laws, which pre-date the Freedom of Information Act, still have an impact on what can be released. This exemption is intended to allow an authority to say it cannot release information in response to an FOI request when, in doing so, it would break another Act or law. The ICO (2006f, p.2) says that there are 'still hundreds of statutory provisions preventing the release of information'. Examples of some of these include the Communications Act 2003 (Disclosure of Information) Order 2010 and the Animal (Scientific Procedures) Act 1986.

As it relates to the provisions of other legislation, statutory instruments and more, the exemption is an absolute one and, as such, there is no PIT needed when an authority wants to rely on it. The authority can NCND under Section 44(2).

Chapter 4 top tips

- There are broadly two types of exemptions. These are absolute exemptions and qualified exemptions.
- There are more qualified exemptions and for a public authority to correctly apply one of these they must conduct a PIT.
- For an authority to withhold information when completing a PIT the reasons for keeping information secret must outweigh the public interest in disclosure in all the circumstances of the request.
- When considering challenging a qualified exemption that has been refused because of the public interest being outweighed, try and think of as many varied public interests that are in favour of disclosure.
- When refusing any FOI request a public authority must explain what exemption it is relying on and why it applies; this is unless in doing so it reveals the information that is exempt.
- It is possible to challenge any refusal of a request and a refusal notice by a public authority should include the requester's right to complain.
- Authorities can refuse to respond to a request when the cost of providing the information would exceed the appropriate limits under Section 12 of the Act.
- It is always worth taking a professional manner when corresponding with a public authority. If requesters are abusive or rude, it may result in a public authority calling the request vexatious under Section 14 of the Act.
- One of the most used FOI exemptions is Section 40 which covers people's personal data. This can be a complex exemption that also heavily interacts with the Data Protection Act.

References

Alistair Mitchell v IC (2005) EA/2005/0002.
All Party Parliamentary Group on Extraordinary Rendition v Information Commissioner and FCO (2012) EA/2011/0049–0051.
All Party Parliamentary Group on Extraordinary Rendition v Information Commissioner and FCO (2013) UKUT 560 (AAC).
Ames v Information Commissioner and Cabinet Office (2008) EA/2007/0110.
APG v Information Commissioner and Ministry of Defence (2011) UKUT 153 (AAC).

Baines, J., 2014. *Interview*. Interviewed by Matt Burgess *[Telephone]* 22 May 2014.

BBC News, 2009. Straw vetoes Iraq minutes release, 25 February. Available at: http://news.bbc.co.uk/1/hi/uk_politics/7907991.stm [Accessed 20 September 2014].

Cabinet Office v Information Commissioner (2010) EA/2010/0031.

Calland v Information Commissioner and Financial Services Authority (2008) EA/2007/0136.

Chris Cole v IC and Ministry of Defence (2013) EA/2013/0042; 0043.

Common Services Agency v Scottish Information Commissioner (Scotland) (2008) UKHL 47.

Dadswell v ICO (2012) EA/2012/0033.

Data Protection Act 1998 (c.29). London: HMSO.

Department for Business, Enterprise and Regulatory Reform v Information Commissioner and Friends of the Earth (2008) EA/2007/0072.

Department for Culture, Media and Sport v Information Commissioner (2010) EA/2009/0038.

Department of Education and Skills v Information Commissioner and the *Evening Standard* (2007) EA/2006/0006.

Derrick Lawton v IC and NHS Direct (2008) EA/2007/0081.

Derry City Council v IC (2006) EA/2006/0014.

Dowling v Information Commissioner and Police Service for Northern Ireland (2012) EA/2011/0118.

Edem v Information Commissioner and Anor (2014) EWCA Civ 92.

Evans v Information Commissioner (2012) UKUT 313 (AAC).

Fatal Accidents and Sudden Deaths Inquiries (Scotland) Act 1976 (c.14). London: HMSO.

Freedom of Information Act 2000 (c.36). London: HMSO.

Freedom of Information and Data Protection (Appropriate Limit and Fees) Regulations 2004 (SI 2004/3224). London: HMSO.

Ganesh Sittampalam v Information Commissioner and Crown Prosecution Service (2014) EA/2014/0001.

Ghafoor, B., 2014. *Interview*. Interviewed by Matt Burgess *[In person]* London: 31 May 2014.

Gibbons, P., 2013a. *The Exemption Index: Section 12 – refusing on grounds of cost*. Available at: www.foiman.com/archives/802 [Accessed 18 August 2014].

Gibbons, P., 2013b. *The Exemption Index: Section 21 – information reasonably accessible by other means*. Available at: www.foiman.com/archives/782 [Accessed 22 June 2014].

Gibbons, P., 2014. *Interview*. Interviewed by Matt Burgess *[In person]* London: 22 May 2014.

Graham, C., 2014. *Interview*. Interviewed by Matt Burgess *[In person]* Wilmslow: 20 May 2014.

Guardian Newspapers Ltd and Heather Brooke v IC and BBC (2007) EA/2006/0011; EA/2006/0013.

HM Government, 2012 (Parliamentary Privilege) (Cmnd. 8318). London: HMSO.

House of Commons Library, 2004. *Research paper 04/82: The collective responsibility of Ministers – an outline of the issues*. Available at: www.parliament.uk/briefing-papers/RP04-82.pdf [Accessed 22 September 2014].

Ian Benson v Information Commissioner and Governing Body of the University of Bristol (2011) EA/2011/0120.

Independent, 2014. Royal family expenses: Taxpayers pay 56p each for upkeep of monarchy – and royals insist it's 'value for money', 26 June. Available at: www.independent.co.uk/news/uk/politics/cost-of-royal-family-rises-twice-as-fast-as-inflation-9563293.html [Accessed 15 August 2014].

Information Commissioner v Devon CC and Dransfield (2012) UKUT 440 (AAC).

Information Commissioner v Magherafelt District Council (2012) UKUT 263.

Information Commissioner's Office (ICO), 2006a. *Decision Notice FS50075171.* Available at: https://ico.org.uk/media/action-weve-taken/decision-notices/2006/367920/DECISION_NOTICE_FS50075171.pdf [Accessed 7 March 2015].

Information Commissioner's Office (ICO), 2006b. *Freedom of Information Act Awareness Guidance No. 10 – The defence exemption.* Available at: https://ico.org.uk/media/for-organisations/documents/1181/awareness_guidance_10_-_the_defence_exemption.pdf [Accessed 7 March 2015].

Information Commissioner's Office (ICO), 2006c. *Freedom of Information Act Awareness Guidance No. 14.* Available at: http://ico.org.uk/for_organisations/guidance_index/~/media/documents/library/Freedom_of_Information/Detailed_specialist_guides/awareness_guidance_14_-_international_relations.ashx [Accessed 14 June 2014].

Information Commissioner's Office (ICO), 2006d. *Decision notice FS50070878.* Available at: https://ico.org.uk/media/action-weve-taken/decision-notices/2006/384972/FS_50070878.pdf [Accessed 7 March 2015].

Information Commissioner's Office (ICO), 2006e. *Freedom of Information Act Awareness Guidance No. 19 – Health and safety.* Available at: http://ico.org.uk/~/media/documents/library/Freedom_of_Information/Detailed_specialist_guides/AWARENESS_GUIDANCE_19_-_HEALTH_AND_SAFETY.ashx [Accessed 28 July 2014].

Information Commissioner's Office (ICO), 2006f. *Freedom of Information Act Awareness Guidance No. 27 – Prohibitions on disclosure.* Available at: http://ico.org.uk/for_organisations/guidance_index/~/media/documents/library/Freedom_of_Information/Detailed_specialist_guides/AWARENESS_GUIDANCE_27_-_PROHIBITIONS_ON_DISCLOSURE.ashx [Accessed 20 June 2014].

Information Commissioner's Office (ICO), 2006g. *Decision Notice FS50089784.* Available at: https://ico.org.uk/media/action-weve-taken/decision-notices/2006/368998/DECISION_NOTICE_FS50089784.pdf [Accessed 8 March 2015].

Information Commissioner's Office (ICO), 2007a. *Decision Notice FS50080115.* Available at: https://ico.org.uk/media/action-weve-taken/decision-notices/2007/394674/FS_50080115.pdf [Accessed 7 March 2015].

Information Commissioner's Office (ICO), 2007b. *Decision Notice FS50122063.* Available at: https://ico.org.uk/media/action-weve-taken/decision-notices/2007/421820/FS_50122063.pdf [Accessed 7 March 2015].

Information Commissioner's Office (ICO), 2007c. *Decision Notice FS50118873.* Available at: https://ico.org.uk/media/action-weve-taken/decision-notices/2007/411922/FS_50118873.pdf [Accessed 7 March 2015].

Information Commissioner's Office (ICO), 2007d. *Decision Notice FS50103691*. Available at: https://ico.org.uk/media/action-weve-taken/decision-notices/2007/413980/FS_50103691.pdf [Accessed 7 March 2015].

Information Commissioner's Office (ICO), 2008a. *Decision Notice FS50104541*. Available at: https://ico.org.uk/media/action-weve-taken/decision-notices/2008/443184/FS_50104541.pdf [Accessed 7 March 2015].

Information Commissioner's Office (ICO), 2008b. *Decision Notice FS50093000*. Available at: https://ico.org.uk/media/action-weve-taken/decision-notices/2008/442988/FS_50093000.pdf [Accessed 7 March 2015].

Information Commissioner's Office (ICO), 2008c. *Decision Notice FS50140872*. Available at: https://ico.org.uk/media/action-weve-taken/decision-notices/2008/426034/FS_50140872.pdf [Accessed 7 March 2015].

Information Commissioner's Office (ICO), 2008d. *Decision Notice FS50134744*. Available at: https://ico.org.uk/media/action-weve-taken/decision-notices/2008/439068/FS_50134744.pdf [Accessed 7 March 2015].

Information Commissioner's Office (ICO), 2008e. *Freedom of Information Act Awareness Guidance No. 13*. Available at: http://ico.org.uk/for_organisations/guidance_index/~/media/documents/library/Freedom_of_Information/Detailed_specialist_guides/RELATIONSWITHINTHEUK.ashx [Accessed 16 June 2014].

Information Commissioner's Office (ICO), 2008f. *Decision Notice FS50121252*. Available at: https://ico.org.uk/media/action-weve-taken/decision-notices/2008/428092/FS_50121252.pdf [Accessed 7 March 2015].

Information Commissioner's Office (ICO), 2008g. *Freedom of Information Act Awareness Guidance No. 15 – The economy*. Available at: http://ico.org.uk/for_organisations/guidance_index/~/media/documents/library/Freedom_of_Information/Detailed_specialist_guides/THEECONOMY.ashx [Accessed 12 July 2014].

Information Commissioner's Office (ICO), 2008h. *Decision Notice FS50142678*. Available at: https://ico.org.uk/media/action-weve-taken/decision-notices/2008/435736/FS_50142678.pdf [Accessed 7 March 2015].

Information Commissioner's Office (ICO), 2008i. *The Duty of Confidence and the Public Interest*. Available at: http://ico.org.uk/for_organisations/guidance_index/~/media/documents/library/Freedom_of_Information/Detailed_specialist_guides/SEC41_CONFIDENCE_PUBLIC_INTEREST_TEST_V1.ashx [Accessed 25 June 2014].

Information Commissioner's Office (ICO), 2008j. *Freedom of Information Act Awareness Guidance No. 2 – Information provided in confidence*. Available at: http://ico.org.uk/for_organisations/guidance_index/~/media/documents/library/Freedom_of_Information/Detailed_specialist_guides/CONFIDENTIALINFORMATION_V4.ashx [Accessed 25 June 2014].

Information Commissioner's Office (ICO), 2008k. *Freedom of Information Act Awareness Guidance No. 5 – Commercial interests*. Available at: http://ico.org.uk/for_organisations/guidance_index/~/media/documents/library/Freedom_of_Information/Detailed_specialist_guides/AWARENESS_GUIDANNCE_5_ANNEXE_V3_07_03_08.ashx [Accessed 30 July 2014].

Information Commissioner's Office (ICO), 2009a. *Decision Notice FS50209662*. Available at: https://ico.org.uk/media/action-weve-taken/decision-notices/2009/474936/FS_50209662.pdf [Accessed 7 March 2015].

Information Commissioner's Office (ICO), 2009b. *Decision Notice FS50121803.* Available at: https://ico.org.uk/media/action-weve-taken/decision-notices/2009/ 465528/FS_50121803.pdf [Accessed 7 March 2015].

Information Commissioner's Office (ICO), 2009c. *Decision Notice FS50178276.* Available at: https://ico.org.uk/media/action-weve-taken/decision-notices/2009/ 505218/FS_50178276.pdf [Accessed 7 March 2015].

Information Commissioner's Office (ICO), 2009d. *Decision Notice FS50227776.* Available at: https://ico.org.uk/media/action-weve-taken/decision-notices/2012/ 701682/fs_50415840.pdf [Accessed 7 March 2015].

Information Commissioner's Office (ICO), 2010a. *Decision Notice FS50260346.* Available at: https://ico.org.uk/media/action-weve-taken/decision-notices/2010/ 570388/fs_50260346.pdf [Accessed 7 March 2015].

Information Commissioner's Office (ICO), 2010b. *Decision Notice FS50209659.* Available at: http://web.archive.org/web/20111213165929/http://www.ico.gov.uk /~/media/documents/decisionnotices/2010/FS_50209659.ashx [Accessed 7 March 2015].

Information Commissioner's Office (ICO), 2011a. *Decision Notice FS50308040.* Available at: https://ico.org.uk/media/action-weve-taken/decision-notices/2011/ 598612/fs_50308040.pdf [Accessed 7 March 2015].

Information Commissioner's Office (ICO), 2011b. *Decision Notice FS50347714.* Available at: https://ico.org.uk/media/action-weve-taken/decision-notices/2011/ 646802/fs_50347714.pdf [Accessed 7 March 2015].

Information Commissioner's Office (ICO), 2011c. *Decision Notice FS50297517.* Available at: https://ico.org.uk/media/action-weve-taken/decision-notices/2011/ 596358/fs_50297517.pdf [Accessed 7 March 2015].

Information Commissioner's Office (ICO), 2011d. *Decision Notice FS50296349.* Available at: https://ico.org.uk/media/action-weve-taken/decision-notices/2011/ 595966/fs_50296349.pdf [Accessed 7 March 2015].

Information Commissioner's Office (ICO), 2011e. *Decision Notice FS50207235.* Available at: https://ico.org.uk/media/action-weve-taken/decision-notices/2009/ 496398/FS_50207235.pdf [Accessed 7 March 2015].

Information Commissioner's Office (ICO), 2012a. *Refusing a Request: Writing a Refusal Notice.* Available at: https://ico.org.uk/media/for-organisations/ documents/1211/refusing_a_request_writing_a_refusal_notice_foi.pdf [Accessed 7 March 2015].

Information Commissioner's Office (ICO), 2012b. *Requests where the Cost of Compliance with a Request Exceeds the Appropriate Limit.* Available at: http://ico.org.uk/for_organisations/guidance_index/~/media/documents/library/ Freedom_of_Information/Detailed_specialist_guides/costs_of_compliance_ exceeds_appropriate_limit.pdf [Accessed 29 June 2014].

Information Commissioner's Office (ICO), 2012c. *Decision Notice FS50425762.* Available at: https://ico.org.uk/media/action-weve-taken/decision-notices/2012/ 727652/fs_50425762.pdf [Accessed 7 March 2015].

Information Commissioner's Office (ICO), 2012d. *Safeguarding National Security (Section 24).* Available at: http://ico.org.uk/~/media/documents/library/ Freedom_of_Information/Detailed_specialist_guides/safeguarding_national_ security_section_24_foi.ashx [Accessed 23 June 2014].

Information Commissioner's Office (ICO), 2012e. *Decision Notice FS50421919*. Available at: https://ico.org.uk/media/action-weve-taken/decision-notices/2012/726770/fs_50421919.pdf [Accessed 7 March 2015].

Information Commissioner's Office (ICO), 2012f. *Decision Notice FS50488287*. Available at: https://ico.org.uk/media/action-weve-taken/decision-notices/2013/900380/fs_50488287.pdf [Accessed 7 March 2015].

Information Commissioner's Office (ICO), 2012g. *The Exemption for Legal Professional Privilege (s42)*. Available at: http://ico.org.uk/for_organisations/guidance_index/~/media/documents/library/Freedom_of_Information/Detailed_specialist_guides/legal_professional_privilege_exemption_s42.pdf [Accessed 12 July 2014].

Information Commissioner's Office (ICO), 2012h. *Decision Notice FS50449512*. Available at: https://ico.org.uk/media/action-weve-taken/decision-notices/2012/755190/fs_50449512.pdf [7 March 2015].

Information Commissioner's Office (ICO), 2013a. *The Prejudice Test*. Available at: http://ico.org.uk/for_organisations/guidance_index/~/media/documents/library/Freedom_of_Information/Detailed_specialist_guides/the_prejudice_test.pdf [Accessed 29 July 2014].

Information Commissioner's Office (ICO), 2013b. *When to Refuse to Confirm or Deny Information is Held*. Available at: http://ico.org.uk/for_organisations/guidance_index/~/media/documents/library/Freedom_of_Information/Detailed_specialist_guides/when_to_refuse_to_confirm_or_deny_section_1_foia.pdf [Accessed 29 June 2014].

Information Commissioner's Office (ICO), 2013c. *Dealing with Vexatious Requests (Dection 14)*. Available at: http://ico.org.uk/~/media/documents/library/Freedom_of_Information/Detailed_specialist_guides/dealing-with-vexatious-requests.pdf [Accessed 6 September 2014].

Information Commissioner's Office (ICO), 2013d. *Information Reasonably Accessible to the Applicant by Other Means (Section 21)*. Available at: http://ico.org.uk/for_organisations/guidance_index/~/media/documents/library/Freedom_of_Information/Detailed_specialist_guides/information-reasonably-accessible-to-the-applicant-by-other-means-sec21.pdf [Accessed 15 June 2014].

Information Commissioner's Office (ICO), 2013e. *Model Publication Scheme*. Available at: http://ico.org.uk/~/media/documents/library/Freedom_of_Information/Detailed_specialist_guides/model-publication-scheme.pdf [Accessed 17 June 2014].

Information Commissioner's Office (ICO), 2013f. *Security Bodies*. Available at: https://ico.org.uk/media/for-organisations/documents/1182/security_bodies_section_23_foi.pdf [Accessed 7 March 2015].

Information Commissioner's Office (ICO), 2013g. *Decision Notice FS50498917*. Available at: https://ico.org.uk/media/action-weve-taken/decision-notices/2013/913904/fs_50498917.pdf [Accessed 7 March 2015].

Information Commissioner's Office (ICO), 2013h. *Decision Notice FS50464968*. Available at: https://ico.org.uk/media/action-weve-taken/decision-notices/2013/817910/fs_50464968.pdf [Accessed 7 March 2015].

Information Commissioner's Office (ICO), 2013i. *Investigations and Proceedings (Section 30)*. Available at: http://ico.org.uk/for_organisations/guidance_index/~/media/documents/library/Freedom_of_Information/Detailed_specialist_guides/

investigations-and-proceedings-foi-section-30.ashx [Accessed 20 September 2014].

Information Commissioner's Office (ICO), 2013j. *Decision Notice FS50504403*. Available at: https://ico.org.uk/media/action-weve-taken/decision-notices/2013/922332/fs_50504403.pdf [Accessed 7 March 2015].

Information Commissioner's Office (ICO), 2013k. *Public Audit Functions (Section 33)*. Available at: http://ico.org.uk/for_organisations/guidance_index/~/media/documents/library/Freedom_of_Information/Detailed_specialist_guides/public-audit-functions-s33-foi-guidance.pdf [Accessed 13 July 2014].

Information Commissioner's Office (ICO), 2013l. *Parliamentary Privilege (Section 34)*. Available at: https://ico.org.uk/media/for-organisations/documents/1161/section_34_parliamentary_privilege.pdf [Accessed 7 March 2015].

Information Commissioner's Office (ICO), 2013m. *Government Policy (Section 35)*. Available at: http://ico.org.uk/for_organisations/guidance_index/~/media/documents/library/Freedom_of_Information/Detailed_specialist_guides/government-policy-foi-section-35-guidance.ashx [Accessed 20 July 2014].

Information Commissioner's Office (ICO), 2013n. *Decision Notice FS50451254*. Available at: https://ico.org.uk/media/action-weve-taken/decision-notices/2013/802426/fs_50451254.pdf [Accessed 7 March 2015].

Information Commissioner's Office (ICO), 2013o. *Prejudice to the Effective Conduct of Public Affairs (Section 36)*. Available at: http://ico.org.uk/~/media/documents/library/Freedom_of_Information/Detailed_specialist_guides/section_36_prejudice_to_effective_conduct_of_public_affairs.pdf [Accessed 23 July 2014].

Information Commissioner's Office (ICO), 2013p. *Personal Information (Section 40 and Regulation 13)*. Available at: http://ico.org.uk/~/media/documents/library/Freedom_of_Information/Detailed_specialist_guides/personal-information-section-40-and-regulation-13-foia-and-eir-guidance.pdf [Accessed 16 June 2014].

Information Commissioner's Office (ICO), 2013q. *Decision Notice FS50480452*. Available at: https://ico.org.uk/media/action-weve-taken/decision-notices/2013/891266/fs_50480452.pdf [Accessed 7 March 2015].

Information Commissioner's Office (ICO), 2013r. *Decision Notice FS50443286*. Available at: https://ico.org.uk/media/action-weve-taken/decision-notices/2013/813598/fs_50443286.pdf [Accessed 7 March 2015].

Information Commissioner's Office (ICO), 2014a. *The Guide to Freedom of Information*. Available at: http://ico.org.uk/for_organisations/freedom_of_information/~/media/documents/library/Freedom_of_Information/Detailed_specialist_guides/guide_to_freedom_of_information.pdf [Accessed 27 July 2014].

Information Commissioner's Office (ICO), 2014b. *Decision Notice FS50522278*. Available at: https://ico.org.uk/media/action-weve-taken/decision-notices/2014/1010448/fs_50522278.pdf [Accessed 7 March 2015].

Information Commissioner's Office (ICO), 2014c. *The Exemption for Information Intended for Future Publication*. Available at: https://ico.org.uk/for_organisations/guidance_index/~/media/documents/library/Freedom_of_Information/Detailed_specialist_guides/section_22_information_intended_for_future_publication.pdf [Accessed 26 July 2014].

Information Commissioner's Office (ICO), 2014d. *Decision Notice FS50512927*. Available at: https://ico.org.uk/media/action-weve-taken/decision-notices/2014/967762/fs_50512927.pdf [Accessed 7 March 2015].

Information Commissioner's Office (ICO), 2014e. *Decision Notice FS50530384*. Available at: https://ico.org.uk/media/action-weve-taken/decision-notices/2014/1020822/fs_50530384.pdf [Accessed 7 March 2015].

Information Commissioner's Office (ICO), 2014f. *Decision Notice FS50518770*. Available at: https://ico.org.uk/media/action-weve-taken/decision-notices/2014/971654/fs_50518770.pdf [Accessed 7 March 2015].

Information Commissioner's Office (ICO), 2014g. *Decision Notice FS50530136*. Available at: https://ico.org.uk/media/action-weve-taken/decision-notices/2014/983596/fs_50530136.pdf [Accessed 7 March 2015].

James and Lynn Case v IC and Colehill Parish Council (2013) EA/2013/0045.

K v Information Commissioner (2014) EA/2014/0024.

Kennedy (Appellant) v Charity Commission (2014) UKSC 20.

Lee v Information Commissioner and King's College Cambridge EA/2012/0015; 0049; 0085.

London Borough of Bexley and Mr Colin P. England v IC (2007) EA/2006/0060; 0066.

Ministry of Justice (MoJ), 2008a. *Section 21: Information Available by Other Means*. Available at: www.justice.gov.uk/downloads/information-access-rights/foi/foi-exemption-s21.pdf [Accessed 17 June 2014].

Ministry of Justice (MoJ), 2008b. *Section 22: Information Intended for Future Publication*. Available at: www.justice.gov.uk/downloads/information-access-rights/foi/foi-exemption-s22.pdf [Accessed 17 June 2014].

Ministry of Justice (MoJ), 2008c. *Section 26: Defence*. Available at: www.justice.gov.uk/downloads/information-access-rights/foi/foi-exemption-s26.pdf [Accessed 20 July 2014].

Ministry of Justice (MoJ), 2008d. *Section 27: International Relations*. Available at: www.justice.gov.uk/downloads/information-access-rights/foi/foi-exemption-s27.pdf [Accessed 30 July 2014].

Ministry of Justice (MoJ), 2008e. *Section 28: Relations within the United Kingdom*. Available at: www.justice.gov.uk/downloads/information-access-rights/foi/foi-exemption-s28.pdf [Accessed 7 August 2014].

Ministry of Justice (MoJ), 2008f. *Section 30: Investigations and Proceedings Conducted by Public Authorities*. Available at: www.justice.gov.uk/downloads/information-access-rights/foi/foi-exemption-s30.pdf [Accessed 7 August 2014].

Ministry of Justice (MoJ), 2008g. *Section 34: Parliamentary Privilege*. Available at: www.justice.gov.uk/downloads/information-access-rights/foi/foi-exemption-s34.pdf [Accessed 9 August 2014].

Ministry of Justice (MoJ), 2008h. *Section 36: Prejudice to Effective Conduct of Public Affairs*. Available at: www.justice.gov.uk/downloads/information-access-rights/foi/foi-exemption-s36.pdf [Accessed 24 August 2014].

Ministry of Justice (MoJ), 2008i. *Section 40: Personal Information*. Available at: www.justice.gov.uk/downloads/information-access-rights/foi/foi-exemption-s40.pdf [Accessed 24 August 2014].

Ministry of Justice (MoJ), 2008j. *Section 41: Information Provided in Confidence.* Available at: www.justice.gov.uk/downloads/information-access-rights/foi/foi-exemption-s41.pdf [Accessed 7 March 2015].

Ministry of Justice (MoJ), 2008k. *Section 41: Legal Professional Privilege.* Available at: www.justice.gov.uk/downloads/information-access-rights/foi/foi-exemption-section42.pdf [Accessed 8 March 2015].

Ministry of Justice (MoJ), 2012a. *Section 24: National Security Information Available by other Means.* Available at: www.justice.gov.uk/downloads/information-access-rights/foi/foi-exemption-s24.pdf [Accessed 23 June 2014].

Ministry of Justice (MoJ), 2012b. *Section 35: Formulation of Government Policy.* Available at: www.justice.gov.uk/downloads/information-access-rights/foi/foi-exemption-s35.pdf [Accessed 9 August 2014].

Ministry of Justice (MoJ), 2012c. *Section 43: Commercial Interests.* Available at: www.justice.gov.uk/downloads/information-access-rights/foi/foi-exemption-s21.pdf [Accessed 18 October 2014].

Ministry of Justice (MoJ), nda. *Section 29: The Economy.* Available at: www.justice.gov.uk/downloads/information-access-rights/foi/foi-exemption-s29.pdf [Accessed 7 August 2014].

Ministry of Justice (MoJ), ndb. *Section 30: Law Enforcement.* Available at: www.justice.gov.uk/downloads/information-access-rights/foi/foi-exemption-s31.pdf [Accessed 10 August 2014].

Newcastle upon Tyne NHS Foundation Trust v Information Commissioner (2012) EA/2011/0236.

Norman Baker v Information Commissioner and Cabinet Office (2007) EA/2006/0045.

O'Brien v Information Commissioner and Department for Business, Enterprise and Regulatory Reform (2008) EA/2008/0011.

Office of Government Commerce v Information Commissioner (Rev 1) (2008) EWHC 737 (Admin).

OFSTED v Information Commissioner (2012) EA/2009/0121.

Oxford City Council and Christopher Martin Hogan v IC (2006) EA/2005/0026; EA/2005/0030.

Oxford Dictionaries, nd. *Oxford Dictionaries.* Available at: www.oxforddictionaries.com/definition/english/vexatious [Accessed 6 September 2014].

Panopticon, 2012. *UK Freedom of Information Blog*, 17 August. Available at: www.panopticonblog.com/2012/08/17/commercial-prejudice-the-importance-of-precise-and-limited-redactions [Accessed 18 October 2014].

Pauline Reith v IC and London Borough of Hammersmith and Fulham (2007) EA/2006/0058.

Peter Burt v Information Commissioner and Ministry of Defence (2011) EA/2011/0004 20.

R H Coggins v ICO (2008) EA/2007/0130.

Salmon v Information Commissioner and King's College Cambridge (2008) EA/2007/0135.

Scotland Office v Information Commissioner (2008) EA/2007/0070.

Secretary of State for the Home Department v Rehman (2001) UKHL 47.

South Yorkshire Police v Information Commissioner (2011) EWHC 44 (Admin).

Thackeray v ICO (2012) EA/2011/0082.

Toms v Information Commissioner (2006) EA/2005/0027.

UK Coal Mining v IC, Nottinghamshire County Council and Veolia (2012) UKUT 212 AAC.

University of Central Lancashire v Information Commissioner and David Colquhoun (2009) EA/2009/0034.

Vaithilingam Ahilathirunayagam v ICO and London Metropolitan University (2007) EA/2006/0070.

Wadham, J., Harris, K. and Metcalfe, E., 2013. *Blackstone's Guide to the Freedom of Information Act 2000*. 5th edition. Oxford: Oxford University Press.

WS v Information Commissioner and North Lancashire PCT (2013) UKUT 181 (AAC).

Chapter 5

How to write a successful FOI request

The fundamental principles behind making a request under the Freedom of Information Act 2000 are easy to understand and no knowledge of the law is needed to make a request. The Act was designed this way so that as many people as possible could exercise their right to ask for information. As such, making an FOI request comes at no cost, in the vast majority of cases.

However, for journalists to use the Act in an effective way there are some key steps that can be taken to increase the likelihood of receiving information that is useful, rather than being a waste of time. Preparation before making requests, and making them in an appropriate way, can significantly increase the chances of the request being successful.

As FOI officer Bilal Ghafoor (2014) says, there are common problems with requests from journalists. 'The biggest problem with FOIs from the media, I think, is that the requests are usually not very well written. They are not very clear, and there's just not enough communication.'

The sections below explore areas that can make a request more likely to reap the information asked for. It covers areas that are related to writing a request. More details are provided on the types of information and requests that can be made in Chapter 6. Templates for requests can be found in the Appendix.

What is needed and how to make a request

Under Section 8, requests must be made in writing, as long as they are legible and the authority can use it for future reference, including via email, post, Twitter or the WhatDoTheyKnow.com website (ICO, 2014, p.5). A request can be made to any person in a public authority but most have dedicated staff who will answer the requests, so it is best to direct the requests to them. This will increase the likelihood of it being answered as soon as possible.

Authorities are advised by the Information Commissioner' Office (nda) that it is good practice to provide contact details for FOI officers or FOI teams who respond to requests. And doing so helps them to meet their Section 45 Code of Practice obligations.

Authorities do not always display FOI email addresses on their websites, let alone telephone numbers. Many display web forms, which specify the fields that can be entered for those making requests. Lists of email addresses for public authorities are available to download on the FOI Directory (2015) website: www.foi.directory.

The request must include your real name and an address for correspondence. This address can be an email address and does not have to be a postal address. A request must also describe the information that is being requested from the public authority as specifically as possible (s.8).

Guardian journalist Ian Cobain (2014) emphasised the importance of asking information. He says: 'Make sure you know basic things like the fact that you're seeking information, not documents. Seeking what's in the documents rather than the documents themselves – although very often you'll get the document if that's what you've asked for.'

Research the request

Carrying out research prior to making a request is one of the most important, if not the most important, aspects to making an FOI request, as it can directly impact whether the request successful or not. The Campaign for Freedom of Information (2014) says that making a request should not be the first thing that a journalist does, it says it should be used 'to penetrate the secrecy'.

A poorly researched request from a journalist for information that is accessible in the public domain will result in the authority applying Section 21. This allows them to direct you to where the information is, but not provide it directly. Journalists should not make requests until they know that the information is not already in the public domain.

If a request takes the full 20 working days that the authority is allowed, or if it takes longer and the response is that the information could have been found elsewhere, not carrying out sufficient research has lost the requester a month. The issues the information relates to may also not be newsworthy anymore.

The Information Commissioner's Office (nda) states that you should check to see if the information is already available before making your request, while the Scottish Information Commissioner's Office (nd) advises it is possible to phone authorities to see if the information is already published.

Scottish journalist Rob Edwards (2013) says in his advice for making request:

> Use Google to check what's online. Look at the information already released, and work out which public agencies might have the information you're after. Talk to experts, insiders, academics,

campaigners, politicians – anyone who might have insight into the issue you are researching.

Paul Gibbons (c2014), on his 'FOIMan' blog, says that effective research before making a request could help to refine what is asked for. Also he says to check WhatDoTheyKnow.com, which allows requests to be made and answered publicly, for previous requests on the issue.

A crucial step in researching a request is working out which authority holds, or is likely to hold, the information that you are seeking. Correctly identifying the authority will mean your request does not go to the wrong one and wastes time.

Heather Brooke (2014) says:

> You have got to be thinking about who precisely holds the information, and I don't just mean the police, I mean exactly which police force and even which unit within each police force. Then you have got to figure out how do they record it because that's really crucial as you've got to understand how they define and categorise different things.

One example of a request that wastes time for an authority and journalist comes from Gibbons (2014), who has previously worked at the School of Oriental and African Studies (SOAS), part of the University of London.

> I remember getting requests at SOAS, which is a humanities-based university, getting these round robin requests which were asking about how many animals did we use in research, funnily enough, none. We are a humanities based institution, if you're going to send FOI requests around at least check which organisations you should send them to. I think a lot of journalists when they are doing it for the first time they don't really do that, they just fire it off.

This highlights the importance of researching who the request is being made to, as well as the content of what is being asked for. Mark Hanna (2014), senior journalism lecturer at the University of Sheffield and co-author of *McNae's Essential Law for Journalists*, says he imparts the importance of the pre-request research to those he teaches.

> What I try and convey is that it is a whole process, it is not just thinking of a request and firing it off, it is doing some pre-research into the subject to know the landscape and what data is likely to be kept and by who, making contact with that organisation with a pre-request phone call ideally and seeing if you can get any feel as to whether that request is likely to be successful or your idea should be amended.

The press office

One method of finding out if information is held before making an FOI request is to contact the press office to see if it is able to provide the information that is being asked for – outside of FOI. This method, when successful, circumvents the formality of the requesting process, as well as providing faster results. At the very least it may provide a clue as to whether the authority does hold the information required, or how it is held.

Cynthia O'Murchu (2014), from the *Financial Times*, says that it can make the process quicker and allows you to anticipate potential problems with the request before it is made. She says: 'I will try through the press office just to get the basics and I'll do my research in advance to figure out, in the case of data, how data is held, or how the information is held.' Gibbons (2014) says that better-equipped press offices will be 'able to help and if you can use those to get the quick queries out of the way then that will help in better defining the FOI requests you need to make to fill in the gaps'.

It is generally accepted that an FOI request should only be made after a journalist has attempted, unsuccessfully, to get information from other sources. Journalist Alex Homer (2014) says that if the information is not in the public domain,

> ask a public official – whether it be a primary source who might be able to supply accurate information, or a press office. I think FOI should be a last resort because it is an excellent tool for journalists and it should not be over-used out of laziness as that will only give weight to the arguments of those who would restrict the remit of FOI.

Giving public officials the impression that journalists are over-using the Act, or not using it responsibly when making requests, may prompt government officials to try to cut back on it. Scottish journalist Paul Hutcheon (2014) says he feels it is important that an official's time should not be wasted and therefore when he makes requests, 'I do always ask myself: "Can I get this from the press office? Can I get this from the source? Is it otherwise available?"'

Gavin Aitchison (2014), from *York Press*, says that the Act is increasingly important in a time when it is harder to get information from officials. He says:

> In particular in these days when so many public authorities are so keen on managing the message that they issue and controlling their public image. It does get difficult at times to find information that you believe is inherently in the public interest.

This view is shared outside of the UK. American journalist Jason Leopold (2014) says he uses the Act when there is no other solution.

> The point being that every request that I file is due to the fact that I can't obtain answers, I can't obtain documents, I mean there are some classified documents that shouldn't even be classified but they are so worried about releasing material that they over classify.

However, FOI officer Lynn Wyeth (2014) says at times journalists gets better treatment:

> Sometimes we will put more context in, we will ring them directly, our press office might go direct to them to get them faster answer. I personally don't see evidence, with people that I know, that offices treat them in a worse way if they are a journalist.

FOI officers

Most organisations employ staff to specifically ensure they comply with the responsibilities of the FOI legislation. For the purpose of this book they are referred to as FOI officers but can often be given different titles and responsibilities by the organisations they work for. Their roles are often integrated with complaints processes and also data protection obligations.

When writing a request, it should be done in a professional manner that would be afforded to contacting any person, or organisation. Gibbons (2014), who has been working in FOI since the Act came into force, says that quite often those who are responding to the requests are doing so because they have had it 'dumped on them' as part of their jobs. He says this can affect the quality of responses that are provided to requesters.

> If the organisation sees it as an admin role, then that sort of colours the view of the FOI officer, because quite often they are quite low paid, junior and all the rest of it. Other organisations take it really seriously; they have people who know what they are talking about. It has gone in two different directions, from those who are very switched on and people who it's kind of just a chore for.
>
> (Gibbons, 2014)

A job advert for an FOI officer for Dorset County Council confirms how junior some FOI staff can be considered and how low the levels of pay can be. The advertisement, which closed on 14 September 2014, listed a salary between £15,598 and £16,998 (Dorsetforyou.com, 2014). The level of pay and responsibility for dealing with a complex piece of legislation and where staff may often be at loggerheads with more senior colleagues, indicates why officers may sometimes be apprehensive about their jobs.

It is a widely held view that the attitudes of FOI officers are often not the reason why FOI requests are denied and that many of them are pro-transparency and openness. In submitting evidence to the Justice Select Committee's review of the Freedom of Information Act, the *Financial Times* (2012) says officials who are new to the public sector in central government are often more willing to embrace the Act and its aims. The paper says: 'In our experience, junior officials who have never known the civil service before the Act are comfortable with it. Complaints – and resistance to the Act – come from senior officials, special advisers, press officers and ministers.'

Newsquest Somerset (2012) says it believes that if journalists can make strong relationships with FOI officers then the perception that they are using requests for fishing expeditions can be reduced.

The Act, and attitudes towards it, have settled down as the number of decisions on controversial cases have been made, says Matt Davis (2014). He believes the relationship between FOI officers and journalists can be more relaxed.

> I would also think it is fair to say the Freedom of Information officers, or certainly the ones that I know, or have some sort of correspondence with, they tend to be advocates of the Freedom of Information Act so they can be quite positive and helpful and on the other side you have got journalists who are more realistic [in what they will receive].
>
> (Davis, 2014)

American journalist Kevin Craver echoed this approach based on his experiences of making requests in the USA: 'Read up on what documents are available, and call the department's compliance officer. A little bit of homework and phoning first will save a lot of time and frustration.'

When writing a request it should not be assumed that the person at the end of the request is there to reject it. FOI officers can often be transparency advocates, which will make them more likely to be positive in disclosing information. In line with the view that FOI officers can, in some cases, be pro-disclosure, it often follows that in some situations it is possible to receive the information you want without putting in a formal request.

Journalist Rob Edwards (2014) says that FOI officers are not the 'enemy' as in a lot of cases they are 'the ones who are trying to persuade the bureaucracies, in which they operate, to comply'. Ghafoor (2014) says that in some cases trying to speak to the officers after a request has been put in, or around the time one is going to be made, will be beneficial to help journalists understand how information is held. He says if journalists 'treated FOI team[s] a bit like the media team where they just phoned up for a chat or a conversation then actually there would be a much better flow of more useful information'.

Ringing the FOI officers detailing what the request you are thinking of making could lead to the officer making suggestions about the best way to make the request, and how to access what you are after (Baines, 2014). A lack of hostility, a willingness to communicate and a general professional attitude towards FOI officers when making initial contact with them is more likely to lead to receiving help in creating requests, and refining them.

Wording

Although an FOI request does not need to be clearly labelled as one, journalists should ensure that it is clear they are asking for information under the Act. This will remove the need for any unnecessary questions from the authority over whether the request is to be treated as being under the Act. Making a request to a specific FOI-related contact will also help to reduce the chance of it being misconstrued.

Being as clear and concise as possible will enable FOI officials to interpret a request in the fastest possible time, as crafting the request for information in a succinct way, where possible, will convey meaning more effectively. It will also allow them to assess if they could provide any advice or assistance (a duty under Section 16).

In almost all cases, asking directly for the information is the most likely way to reap rewards. Requests that attempt to allude to some information without saying what it is are likely to be deemed insufficiently specific for the authority to identify the information.

The authority will either disclose or withhold the information on the basis of its content. It is unlikely that it will be tricked into releasing information that it has not been asked for, or information that you mention in passing without asking for it to be specifically disclosed. Therefore in routine requests you should be as upfront as possible when asking for information, and not try to trick the official as it is most likely this method will be ineffective.

It is also important to continue to be polite to the authority even when it has rejected a request or may seem to be trying to avoid the request and be difficult. This includes not making unsubstantiated accusations of wrongdoing in requests, which may lead to a lightning fast decision, from an official, to reject the request.

There are comprehensive complaint procedures that are available for requesters to pursue. These will often provide more effective routes for getting access to information than being difficult with the authority. Being unduly difficult with an authority may lead to complexities during the complaints process, which could undermine the overall complaint. Template examples of requests can be found in the Appendix.

Being specific

When writing a request for information, it is vital the request is being specific about the subject, so the information can be found. The more focused and narrowed down, to a topic, set of data or piece of information, a request is, the higher the likelihood of a staff member being able to easily locate that information. This will be aided by knowing the correct authority and department that holds the information.

Although requests do not have to be specific, or even ask for information which is known to the requester, it is beneficial to be as specific as possible, where feasible. This is because the FOI officers who are dealing with the request are unlikely to know, without research, what information an authority holds. They are not specialists in the day-to-day working areas of the organisation. They are trained in information management and how to apply the law to information to decide whether it should be disclosed or not.

The person who knows what information is recorded, and how it is recorded, will often be the person who gathers or inputs the information. Being more specific gives the authority a greater chance of being able to find what is being asked for. Public authorities can be very large and hold reams of information and documents relating to policies, decisions, investigations and their day-to-day working.

The BBC's FOI expert, Martin Rosenbaum (2014), says journalists should be as precise as possible when making requests: 'If you do have to put in an FOI request, be specific, think clearly about the information you want and spell it out very clearly in your request, avoid all ambiguity.' This, he says, can include considering aspects such as when asking about staffing numbers and levels, if the staff numbers you want are full-time equivalent or the overall number of staff. He went on to say:

> Unless you spell it out you don't know what you are going to get and different information is incompatible, so you would see a request where people have said 'How many kids have you placed in children's homes in 2013?' is ambiguous, does this mean on a particular date, or what was the kind of throughput of numbers within a particular time.
>
> (Rosenbaum, 2014)

Trinity Mirror data journalist Claire Miller (2014) says that, in some cases, it is 'almost better to ask for less' in a request as 'you will get back something that you can actually use'. Tim Turner (2014), a Data Protection and Freedom of Information trainer, says success can all come down to the precision of what is asked for. He gives the example of people asking for information about a 'management team', without defining what that team is, or what it means.

It may be clear in the journalist's head what they are asking for but the terms used will only be helpful to the official if it is something that is understandable in the language of the bureaucracy. Using journalistic phrases or slang when asking for information will give the authority an easy way to reject the request.

This is also the approach of Canadian investigative journalist Dean Beeby (2014), when he makes requests in Canada.

> My other piece of advice is for journalists to become closely acquainted with document types, to speak the language of bureaucrats, to better focus and narrow the request to those document types most likely to escape the exemption process and still contain useful information.

Dave West (2014), who works at the *Health Service Journal*, says being specific when making requests is crucial as it can help the journalist to understand what information the authority has.

> The more background work you can do to convince yourself first that they actually have that information, and then you can demonstrate in your request that you know for a fact that they have that information then it will give you a much better chance of getting what you want.

Information chaos

The management of government files can be haphazard and unintentionally thwart even the most researched and succinct requests. Poor storage and filing systems from years gone by can mean that it is impossible to locate a specific piece of requested information.

For example, there are 260 crates of documents on police corruption in one corner of London (*Independent*, 2014) and the Metropolitan Police may never know which files they shredded relating to the murder of Stephen Lawrence, a review found (*BBC News*, 2014a).

Additionally, the Home Office lost 114 files on historical child abuse cases (*Guardian*, 2014a), while the government lost the personal data of more than 17,000 asylum seekers (*Observer*, 2009). While they eventually did turn up, the Serious Fraud Office sent 32,000 pages of documents to a warehouse in East London (*Exaro News*, 2013).

Ghafoor (2014) says:

> Records essentially are in a complete mess, all through every organisation I have worked for and for every organisation I will ever work for, and that almost cannot be avoided because of the nature of the amount of data there is and because people keep the data in a form that is useful for them to be able to carry out their job.

In short, the information has not been created for the purposes of answering FOI requests and this makes requests harder for officials to respond to.

Emily Martin (2014), who works in information rights, says that it is important that authorities put their records into as sensible order as possible as it will help them to respond to FOI requests, 'otherwise you are chucking your records into a bin, and for FOI you just can't find any information.'

> For journalists putting in an FOI request, I think it would be giving them as much information as possible when selecting the records that they want because the more information they give them, the more likely they are going to be able to find it and the less likely they are going to be to come back to them to say can I have some clarification.
>
> (Martin, 2014)

Beat the bureaucrat

It may often be the case that using the language of civil servants will result in the information being able to be found, so where possible it is always worth attempting to speak in the language of the official.

A prime example of the importance of selecting the correct jargon is requests relating to the government's Work Programme, which was started to help people get back to work (Gov.uk, 2014), although it only created 48,000 jobs (*Guardian*, 2014b). The programme is often referred to by campaigners as being part of a 'Workfare' scheme as it involves unpaid work to receive benefits (Unite, nd).

However, if you were to make a request for information about 'Workfare' schemes to the Department of Work and Pensions, it will not yield any results as the term is not used in official policies. One response says: 'DWP does not use the term Workfare in any of our policies as such we have no need to hold or create a definition for it, and as such do not hold it' (WhatDoTheyKnow.com, 2012).

Another case of bureaucratic language is police forces calling open places where people have sex, 'Public Sex Environments' (*BBC News*, 2014b). Unless a journalist has researched this thoroughly, they would not know that incidents get recorded using this terminology.

Journalist Matt Davis (2014) says for colleagues to get successful results they should try to put themselves in the position of the officials, and bear in mind that the information collected by authorities is not kept for the benefit of the press, but it is needed for the authority to fulfill its duties. He says, for example, when trying to get information on prisoners' day release from the Ministry of Justice, he had to request information about people who were given 'release on temporary licence'. 'They are collating information for their organisation for whatever reason that might be. We, i.e. journalists, want to be successful; we have to then try and tailor the information that they are holding to then use for our benefit', Davis (2014) says.

If it is possible to work out the official terminology used by officials, then this will help an FOI request to be interpreted and the information searched for in relevant databases and computer systems.

A starting point for finding official names for programmes or schemes can be found through government departments or the authority websites. Other sources for finding them will be official reports, media cuttings and legislation. Press offices may also be able to provide assistance when searching for official names of schemes. Or, it is always possible to ring authorities to ask about the schemes they run. FOI officers also have a duty to advise and assist requesters, even before they make a request.

It should be argued, if a response to a request is received that says the information is not held under that name, that under their Section 16 (Freedom of Information Act 2000) duty to advise and assist, the officials should provide help to find the appropriate phraseology for what has been requested.

Check your variables

When asking for information under the Act with the intention to compare it with that of other authorities, it is always important to work out how the information may be held by timescale and other variable factors. Clearly spelling out variables will increase the chances of information that is the same, and thus comparable, being returned. It is unfair upon authorities to compare data from different dates, times, contexts and anything else that may be misinterpreted.

Asking for information from the past three years leaves the request open to be interpreted. One authority may provide information from the past three financial years, while another may give information from the past three calendar years, while a third may provide it on a monthly rolling year.

Ibrahim Hasan (2014), from Act Now Training, which specialises in information and surveillance law, says: 'Try and be precise in what you want including dates, times and document version.' Where this occurs the information that has been provided will not be comparable as it covers different periods. A better request should be specific to state the time period for which information is sought, i.e. 'the previous three complete calendar years'. A well-performing public authority should ask in which form the data would be preferred, if it is not specified, but many will just give the information in the way it has been recorded.

Caveats

Including caveats to the requested information may also increase the chance of the information being provided by the public authority. For example, when asking for information across a period of five financial years, it may also be worth including that if it is not possible to provide the information within the cost limits of the Act, then it would be acceptable to receive the information for three financial years instead. This may preempt a clarification coming back from the authority and save some time in the overall process.

Format to be received in

When making a request, the legislation allows for the requester to determine the format in which they wish to receive the information. This also means that the requester can ask for the format of the file to be a specific one, for example, he/she can request data that is held in an Excel file and expect to receive it in an Excel file. It can be common practice for a public authority to print an Excel table and then scan it into the computer before sending it as a PDF file.

The ability to receive information in a particular way is covered by Section 11 of the Act and the requesters' rights were enhanced thanks to a court decision. Section 11, 'Means by which communication to be made', states that when making a request you are able to express a preference for communication by a form that is acceptable to the applicant (s.11(1)(a)). The section also gives the chance to inspect the information (s.11(1)(b)) and if required by the requester to provide a digest or summary of what they have asked for (s.11(1)(c)). The first part of Section 11 clarifies that the authority only has to do this when it is 'reasonably practical' to do so.

An interpretation of the section in the Court of Appeal in the case of Innes v Information Commissioner (2014) EWCA Civ 1086 says that if someone asks for information in a specific file type, then it has to be given to them in that file type, as long as it is reasonably practical to do so. In this case, Lord Justice Underhill concluded that one of the central points of the Freedom of Information Act is to give members of the public access to information so they can make use of it.

As summed up by the information law blog of legal practice 11KBW, the judgment also stipulated that the query for file type must be made at the time of the request, although a follow-up to the request stating the file type can be considered as a new request (Panopticon, 2014). It was said by the Innes tribunal (par 40) that if an authority is asked to provide the information in a format that it is not already held in, or that it cannot easily convert, then it may be able to rely on the reasonably practical grounds. Lord Justice Longmore, summing up the Innes tribunal, says:

> To my mind the words of Section 11(1) of the 2000 Act are not intended to give the person requesting information only a choice between being provided with the information in permanent form or being provided with the information in another (non-permanent) form. That would be a restriction on the requester's ability to say what was or was not acceptable which would be surprising to find a statute intended to open up channels of information in bureaucracies which had hitherto been closed.

Show what you know

While FOI officers have expressed in interviews for this book that being overly demanding when making requests can frustrate them, it is always useful for journalists to show that they do have an idea what they are talking about when putting in requests for information. Filling an email with basic facts may appear hostile and suspicious of their actions, or attitude, before they have even had a chance to consider the request in front of them.

However, if the requester shows some knowledge in an astute way, the public authority may be less likely to handle a request in an inappropriate way. Examples of this may include:

- Asking for the authority to provide advice and assistance under Section 16 in relation to your request.
- Asking for any clarifications to the request to be made as soon as possible within the 20 working day period.
- If asking for a specific file type for the information to be returned in then it may be worthwhile stating the Innes decision (above).
- When asking for an internal review, mention that the Commissioner expects internal reviews to be completed within 40 working days at the very most.
- If requesting information from a council that may not often receive FOI requests, i.e. a Parish Council or a school, it can be worth saying that the authority has to reply within the 20 working day period outlined by the Act.

There is also the chance that, in some cases, the FOI official, who may have had the job forced upon them, is not keeping up to date with case law, or has not had a request of a specific nature sent to them before.

When requesting it is important to remain courteous and polite to the officials, even if they are being difficult, or trying to avoid answering the request. Any complaints to the Information Commissioner will assess all correspondence relating to a request and the Commissioner may not look favourably on a journalist who is requesting in an unreasonable way.

Chapter 5 top tips

- A request has to be made in writing and can be in any of the following forms: letter, fax, email, social media.
- All information that is intended to be requested should be thoroughly researched to ensure the information is not already in the public domain.
- Research should also be completed to make sure you are asking the right authority for the information, and if possible which department of the authority may hold the information.
- Where possible speak in the language of the bureaucrat.
- Ensure requests that contain variables, such as dates, are written so that they are specific, non-ambiguous and will not need to be clarified by the public authority.
- Journalists can contact the press office before they make a request to see if they are able to provide the information outside of the realms of FOI.
- FOI officers, in most cases, are pro-transparency and openness and have a duty to provide advice and assistance (s.16) to a requester even before they have made a request.
- Include caveats, where appropriate, in cases where it may be possible that the information requested will go over the cost estimates.
- Include the format you want the response to be provided in, i.e. if it is data say that you want it in a spreadsheet.
- Provide contact details for the authority and be open to them contacting you where a clarification to the request may be required.

References

Aitchison, G., 2014. *Interview*. Interviewed by Matt Burgess *[Telephone]* 12 May 2014.

Baines, J., 2014. *Interview*. Interviewed by Matt Burgess *[Telephone]* 22 May 2014.

BBC News, 2014a. Met Police corruption probe document shredding extent 'unknown', 10 June. Available at: www.bbc.co.uk/news/uk-27786043 [Accessed 25 September 2014].

BBC News, 2014b. The tricky business of policing sex in public, 16 September. Available at: www.bbc.co.uk/news/magazine-29205198 [Accessed 26 September 2014].

Beeby, D., 2014. *Interview*. Interviewed by Matt Burgess *[Email]* 4 November 2014.

Brooke, H., 2014. *Interview*. Interviewed by Matt Burgess *[In person]* London: 23 May 2014.

Campaign for Freedom of Information, 2014. *Interview*. Interviewed by Matt Burgess *[In person]* London: 19 May 2014.

Cobain, I., 2014. *Interview*. Interviewed by Matt Burgess *[Telephone]* 2 June 2014.

Craver, K., 2014. *Interview*. Interviewed by Matt Burgess *[Email]* 4 November 2014.

Davis, M., 2014. *Interview*. Interviewed by Matt Burgess *[Telephone]* 21 May 2014.

Dorsetforyou.com, 2014. *Freedom of Information Officer (Internal and External applicants may apply)*. Available at: http://jobs.dorsetforyou.com/legal-political-dorset-county-council-freedom-of-information-officer-internal-and-external-applicants-may-apply/13103.job [Accessed 5 September 2014].

Edwards, R., 2013. *16 Tips for Using Freedom of Information Law in the UK*. Available at: www.robedwards.com/2013/04/exercising-your-right-to-know-.html [Accessed 4 August 2014].

Edwards, R., 2014. *Interview*. Interviewed by Matt Burgess *[Telephone]* 14 May 2014.

Exaro News, 2013. Found: BAE files lost in SFO blunder ended up in this warehouse, 19 August. Available at: www.exaronews.com/articles/5074/found-bae-files-lost-in-sfo-blunder-ended-up-in-this-warehouse [Accessed 25 September 2014].

Financial Times, 2012. *Written Evidence from the Financial Times*. Available at: www.publications.parliament.uk/pa/cm201213/cmselect/cmjust/96/96vw39.htm [Accessed 10 July 2014].

FOI Directory, 2015. *About FOI Directory* Available at: www.foi.directory/what-is-foi/about-foi-directory [Accessed 14 April 2015].

Freedom of Information Act 2000 (c.36). London: HMSO.

Ghafoor, B., 2014. *Interview*. Interviewed by Matt Burgess *[In person]* London: 31 May 2014.

Gibbons, P., 2014. *Interview*. Interviewed by Matt Burgess *[In person]* London: 22 May 2014.

Gibbons, P., c2014. *FOI Man's Guide to Making FOI Requests*. Available at: www.foiman.com/resources/foiguide1 [Accessed 18 September 2014].

Gov.uk, 2014. *Help with Moving from Benefits to Work*. Available at: www.gov.uk/moving-from-benefits-to-work/job-search-programmes [Accessed 26 September 2014].

Guardian, 2014a. Child abuse files lost at Home Office spark fears of cover-up, 10 June. Available at: www.theguardian.com/politics/2014/jul/05/lost-child-abuse-files-home-office [Accessed 25 September 2014].

Guardian, 2014b. Work programme creates just 48,000 long-term jobs in three years, 21 March. Available at: www.theguardian.com/society/2014/mar/21/work-programme-creates-48000-long-term-jobs-three-years [Accessed 25 September 2014].

Hanna, M., 2014. *Interview*. Interviewed by Matt Burgess *[In person]* Sheffield: 27 April 2014.

Hasan, I., 2014. *Interview*. Interviewed by Matt Burgess *[Email]* 13 June 2014.

Homer, A., 2014. *Interview*. Interviewed by Matt Burgess *[Email]* 8 August 2014.

Hutcheon, P., 2014. *Interview*. Interviewed by Matt Burgess *[Telephone]* 4 June 2014.

Independent, 2014. Police files reveal 'endemic corruption' at the Met, 3 August. Available at: www.independent.co.uk/news/uk/crime/police-files-reveal-endemic-corruption-at-the-met-9644667.html [Accessed 25 September 2014].

Information Commissioner's Office (ICO), 2014. *Recognising a Request Made Under the Freedom of Information Act (Section 8)*. Available at: http://ico.org.uk/~/media/documents/library/Freedom_of_Information/Research_and_reports/recognising-a-request-made-under-the-foia.pdf [Accessed 18 July 2014].

Information Commissioner's Office (ICO), nda. *What Should we do When we Receive a Request for Information?* Available at: http://ico.org.uk/for_organisations/freedom_of_information/guide/receiving_a_request [Accessed 25 September 2014].

Information Commissioner's Office (ICO), ndb. *How to Access Information from a Public Body* Available at: http://ico.org.uk/for_the_public/official_information [Accessed 18 September 2014].

Innes v Information Commissioner (2014) EWCA Civ 1086.

Leopold, J., 2014. *Interview*. Interviewed by Matt Burgess *[Telephone]* 28 May 2014.

Martin, E., 2014. *Interview*. Interviewed by Matt Burgess *[Telephone]* 12 June 2014.

Miller, C., 2014. *Interview*. Interviewed by Matt Burgess *[Telephone]* 22 May 2014.

Newsquest Somerset, 2012. *Written Evidence from Newsquest Somerset*. Available at: www.publications.parliament.uk/pa/cm201213/cmselect/cmjust/96/96vw72.htm [Accessed 11 July 2014].

Observer, 2009. 17,000 asylum seekers' files lost, 1 February. Available at: www.theguardian.com/uk/2009/feb/01/refugees-asylum [Accessed 25 September 2014].

O'Murchu, C., 2014. *Interview*. Interviewed by Matt Burgess *[Telephone]* 23 May 2014.

Panopticon, 2014. Section 11 FOIA and the Form of a Request. *Panopticon*, 1 August. Available at: www.panopticonblog.com/2014/08/01/section-11-foia-and-the-form-of-a-request [Accessed 6 September 2014].

Rosenbaum, M., 2014. *Interview*. Interviewed by Matt Burgess *[In person]* London: 30 May 2014.

Scottish Information Commissioner's Office, nda. *Make the Most of Your Right to Know* Available at: www.itspublicknowledge.info/YourRights/Tipsforrequesters.aspx#already-published [Accessed 18 September 2014].

Turner, T., 2014. *Interview*. Interviewed by Matt Burgess *[Telephone]* 21 May 2014.

Unite, nd. *Workfare*. Available at: www.unitetheunion.org/campaigning/workfare [Accessed 26 September 2014].

West, D., 2014. *Interview*. Interviewed by Matt Burgess *[Telephone]* 10 June 2014.

WhatDoTheyKnow.com, 2012. FOI Act response from DWP Central Freedom of Information Team. Available at: www.whatdotheyknow.com/request/108541/response/274471/attach/html/2/FoI%20IR%20185%2018.04.12.pdf.html [Accessed 26 September 2014].

Wyeth, L., 2014. *Interview*. Interviewed by Matt Burgess *[Telephone]* 10 July 2014.

How to utilise FOI

Why is FOI important for the media?

Since the Act came into force in 2005, it has provided an invaluable tool for enabling journalists, from reporters on a daily beat to investigative journalists, to access information. FOI requests have successfully produced a raft of significant stories, on topics such as the RAF relying on drones in Afghanistan (*Guardian*, 2010a), how £400,000 was spent on trees for MPs' offices (*London Evening Standard*, 2012), how bosses of contractors take officials out for dinner (*Guardian*, 2010b) and the hundreds of children being detained in police cells under the Mental Health Act (*BBC News*, 2014).

The importance of the Act can often be downplayed, with its many flaws being highlighted, but it has allowed journalists more access to information than ever before. *The Guardian*'s Rob Evans (2014) says that the Act's value is evident from the government's attempts to curtail what can be accessed as early as 2006.

> They tried to tighten up the Act but they were beaten off, why that was, I always thought was that a lot of people across the media and lots of other people were using the Act so they saw that it was something of value and they wanted to keep it. If it had just been *The Guardian* then that battle wouldn't have been won.
>
> (Evans, 2014)

Investigative journalist David Hencke (2014) says he believes the Act is important for the media as there's a lot of information that does not get dug up, although he attributes this in part to declining numbers of staff employed on national newspapers.

> I find it is rather sad given we have got a law that can be used to obtain a lot more information than was ever available before and if you combine

that with the use of the internet and you start digging around you can get quite a lot of information. Your chances to get bigger stories and more information is much higher.

(Hencke, 2014)

How much?

It is not possible to put a figure on how much journalists should be using the Act. There is no set number of requests that should be made each day, week or month. Some authorities collate the number of requests that journalists make, although there is no requirement for them to do this. Journalists do not always state their profession when making a request, and they may use a private e-mail account so the authority will not treat them differently from any other requester.

The Act should be used proportionately for issues that are important to members of the public. Maurice Frankel, from the Campaign for Freedom of Information (2014), says that requests such as those made for the amount councils spend on biscuits, as the *Daily Mail* (2009) reported, are a waste of time and can give the press a bad name for not using the Act maturely, leaving it vulnerable to attack from those opposed to the Act.

Although Information Commissioner Chris Graham (2014) says that instances where journalists misuse the Act are very rare, they should not make requests 'to just play this for laughs'. He went on to say that he believes journalists should use the Act for the things that 'really matter', as readers of newspapers, who are paying taxes to help run public services, are paying for requests to be answered.

Academic Ben Worthy (2014) says that from his work he has seen that the use of the Act by journalists can be contained to a specific group.

I think there is only a small group of journalists who use Freedom of Information regularly, they are extraordinarily knowledgeable, they are extraordinarily intelligent and they use the Act very, very well. And then there's a large group of journalists who perhaps chance their arm every now and again, and they are possibly the ones that get a kind of bad reputation.

(Worthy, 2014)

Journalist Alex Homer (2014) says: 'Personally, I have tried to use FOI predominantly to request exclusive material, and follow-up self-generated ideas, and check out information I have heard but could not "stand up" by other means than FOI, rather than for background.'

FOI gives a cleaner journalism

The Freedom of Information Act creates the potential for a better quality of journalism. One that is based on access to official documents, from an official source. Although it may be difficult to extract high-profile, damning documents that reveal high-level corruption, the Act does make it possible to show readers the story's source. This is not the case for stories that come from anonymous sources, or questionable sources.

Although they were not revealed as a result of FOI requests, the power of official documents can be seen from the publication of more than 250,000 WikiLeaks US embassy cables (WikiLeaks, c2010), the disclosure of official NSA documents by Edward Snowden (*Guardian*, 2013) and even the Hillsborough Independent Panel's (2012) publishing of 25,000 documents it unearthed about the tragedy.

An American survey showed that more than one-quarter of journalists it surveyed wanted to learn more about documents and records utilisation (Willnat and Weaver, 2014, p.23). Official documents are worth more than an investigative interview as they are useful for providing 'tangible evidence of wrongdoing', while quotes from interviews may sound self-serving, says Protess (1992, p.217).

Heather Brooke (2014), whose requests helped to expose the MPs' expenses scandal, says FOI is important as it allows journalism that is free from spin. This hands the truth, as seen by officials at the time, to the journalist. She says that the view from senior officials that being as 'obstructive as possible on FOI can shut down critical stories' creates a worse quality of journalism.

> But actually what ends up happening is that it incentivises a type of journalism that is really reactionary, salacious and scandal based because it is going to be a journalism that is based on leaks. When people leak, the information is coming out with a really hard spin on it generally. The thing about FOI, it creates a culture of mature journalism because the information comes out with no spin on it, I mean it shouldn't unless the press office has got hold of it which does happen, especially in Britain.
>
> (Brooke, 2014)

Guardian investigative journalist Ian Cobain (2014) shares this view, as it allows journalists to have access to the raw material, which can reveal the truth of what happened, or what a particular official's view on an incident actually was, rather than a perspective engineered by a public authority. Cobain (2014) says: 'The versions that these legions of government press officers like to peddle is very often at odds with that which the documents themselves contain. You're more likely to get accurate, true information from the documents themselves.'

The ability to access documents that have not be changed from their original state can give an insight into the true thoughts of officials as well as providing data that has not been altered to fit a political agenda. Official documents that may be obtained by FOI can confirm suspicions that may then be investigated in conjunction with other sources: 'If so, consult them first. You will have a better understanding of the story before you speak to people, and they will appreciate it' (Hunter, 2011, p.21).

Hencke (2014) says that FOI-based stories give journalists an advantage of documents acting as indisputable evidence, as they have been officially produced. He says: 'With a story that is based on leaks, you might get a political dossier story, but that wouldn't use FOI, it can just be said that it's someone's nasty views. It can be challenged.'

Michael Morisy (2014), from USA investigative website Muckrock, which allows people to pay for and crowdfund requests that are made by experienced professionals, says that being able to access official documents gives a clearer picture. He says that when a controversial event takes place,

> people can spin, add to the fact that memories are blurry and a lot of the time those documents provide the best window into what was actually going on when an ill-conceived programme was being put together or in the aftermath when people are sharing emails about what happened and the best way to access that is through the Freedom of Information Act.
>
> (Morisy, 2014)

Meanwhile, Jules Mattsson (2014), from *The Times*, says that getting documents from FOI requests allows journalists to have an accountable source for the information. This gives any story produced from it 'balanced facts', Mattsson (2014) says. 'If you have to rely on skulking around behind the scenes to get information it effects how the information gets to the public because it has come through certain ways rather than coming officially', he continued.

Publishing the original documents also creates trust between the journalist and the media organisation. John Cook, the editor of *Gawker*, says: 'People get a kick out of seeing the original material' (*Poynter*, 2014).

Brooke (2014) agreed with this view and says when documents are not widely available stories are not accountable. She says: 'Very few stories come as objective, it is kind of an educational fact. And a lot of that is because nobody can go back to the raw resource documents to check on anything.'

However, even a document that has been obtained from an authority using an FOI request may not be completely trustworthy. FOI responses can be wrong and if all the information contained in the document is incorrect, the result may be misleading.

Common requests

There are some frequently asked FOI requests on certain areas of public life. Some common areas that are covered by journalists making FOI requests are:

- parking fines and top earning car parks;
- compensation payments to staff;
- bonuses paid to staff members;
- money spent on consultants;
- the number of drivers with more than 12 points on their licence;
- cautions used by police to deal with serious crimes.

These are a flavour of potential issues that are often covered by local, regional and national newspapers. These types of requests, which concern areas of public spending and items of excess, will generally throw up one or two newsworthy figures that are larger than the others, and there is also the overall figure/amount that comes with them.

Those requests that are frequently made and covered slowly lose their value, even though they may occasionally bring out new details or extremes in a story. The most effective requests, however, often relate to current issues, follow up on developments, cover events that have happened or look to shed light on something new that is in the public interest. Requests can be powerful and make strong stories without requiring the clout of wrongdoing.

Paul Bradshaw (2014) says that there is often an impression with FOI that journalists have to be completely original and try to find a huge scoop every time. He says that this does not have to be the case.

> People try and be creative and do something completely original because they are not wanting to be derivate but actually there is a very rich history of starting off by being derivative and repetitive, but learning from that and developing the kind of confidence and the muscles to do something quite striking.
>
> (Bradshaw, 2014)

By making requests that have previously been made, it allows those new to the Act to discover what works and what does not work. Making requests is the fastest way to learn the limitations, quirks and working practices of the legislation.

Ideas for requests

Ideas and sources for FOI requests can be found almost anywhere, as long as they have a connection to a public authority. The idea for the request will be what makes a newsworthy story. To help the process, journalist and lecturer Phil Chamberlain (2014) says that FOI requests should be part of the newsroom's general operation. 'I think you should build it into the everyday newsgathering process', he says.

Bradshaw (2014) says ideas for FOI requests can be inspired or informed by others that have already been made and applied to a different sector or patch. Previous requests may also highlight areas of conflict regarding which correspondence may be obtainable.

As stated in Chapter 5, it is crucial that requests are fully researched before they are made. If the same request has been made to the public authority, or the information is already in the public domain, they will easily be able to refuse it, wasting your and the authority's time.

General sources that you may speak to for diary or off-diary stories may also inadvertently inspire ideas for potential FOI requests, by highlighting a specific issue that could be investigated using FOI. Chamberlain (2014) adds: 'Every time a story comes up locally or nationally it's about thinking what documents could I request about that.'

Asa Bennett (2014), a journalist at the *Huffington Post UK*, says: 'Sometimes I think of trying to run ahead of a story. So what the main story is now to then think what are people not quite getting yet, or what is the story beneath the story.' He added one example where John Bercow, the speaker of the House of Commons, announced that he received complaints about Prime Minister's Questions and the behavior of MPs. A few weeks later there were stories from FOI requests on the number of complaints Bercow received (*Huffington Post UK*, 2013) and details of the complaints calling MPs 'braying donkeys' (*Daily Mail*, 2013).

Bradshaw (2014) gives the following example:

> Say you're asked to interview someone who had an operation and a surgical implement was left in their body and they had to go back in to get it removed, or someone who died through a lack of care, then that should give you the idea to think that's one person's story but I can use FOI to get the bigger context around this. I can use FOI to find out how many other people have also been affected by this. So often it is very good for that bigger picture.

Leaks for requests

In many ways the results of information obtained by FOI requests and leaked information are similar. In both cases the details can be embarrassing and highlight wrongdoing, which officials would not have wanted published in the first place. Multiple journalists during the production of this book, some off the record, have said information requested via FOI has been leaked to them instead.

Generating ideas for FOI requests

- Follow-ups: asking more information about stories you have already published.
- Official meetings (including their minutes): details of schemes or problems may be mentioned in this, which can be followed up with FOI requests.
- Events taking place, i.e. a special celebration that would incur costs – for example, Tower Hamlets Council spent £47,000 on curry awards with Ainsley Harriott (*Hackney Gazette*, 2014).
- Crime sprees: requests can help to see if there are any trends, in specified areas or time periods, regarding particular crimes.
- Press releases: asking for the data and information behind press releases issued that may not quite add up.
- Fact checking claims: asking for the details behind a claim a politician or official makes. For example, if a police boss claims they have put more officers on the streets, a request could find the underlying figures.
- Central government decisions: for local media organisations more information can be obtained on decisions that are made by central government and are specific to the organisation's patch.
- Requests about requests: asking for the details, and correspondence, that led to a request being refused may uncover authorities trying to cover up what you have asked for.

Pulitzer prize winner James Grimaldi (2014) says, in the USA, he has experienced documents being leaked when they have been requested:

> I think the existence of FOIA and the idea that governments like to keep secrets may actually be propelling the leak function so that tension may actually be forcing things to be released. It's been a while since this happened so I can't think off the top of my head, but I've had instances where I've FOIA'd the documents and instead they showed up in a plain envelope in the mail.
>
> (Grimaldi, 2014)

Grimaldi (2014) went on to say that the concept of openness, and that more should be published, might ultimately drive people to leak details that they cannot disclose via official channels.

Guardian journalist Ian Cobain says: 'You could say that occasionally I've found the people I've been dealing with to offer up information over and above that which I've been seeking, which has been surprising and most welcome, of course.'

The BBC's Martin Rosenbaum (2014) says he does not think that FOI and leaks are completely connected, or will wipe each other out; however, he goes on to say that he has been given tip-offs from sources and contacts about making requests: 'I have certainly had the experience, sometimes of people, a source has said, this is a key document why don't you put in an FOI request I think you will get it.'

FOI laws cannot replace leaks, but they can complement them, and some believe that there are links between the two. 'People don't see WikiLeaks and Snowden as being creatures of the FOIA but in a way they are, they're creatures of the failure of FOIA because the information they are releasing is staggering', says Gavin MacFadyen (2014) from the Centre for Investigative Journalism. He went on to say that without the Snowden leaks, the public would not have any knowledge of the scale of the surveillance activities and they would never have been discovered using FOI laws.

Jason Leopold (2014) says that people were already asking for the information leaked by Snowden. He obtained the records of what people were requesting from the National Security Agency (NSA) by using the Freedom of Information Act. 'I have the NSA FOIA logs and before the Snowden leaks I can see that people were asking for records about these programmes, not necessarily by the exact name but about these programmes, and they were not getting it', Leopold (2014) says.

Snowden's leaks prompted US citizens to be more inquisitive about the NSA's actions and what information it held. Many of these turned to the FOI laws to try to gather more information. Leopold found that the leaks promoted thousands of open record requests, leading to the agency struggling to cope with the demand. Ultimately, the NSA acted in the only way that it knew and tried to fight off the requests (*Guardian*, 2014).

Types of requests

A number of varieties of requests allow journalists to access information that will lead them to be able to produce exclusive stories, with each requiring different techniques to be as effective as possible. FOI officer Lynn Wyeth (2014) says that different types of journalists will make use of the Act in different ways. She says that local journalists are more likely to build up relationships with FOI officers but there are also those who 'just want the highest percentage return that they can possibly get and they will make a story out of whoever answers'. She added:

> So there's all the different types of journalists that want to get different things out of Freedom of Information requests and that would depend how you use it. And I am not sure any of them are using it to the best

of their abilities yet, it is still quite new and relatively, I suppose, few
journalists to my knowledge seem to actually make use of it.

(Wyeth, 2014)

Although there are no fool-proof strategies for obtaining information and it
is not always possible to predict which exemption(s), if any, a public authority might rely on to withhold information, there are ways to make requests
more effective and streamlined to reduce the chance of them being kicked
into the long grass.

Round robin

Round robin requests are often ones that journalists use to create many of
the FOI-based stories that appear in the press. They involve making an FOI
request to a large number of public authorities at the same time, asking the
same question. These batch requests can primarily be made to obtain figures
or comparable information from the authorities.

A classic example of the round robin is one that asks for the amounts of
compensation paid out to staff members from a particular type of public
body. For example, a headline by the *Daily Mail* (2012) reads '£120,000
for a BRUISE! Compensation payouts to police officers blasted as forces pay
out £12m to staff'. It was created by asking all the forces how much they
have paid out after staff have had accidents and then using the figures to
find a combined total, as well the 'shocking' payouts picked to be illustrated
alongside the overall figure.

Round robins have been known to frustrate public authorities as they can
take a lot of time to answer, and the results may never be published. Ben
Worthy (2014) says:

> It's that method that winds up FOI officers because they feel like they
> will put together information and it will never be used, it's just a kind
> of super fishing expedition as it were. Journalists do use it but also cam-
> paign groups and others do use it, people like the TaxPayers' Alliance.

This type of request can also be time consuming for the journalist making
the requests. However, there is nothing to stop the requests being made.
The fact that the Information Commissioner's Office (2009a) has guidance
for authorities on these type of requests shows that there have been issues
regarding authorities being irked by requests that lack details about their
particular area. The guidance does not provide authorities with specific
details on how to handle round robins any further than saying that they are
valid requests and should be treated as any other.

Round robin requests can cause problems for the journalist if they are not
written with enough detail to gather comparable information (see Chapter 5

for more). FOI trainer Tim Turner (2014) says that it is always possible for those handling requests to spot whether one is a round robin as 'they are often written rather blandly because there's an awareness that things are dealt with in a different way for organisations'. This, he says, leads to a vagueness in the way the requests are written and, if care is not taken, can lead to an equally vague answer.

To limit this effect, when making mass requests, you can test out the questions on a small number of authorities first. This allows journalists to see if their request will be successful, and gives the potential to identify any flaws in the wording, which will limit the answers that are received. Once it is established that the request can yield the results desired, it can be sent out to a larger number of authorities.

The Association of Chief Police Officers (2014) provides a central hub for advising all the police forces on what their answers should be to round robin requests and other complicated requests (Wise, 2014). Mark Wise (2014), who is in charge of the team that provides advice, says: 'You will get journalists who will test the water in a couple of forces in how they respond and the type and level of information before they go the full honch and send it off to 43 forces.'

Turner (2014) advises journalists that if they are making mass requests to authorities they should be prepared to put the work in to try to respond to any queries that authorities have. He says:

> A big wide ranging request is much more likely to be turned down solely on cost and sometimes you can ask for clarification knowing that if a journalist has made 430 requests and you ask them for clarification then they will never come back. Whereas, if your request is focused and precise then it is much more likely to be answered in whatever its form.
>
> (Turner, 2014)

Fishing expeditions

Public authorities have been known to make a big deal about requests that are considered 'fishing expeditions' from journalists. These are requests in which the journalist does not know what the information they are requesting is and is sending the request in a speculative way. They can often involve making requests for a lot of information in the hope that the request will catch something newsworthy.

All requests could, in some way, be considered a fishing expedition as the journalist does not know exactly what they are asking for. If they did, it would be unlikely that they would be making the request. Also, it can be considered that a journalist's job is to ask questions where there may be no story at the end of it, or where there may be a rumor that needs clarifying. This could translate into the process of making FOI requests as well as day-to-day journalistic inquiries. There will always be requests where there is no information to be provided.

In practice, FOI officials can rely on the cost limit exemption (Freedom of Information Act 2000, Section 12) to deal with requests that ask them to gather too much information. Scottish environmental journalist Rob Edwards (2014) says that fishing expeditions should not be totally disregarded by journalists, but it should be done in a refined manner. He says:

> I have said several times you shouldn't go drift netting you should go angling. I don't think there's anything wrong with fishing for information but you should go angling with a rod and line with a clear idea of what you want rather than drift netting in the hope of catching everything.
>
> (Edwards, 2014)

Schedules

A simple but effective way for journalists to be able to identify what an authority holds is to ask for a list, or schedule, of the information around a particular area. This could be a list of file names on a topic, the subject lines of emails, specific file types held or anything that details the variety of information that is held around what you are asking for.

This approach allows you to see what is held by the authority and then follow this up with a second request for a specific file, email or piece of information. This method not only allows you to find out what the authority holds about a topic but it also reduces the chances of the authority being able to refuse it on cost grounds. As there is a chance to specify a piece of information that you are asking for, it almost wipes out any potential retrieval and locating time the authority has for finding the information.

For data-based requests it is possible to ask for the fields that make up the database. This approach is favoured by *The Times* and *The Sunday Times* data journalist Nicola Hughes. She says:

> Another thing is that sometimes you can't access the data because there is private information in there – which to a certain extent is misleading. The way to get around that is to ask them the schema of the database and then say I want you to extract only these columns because they don't understand you can extract partial parts of the data if it is in a database.
>
> (Hughes, 2014)

Being able to cherry pick the parts of the data, or the particular files that you want, may mean that there is less of a battle to get the information released. Gibbons (2014) says that, although this type of research is an option that is available to requesters, it is not one that he often sees used.

> It goes back to that issue about research, you make a first FOI request about details of what information is actually held, you can then look at that list and actually go 'that request sounds really interesting, I will zero in on that'.
>
> (Gibbons, 2014)

The BBC's Rosenbaum (2014) echoed this view, describing it as being a 'legitimate tactic' to find out how the public authority organises their information.

> If you are interested in a particular area the public authority could have a vast amount of documentation to it, you want to know how to narrow down your request getting that list of files is actually the tool that enables you to narrow down that request because actually you can say I want this one.
>
> (Rosenbaum, 2014)

Even if the authority does not hold the information in a pre-determined list and does not have to create new information for the purposes of a request, it is possible to ask for a summary.

The Commissioner's guidance states that a public authority is not creating new information in the following circumstances.

- Where it presents information it holds in the form of a list or a schedule.
- Where answering a request requires it to complete simple manual manipulation of information.
- Where information is extracted from a database by searching it in the form of a query.

> (ICO, 2009b, p.2)

Correspondence

A very effective request that can be made by a journalist to find out what is really happening, is a request for correspondence. This type of request asks for what a particular official, authority or interested party has been saying behind closed doors. The requests can reveal the intimate details of what has been said on particular issues of public interest, which would not otherwise be made available. Correspondence may also be able to raise awareness of how internal processes and decisions are made.

But requests for correspondence can be some of the most difficult to get results from. In many cases these will contain information that could be embarrassing for officials. Correspondence requests can also contain the personal details of junior public officials who, because of their low-grade role, are entitled to a greater level of privacy than more senior officials.

Where this is the case, their details should be redacted, rather than the entire response refused.

Requesting correspondence revealed that scientists developed a 'reasonable' worst-case scenario for when the Fukushima Daiichi nuclear plant was damaged by earthquake and tsunami. *The Guardian* accessed 30 documents that said teams specially trained in radiation would be deployed to screen passengers coming from Japan to the UK (*Guardian*, 2011a).

After the 2011 riots in the UK, emails were disclosed under the Freedom of Information Act showing courts were encouraged to ignore sentencing guidelines when dealing with those caught rioting (*Guardian*, 2011b).

Gibbons (2014) says when asking for 'all correspondence' it is unlikely that an authority will be able to provide it due to the size of authorities and the time it would take to collate, retrieve and extract the information. His advice for making requests for correspondence is to do the research before making it, 'If you can name some individuals, i.e. this person and that person, it is obviously going to narrow it down quite a bit. Keep the timescale quite tight, say within a six month period, or a defined period' (Gibbons, 2014). For correspondence requests on popular subjects that may be discussed, or within large teams, it may be worth narrowing the request to an even smaller timescale.

Police use of the Regulation of Investigatory Powers Act 2000 (RIPA)

Different authorities, of the same type, will treat the same FOI request in different ways. This was evident when the *Press Gazette* probed police forces on their use of RIPA surveillance powers on journalists, and then followed this up with a request about the correspondence of their rejected responses.

It was revealed from all the requests that the police body ACPO (Association of Chief Police Officers) advised all the forces to reject the original requests either on cost grounds (s.12), aggregate the requests (also under Section 12) or refused to NCND using national security, investigations, law enforcement or personal information.

However, it was reported that forces used all three of the above options to them as well as one claiming that releasing information would be prejudicial to the conduct of public affairs (s.36) and others also said that SARs under the Data Protection Act 1998 would have to be made.

(*Press Gazette*, 2014)

NB: They later began to refuse FOI requests from *Press Gazette* as forces thought they were vexatious.

Data requests

Requests for datasets can be made so that it is possible to analyse the data that an authority holds, including unedited information behind official statistics upon which press releases and official statements are based. There are particular provisions that help to allow the reuse of information that has been collected by the public authority. It is also possible to use the Act to help create your own datasets, which compare the performance of a range of public authorities.

Kathryn Torney (2014), a data journalist with *The Detail* in Northern Ireland, says it gives journalists access to official data that is often not put into the public domain. This then allows them to 'carry out their own analysis of government data using the raw statistics. This allows us to paint a detailed picture of a topic and to go beyond the headline figures of official press releases.' She continued that one of the benefits of requesting data is that often a geographical field can be introduced, which allows for resulting stories to be tailored to the readers in specific areas.

Building datasets

As well as providing the ability to ask for preformed datasets, FOI can also allow journalists to make their own. To do this, requests may need to be made to multiple authorities. Although it may take some more time to collate the results, this can lead to a dataset that nobody else has.

Claire Miller (2014), a data journalist at *Trinity Mirror*, says she often requests information so that she can create her own datasets to compare the performance of multiple authorities at once. The approach of asking for a little information to be combined with other data also may make it easier for the public authority to locate and retrieve the information rather than if a lot was asked for all at once.

> If I am asking lots and lots of public bodies, I ask for small amounts of data and limited pieces of information from them to build into a dataset. So for example asking health boards and hospital trusts how many operations they cancelled due to a lack of beds, so they flood all of them back, each of them is only going to send you a small amount of information but you can build that into a full dataset when you hear back from all of them.
>
> (Miller, 2014)

Nicola Hughes (2014) agreed that asking for less data makes it easier to compare common features. She says that a common mistake that journalists make is trying to compare data that is held in different ways by different authorities:

What I have to say to them is you're comparing apples and oranges if they are not holding the data in the same way, [e.g.] if they are taking the date of offence from arrest or date of arrest from conviction you can't compare them.

(Hughes, 2014)

Raw datasets

The Protection of Freedoms Act 2012 gave public authorities added responsibilities for when they have received a dataset request, in order to ensure that public authorities provide these datasets, through FOI requests or publication schemes, in a way that guarantees the public is able to reuse them.

It says that a 'dataset' means a collection of information held in electronic form where all the information, or most of it, has been collected for informing the authority in relation to its functions. This is added to Section 11 of the Freedom of Information Act. It only applies when the information has not been altered since it was obtained or recorded (added to the Freedom of Information Act by the Freedoms Act, Section 102(3)).

The Information Commissioner's Office (2013a, p.2) guidance on datasets reiterates that if the requester has asked for the dataset in a reusable format then that is how it should be given to them. Also, if a dataset has been requested from a public authority then the authority should publish the dataset under its publication scheme. It should publish any updated versions of the datasets (ICO, 2013a, p.23).

Hughes (2014) says that when asking for datasets it can help to ask for the schema of the database. She says this then allows a second request to be made, which can seek the columns or rows that you are most interested in. She says that she often asks for the technical information first to allow her to ask a question to get the data afterwards.

Paul Bradshaw (2014), journalism lecturer at City University and Birmingham City University, says that by asking for details of which fields are contained in a database it can give you ideas that you might not have already had, as well as 'alert you to the context that you might need for the story, or colour'.

Miller (2014) added that WhatDoTheyKnow.com, which easily allows anybody to make requests online and then publishes the answers, can also be a good source for finding raw data. She says this could then lead to follow-up questions or information that can be used.

Meetings and their minutes

The minutes from most official meetings within public authorities, especially those at a local authority level, are required to be published. The Information Commissioner's Office (2013b) model publication scheme sets out that minutes for certain types of meetings should be published on a routine basis. This includes the minutes and agendas of public meetings, as well minutes of senior-level policy and strategy meetings, and background documents that are referred to in the agendas (ICO, 2013c, p.3).

However, the ICO says this should not affect people who want to make requests and that when a request for minutes is received, it should be based on the circumstances at the time the request was made.

> It [the authority] is obliged to consider these requests in the normal way. It is important for an authority to remember that, even if it has already considered the information and has decided that it cannot be released, on receiving a request it should consider the matter again.
>
> (ICO, 2013c, p.5)

It is possible to request minutes from even the highest level of meetings, although the higher up the political spectrum the meeting was, the harder it will be for the minutes to be successfully disclosed. For example, a tribunal ruled that Cabinet meeting minutes on the Iraq war should be published in response to a request. The tribunal of Cabinet Office and Dr Christopher Lamb v IC (2009) EA/2008/0024 and EA/2008/0029 stated that while it recognised 'the importance of the convention and the damage that may result from the publication of Cabinet minutes' (par 32), the overwhelming public interest of withholding the minutes of the meeting was not outweighed by the public interest in keeping them a secret.

These minutes were not disclosed as Home Secretary Jack Straw decided to use the ministerial veto to block their publication, on the basis that releasing the minutes would do 'serious damage' to the government (*BBC News*, 2009).

The Act also, in theory, allows for the details of those who have attended meetings with officials to be released, although this will depend on the seniority of the officials as well as the nature of the meetings. The Commissioner told the Cabinet Office to reveal the details of all the Prime Minister's official meetings that were held in Downing Street in June 2005, in DN FS50123190 (ICO, 2008a). This case included the ministerial colleagues, officials and advisors that the Prime Minister had held meetings with. The decision found that there would be no significant harm caused. The DN says:

> The Commissioner also does not accept that the meetings list can link civil servants to any particular area of policy. Where individuals are named there is no indication of any subject matter under discussion and even if it were possible to speculate he does not agree that this would affect the impartiality or neutrality of the civil service.
>
> (ICO, 2008a, p.8)

Contracts

In many cases it should be possible to access a contract between a public authority and a service provider, although this will not always be met with a willingness to cooperate from those who may have commercial interests. As Heather Brooke puts it in *Your Right to Know*, it is crucially important that public authorities are able to make contracts available as vast sums of money can be poured into them.

> Information is also available about private companies in two other areas: procurement (companies selling goods or services to public bodies); and public–private partnerships/private finance initiatives. Huge sums or money are often involved in these projects so the possibility for corruption and mismanagement is great. Transparency and direct accountability is essential.
>
> (Brooke, 2006, p.263)

The Information Commissioner's Office (2008b, p.1) highlights the important point that a contract between an authority and a provider will rarely be able to be held because of the legal principle of confidence (s.41). This is because 'a concluded contract agreed between a public authority and another party is not generally information being provided by one party to the other'.

This was outlined in the tribunal of Derry City Council v Information Commissioner (2006) EA/2006/0014. It is possible, as indicated by the tribunal, that in some circumstances there can be information provided in the creation of a contract and that other exemptions can apply.

As the Act is retrospective, the Information Commissioner's Office (2006, p.1) raised the issue that many of the contracts were done so on the agreement that 'most, if not all' the information concerning commercial relationships would remain 'confidential'. But the ICO says where the contractors want to keep all information relating to contracts and its commercial relationship a secret, 'such expectations need revising in light of the Act' (ICO, 2006, p.4).

In relation to new contracts, 'the Commissioner recognises, while a public authority cannot contract out of its FOIA obligations, that there is a place for confidentiality clauses where they serve to identify information that may be exempt' (ICO, 2006, p.3).

For companies that want to write for tender, it is made clear to them on the Gov.uk (2014) website that ordinarily 'all contracts with public bodies are subject to the Freedom of Information Act', unless subject to an exemption.

Meta requests

Requests about requests are not at all uncommon and although they may sound like they could waste authorities' time, they can be a useful tool to ensure that the correct processes are being followed. The requests will, most often, ask for how an authority has handled a particular FOI request. This can be their internal correspondence about how they have decided on the answering of the request, or communications across the authority about the request and who has made it.

The leading tribunal case on this is the decision of Home Office and Ministry of Justice v Information Commissioner (2009) EWHC 1611 (Admin). This tribunal involved the journalist Matt Davis. In this case Davis wanted to find out if his requests were being treated any differently because he was a journalist.

The approach is also shared by American journalist Jason Leopold (2014) who advocated making 'meta-FOIA' requests when an agency is dragging its feet in providing an answer. He says: 'There are ways to find out behind the scenes how various agencies handle FOIA requests, you can actually ask for the documents that showed how your request is being handled, what's being said behind the scenes' (Leopold, 2014) and doing this gives the requester the power to see what is being done by officials, and if they are doing it in accordance with laws.

Refused requests

Even when an authority does not give out what it has been asked for, this can often make a better story than if it had just handed over the information. The ability to expose what a public authority will not reveal, and its attitude behind it, can be more telling about the authority than what it will release.

Whether this is Shropshire Council not disclosing the pay of senior staff (*Shropshire Star*, 2013), or whether voting figures for BBC programmes are confidential (*London Evening Standard*, 2013), every story shows what the authority is prepared to disclose. Even if the information has been withheld correctly with an exemption, the stories that are produced illustrates to members of the public what the Act can, and cannot, achieve. They also serve to put pressure on the authority to correctly answer requests, if they have not done so.

Chamberlain (2014) says when an authority refuses some information it can still be an advantage to those using the Act.

> I think sometimes you're in a win–win, you either find out information in which case there's my kind of story or they refuse to say in which case you've got your secrecy intro kind of written.
>
> (Chamberlain, 2014)

Using rejections of FOI requests to write stories has even progressed to writing requests about non-issued refusals. The story headlined 'NHS staff discuss rejecting FOI request in leaked email' appeared in *The Telegraph* (2012) after one of its reporters was sent an internal email that included the line: 'Can we say that our strategy is commercially sensitive and refuse to disclose?'

This type of story can also include responses that NCND that the information is held, or where organisations are taking too long to respond. This is even a position that is endorsed by the Information Commissioner, Christopher Graham.

> If you are a local newspaper journalist and the council is taking too long to deal with something, again I can think of examples where that itself has been the story, if you look at one of the authorities we have been monitoring recently, which is Wirral Borough Council. I've lost track of the number of stories where the story has been about the inability of the council to turn things around in time.
>
> (Graham, 2014)

Chapter 6 top tips

- Publishing documents that have been received under FOI alongside a story will allow the reader to see the source of the information.
- Ideas for requests can come from almost anywhere, including sources, follow-ups, events, public meetings and more.
- Any fishing expeditions should be treated with caution but there is no reason under the Act why they cannot be made.
- When asking for data, entire datasets can be requested, or smaller pieces of information can be requested that can then be combined to create a new dataset.
- Asking for a schema of a database can reveal the subject/column headings of the data base that can then be followed up with a request for the specific data.
- When sending a round robin request, the chances of it being successful can be increased by testing the request with a couple of authorities first, before refining it and sending to more authorities.
- Schedules of documents held can be requested and these may allow a second request to cherry pick the most important and newsworthy files, or pieces of information.

- Correspondence requests should be specific: where possible they should have a narrower time frame, include the names/groups of people that are involved and in some cases it may be worth including a subject area.
- Requests about requests may reveal more detailed reasons why an authority rejected a request, or if they handled it in a proper manner. Refused requests can make stories about a lack of transparency and obstructiveness from a public authority.

References

Association of Chief Police Officers, 2014. *Update on ACPO Future*, 17 October. Available at: http://news.acpo.police.uk/releases/update-on-acpo-future [Accessed 8 March 2015].

BBC News, 2009. Straw vetoes Iraq minutes release, 25 February. Available at: http://news.bbc.co.uk/1/hi/uk_politics/7907991.stm [Accessed 17 October 2014].

BBC News, 2014. Hundreds of children 'detained in police cells', 26 January. Available at: www.bbc.co.uk/news/uk-25900085 [Accessed 26 September 2014].

Bennett, A., 2014. *Interview.* Interviewed by Matt Burgess *[In person]* London: 21 May 2014.

Bradshaw, P., 2014. *Interview.* Interviewed by Matt Burgess *[Telephone]* 19 May 2014.

Brooke, H., 2006. *Your Right to Know: A Citizen's Guide to the Freedom of Information Act.* London: Pluto Press.

Brooke, H., 2014. *Interview.* Interviewed by Matt Burgess *[In person]* London: 23 May 2014.

Cabinet Office and Dr Christopher Lamb v IC (2009) EA/2008/0024 and EA/2008/0029.

Campaign for Freedom of Information, 2014. *Interview.* Interviewed by Matt Burgess *[In person]* London: 19 May 2014.

Chamberlain, P., 2014. *Interview.* Interviewed by Matt Burgess *[Telephone]* 19 May 2014.

Cobain, I., 2014. *Interview.* Interviewed by Matt Burgess *[Telephone]* 2 June 2014.

Daily Mail, 2009. Revealed: How police forces spend £3m on tea and biscuits, 15 August. Available at: www.dailymail.co.uk/news/article-1206446/A-new-expenses-storm-brewing-Police-forces-spend-3m-tea-biscuits.html [Accessed 25 September 2014].

Daily Mail, 2012. £120,000 for a BRUISE! Compensation payouts to police officers blasted as forces pay out £12m to staff, 27 January. Available at: www.dailymail. co.uk/news/article-2092578/Police-compensation-payouts-12million-including-120-000-bruise.html [Accessed 15 September 2014].

Daily Mail, 2013. 'Buffoons, morons and braying donkeys': What voters REALLY think about MPs' antics at Prime Minister's Questions, 4 December. Available at: www.dailymail.co.uk/news/article-2517966/Buffoons-morons-braying-donkeys-What-voters-REALLY-think-MPs-antics-Prime-Ministers-Questions-revealed.html [Accessed 19 September 2014].

Data Protection Act 1998 (c.29). London: HMSO.

Derry City Council v Information Commissioner (2006) EA/2006/0014.

Edwards, R., 2014. *Interview*. Interviewed by Matt Burgess *[Telephone]* 14 May 2014.

Evans, R., 2014. *Interview*. Interviewed by Matt Burgess *[Telephone]* 29 July 2014.

Freedom of Information Act 2000 (c.36). London: HMSO.

Gibbons, P., 2014. *Interview*. Interviewed by Matt Burgess *[In person]* London: 22 May 2014.

Gov.uk, 2014. *Tendering for Public Sector Contracts*. Available at: www.gov.uk/tendering-for-public-sector-contracts/disclosing-information-in-your-tender [Accessed 23 October 2014].

Graham, C., 2014. *Interview*. Interviewed by Matt Burgess *[In person]* Wilmslow: 20 May 2014.

Grimaldi, J., 2014. *Interview*. Interviewed by Matt Burgess *[Telephone]* 27 May 2014.

Guardian, 2010a. RAF 'relying' on drones in Afghanistan, 7 February. Available at: www.theguardian.com/uk/2010/feb/07/raf-drones-afghanistan [Accessed 4 August 2014].

Guardian, 2010b. Revealed: How BAE Systems wined and dined MoD top brass 52 times, 22 August. Available at: www.theguardian.com/business/2010/aug/22/bae-systems-ministry-of-defence-hospitality [Accessed 4 August 2014].

Guardian, 2011a. UK government's Fukushima crisis plan based on bigger leak than Chernobyl, 20 June. Available at: www.theguardian.com/science/2011/jun/20/japan-earthquake-and-tsunami-japan [Accessed 1 August 2014].

Guardian, 2011b. Magistrates were told to send rioters to crown court, emails show, 14 September. Available at: www.theguardian.com/uk/2011/sep/13/riots-sentencing-justice-system-emails [Accessed 31 July 2014].

Guardian, 2013. Edward Snowden: The whistleblower behind the NSA surveillance revelations, 11 June. Available at: www.theguardian.com/world/2013/jun/09/edward-snowden-nsa-whistleblower-surveillance [Accessed 26 September 2014].

Guardian, 2014. Top NSA officials struggled over surge in Foia requests, emails reveal, 29 May. Available at: www.theguardian.com/world/2014/may/29/nsa-emails-foia-requests-snowden-leaks [Accessed 19 October 2014].

Hackney Gazette, 2014. Tower Hamlets spent £47k on Brick Lane curry awards with Ainsley Harriott, 1 May. Available at: www.hackneygazette.co.uk/news/tower_hamlets_spent_47k_on_brick_lane_curry_awards_with_ainsley_harriott_1_3581664 [Accessed 19 September 2014].

Hencke, D., 2014. *Interview*. Interviewed by Matt Burgess *[Telephone]* 27 May 2014.

Hillsborough Independent Panel, 2012. *Catalogue of all Material Considered for Disclosure*. Available at: http://hillsborough.independent.gov.uk/catalogue/index/organisation/all/outofscope/all/perpage/20/page/1.html [Accessed 25 September 2014].

Home Office and Ministry of Justice v Information Commissioner (2009) EWHC 1611 (Admin).

Homer, A., 2014. *Interview*. Interviewed by Matt Burgess *[Email]* 29 August 2014.

Huffington Post UK, 2013. Rowdy PMQs prompts 61 complaints to speaker John Bercow in five months, 3 December. Available at: www. huffingtonpost.co.uk/2013/12/03/john-bercow-pmqs-letters_n_4377548.html? [Accessed 19 September 2014].

Hughes, N., 2014. *Interview*. Interviewed by Matt Burgess *[Telephone]* 13 May 2014.

Hunter, M., 2011. *Story-Based Inquiry*. France: UNESCO Publishing.

Information Commissioner's Office (ICO), 2006. *Freedom of Information Act Awareness Guidance No. 5 – Annexe*. Available at: www.ljmu.ac.uk/secretariat/docs/ICO_Public_Sector_Contracts.pdf [Accessed 8 March 2015].

Information Commissioner's Office (ICO), 2008a. *Decision Notice FS50123190*. Available at: https://ico.org.uk/media/action-weve-taken/decision-notices/2008/438578/FS_50121390.pdf [Accessed 8 March 2015].

Information Commissioner's Office (ICO), 2008b. *Information Provided in Confidence Relating to Contracts*. Available at: http://ico.org.uk/~/media/documents/library/Freedom_of_Information/Detailed_specialist_guides/CONFIDENCEANDCONTRACTS.ashx [Accessed 7 July 2014].

Information Commissioner's Office (ICO), 2009a. *Circular (or Round Robin) Requests*. Available at: http://ico.org.uk/for_organisations/guidance_index/~/media/documents/library/Freedom_of_Information/Practical_application/foi-guidance-round-robins.pdf [Accessed 20 April 2009].

Information Commissioner's Office (ICO), 2009b. *Do I have to Create Information to Answer a Request*. Available at: http://ico.org.uk/for_organisations/guidance_index/~/media/documents/library/Freedom_of_Information/Detailed_specialist_guides/INFORMATION_FROM_ORIGINAL_SOURCES.ashx [Accessed 16 June 2009].

Information Commissioner's Office (ICO), 2013a. *Datasets (Sections 11, 19 & 45)*. Available at: http://ico.org.uk/for_organisations/guidance_index/~/media/documents/library/Freedom_of_Information/Detailed_specialist_guides/datasets-foi-guidance.pdf [Accessed 11 June 2009].

Information Commissioner's Office (ICO), 2013b. *Model Publication Scheme*. Available at: http://ico.org.uk/for_organisations/freedom_of_information/guide/~/media/documents/library/Freedom_of_Information/Detailed_specialist_guides/model-publication-scheme.pdf [Accessed 16 June 2014].

Information Commissioner's Office (ICO), 2013c. *What Should be Published? Minutes and Agendas*. Available at: http://ico.org.uk/for_organisations/guidance_index/~/media/documents/library/Freedom_of_Information/Detailed_specialist_guides/minutesandagendas.pdf [Accessed 21 October 2014].

Leopold, J., 2014. *Interview*. Interviewed by Matt Burgess *[Telephone]* 28 May 2014.

London Evening Standard, 2012. MPs spend £400,000 of taxpayers' cash on 12 fig trees for their offices, 14 February. Available at: www.standard.co.uk/news/mps-spend-400000-of-taxpayers-cash-on-12-fig-trees-for-their-offices-7443040.html [Accessed 8 March 2015].

London Evening Standard, 2013. Voting figures are strictly confidential, says the BBC, 5 February. Available at: www.standard.co.uk/news/londoners-diary/voting-figures-are-strictly-confidential-says-the-bbc-8481861.html [Accessed 8 March 2015].

Mattsson, J., 2014. *Interview*. Interviewed by Matt Burgess *[Telephone]* 23 June 2014.

MacFadyen, G., 2014. *Interview*. Interviewed by Matt Burgess *[In person]* London: 23 May 2014.

Miller, C., 2014. *Interview*. Interviewed by Matt Burgess *[Email]* 22 May 2014.

Morisy, M., 2014. *Interview*. Interviewed by Matt Burgess *[Telephone]* 22 May 2014.

Poynter, 2014. FOIA lessons from *Gawker* Editor John Cook, 11 February. Available at: www.poynter.org/latest-news/top-stories/238702/foia-lessons-from-gawker-editor-john-cook [Accessed 19 September 2014].

Press Gazette, 2014. ACPO scuppered Press Gazette FoI requests on police use of RIPA by issuing blanket guidance, 10 November. Available at: www.pressgazette.co.uk/acpo-scuppered-press-gazette-foi-requests-police-use-ripa-issuing-blanket-guidance [Accessed 15 November 2014].

Protection of Freedoms Act 2012 (c.9). London: HMSO.

Protess, L. ed., 1992. *The Journalism of Outrage: Investigative Reporting and Agenda Building in America*. New York: Guilford Press.

Regulation of Investigatory Powers Act 2000 (c.23). London: HMSO.

Rosenbaum, M., 2014. *Interview*. Interviewed by Matt Burgess *[In person]* London: 30 May 2014.

Shropshire Star, 2013. Shropshire Council will not disclose pay-offs to senior staff, 8 February. Available at: www.shropshirestar.com/news/2013/02/08/shropshire-council-will-not-disclose-pay-offs-to-senior-staff [Accessed 23 October 2014].

Telegraph, 2012. NHS staff discuss rejecting FOI request in leaked email, 13 November. Available at: www.telegraph.co.uk/news/uknews/9675703/NHS-staff-discuss-rejecting-FOI-request-in-leaked-email.html [Accessed 23 October 2014].

Torney, K., 2014. *Interview*. Interviewed by Matt Burgess *[Email]* 16 June 2014.

Turner, T., 2014. *Interview*. Interviewed by Matt Burgess *[Telephone]* 19 May 2014.

WikiLeaks, c2010. *Secret US Embassy Cables*. Available at: https://wikileaks.org/cablegate.html [Accessed 20 September 2014].

Willnat, L. and Weaver, D., 2014. *The American Journalist in the Digital Age*. School of Journalism, Indiana University. Available at: http://news.indiana.edu/releases/iu/2014/05/2013-american-journalist-key-findings.pdf [Accessed 15 September 2014].

Wise, M., 2014. *Interview*. Interviewed by Matt Burgess *[Telephone]* 31 July 2014.

Worthy, B., 2014. *Interview*. Interviewed by Matt Burgess *[In person]* London: 21 May 2014.

Wyeth, L., 2014. *Interview*. Interviewed by Matt Burgess *[Telephone]* 10 July 2014.

Case studies

The Freedom of Information Act has allowed the public and journalists unprecedented access to information. Its implementation has allowed us to see the bonuses police have received despite missing targets (*Telegraph*, 2008), that there have been oil and gas spills in the North Sea every week (*Guardian*, 2011) and how a council spent almost £50,000 on celebrities to motivate their staff (*London Evening Standard*, 2011). These are just a few of the thousands of issues that FOI has revealed, which would not have been possible without the Act.

However, for every time an exposing story is published from an FOI request, there are countless others that are rejected – whether rightly or wrongly. This has caused battles between journalists, their media organisations and public authorities. Sometimes the media have won, sometimes the bureaucrats came out on top.

The most famous of these was the MPs' expenses scandal that saw data released after FOI requests forced the issue into the public knowledge. But this has not been the only FOI battle between politicians and the media. Ben Worthy (2014), who worked at University College London's Constitution Unit, which researched FOI for four years, says that journalists will always cause tension with politicians, whether they are using the Act or not.

> Another important thing that journalists do is innovate with the Act. They push the boundaries, they put through the case law, they do all sorts of interesting things with it – especially as they start working with data journalists and that is also likely to cause political tension.
>
> (Worthy, 2014)

Below are short studies of some of the most contentious FOI cases the media has been involved in. As well as featuring prominently in the news at the time the battles were fought, they have set a number of FOI precedents and case laws.

MPs' expenses scandal

The revelations of what British MPs were putting on their taxpayer-funded expense claims was a story that rocked cultural, political and journalistic spheres. Although the information was not put into the public domain without controversy surrounding the case, it was one of the biggest stories in modern British history. The spending on the £1,600 duckhouse (*Telegraph*, 2009a), swimming pool boiler repairs and hanging baskets (*Telegraph*, 2009b) helped to change the political landscape and led to trust in politicians falling to an all-time low (*Telegraph*, 2010).

However, it would have been unlikely that the story had ever surfaced without the Freedom of Information Act. Three journalists, Heather Brooke, Ben Leapman and Jonathan Ungoed-Thomas, were responsible for applying the pressure to release the data. They put in the original requests for the information and followed it through all the way to the High Court, where it was ruled to be released. However, before it could be released, in a redacted form with addresses that MPs' had exempted, the information was leaked.

> First to say, the expenses scandal was solely based on FOI because in the past journalists had only ever gone after specific MPs and what I wanted to do was create a situation where not just a few MPs but as a point of principle the entire dataset of all expenses were published pro-actively and that members of the public could go and look at that.
>
> (Brooke, 2014)

For Brooke, the battle was to ensure the data about spending was published, and to try and change the culture of secrecy that was inherent in the system. Little to her, and others', knowledge would it take so long for the information to be published. Attempts to reveal MPs' expenses began almost as soon as the Act came into effect in 2005 and it took until 2009 to come to the fore, when the leak occurred. The decision went all the way through the Tribunal and court system until it reached the High Court.

The High Court, reiterating previous decisions, says the 'system was deeply flawed, public scrutiny of the details of individual claims were inevitable. In such circumstances it would have been unreasonable for MPs to expect anything else.' Ultimately the court, in the case of Corporate Officer of the House of Commons v Information Commissioner, Heather Brooke, Ben Leapman and Jonathan Ungoed-Thomas (2008) EWHC 1084, ruled that there were no legal issues as to why in-depth, although redacted, details of the expenses claimed should be revealed.

The information was sold to *The Telegraph* for between £110,000 (*Guardian*, 2009a) and £150,000 (*Daily Mail*, 2012), but without FOI requests and the journalists' work in pursuing the cause the information may not have ever come to light. There were calls for the leak's legality to be investigated by the Metropolitan Police; however, the police decided that there would be no investigation (*Independent*, 2009a).

On the first day that the expenses were published from the leak, *The Telegraph* revealed that Prime Minister Gordon Brown had paid his brother for cleaning services, Jack Straw had over-claimed for his council tax and Lord Mandelson claimed thousands to improve his constituency home after he announced his resignation as an MP, among other details (*Telegraph*, 2009c).

Eventually, the House of Commons put the requested versions online. They were heavily redacted and contained nowhere near the level of detail as was in the leaked versions. The BBC's Nick Robinson says MPs would not have been forced to resign if the details were not leaked (*BBC News*, 2009). Even after the court rulings, there were attempts to block the publication of the expenses, with Prime Minister Gordon Brown having to back down from plans to block the publication after there were warnings that up to 100 backbenchers would ignore being told to vote with the government (*Independent*, 2009b).

It was said that scanning and redacting cost the Commons around £1 million and the failed legal bid to keep the expenses out of the public views cost around £150,000 (*Daily Express*, 2009). Brooke (2014) says she did not expect the case to win in front of the High Court.

> I went into that High Court, with these three High Court judges who looked like fully paid-up members of the establishment and I had looked at previous cases that had been, or Freedom of Expression cases that had come before the court, and I was not hopeful that they would sort of mark a blow for the people's right to know. When they did make that ruling, I think everybody was shocked, particularly Parliament, I think it really took them by surprise.

Nevertheless the disclosures made a profound difference.

> It has had a significant impact leading to the resignation of the Commons' Speaker, a number of MPs stepping down and with four MPs imprisoned. A Fees Office official was also later imprisoned for fraud after *The Telegraph*'s investigation found he created fake invoices,
>
> (Worthy and Bourke, 2011, p.16)

It also led to reform of the expenses system for MPs with the creation of the Independent Parliamentary Standards Authority, which was formed after the scandal as part of the Parliamentary Standards Act 2009.

The information that was contested for years could have been released much sooner, and at lower cost for all involved, if the Commissioner had stuck with an original DN. A draft decision in 2006 showed that Richard Thomas, the first Commissioner, was due to say that everything should be released, including receipts. But the final decision says that information should be redacted and the receipts should not be disclosed, following a meeting with the Commons leader Jack Straw (*Telegraph*, 2009d).

However, in Scotland, which has a much more liberal Freedom of Information Act (as can be seen in Chapter 11), the expenses of Scottish MPs were published almost immediately. The Conservative leader David McLetchie resigned after his travel expenses were published from the results of an FOI request. It was shown that he claimed £11,500 in taxi claims over a period of five years (*BBC News*, 2005a).

Journalist Paul Hutcheon (2014), who made the request, says of the McLetchie affair:

> That was a very high profile case involving the body that passed the Act in the first place and it also related to the MSPs expenses and so that case led to the Scottish Parliament putting all expenses claims online which then had a knock on effect at Westminster.

As highlighted by Hutcheon (2014), the requests led to the publishing of all Scottish MPs' expenses. In December 2005, less than a year after the Act was implemented, the Scottish Parliament published 700 pages of expense details, up from the usual 12 pages that were published (*BBC News*, 2005b).

There remain sceptics who opine that the FOI requests did not reveal the full details and it came down to a leak to do that, as one writing in *The Guardian* (2009b) says: 'For all the front-page stories on MPs' expenses, the case for journalism by FOI is still to be made.'

Brooke (2014) contested that the leaking process plays in to the hands of journalists who are willing to do anything for the story and that it falls into the hands of the system:

> That is what the powers that be don't understand, if you make it so difficult for journalists like me you actually play right in to the hands of this other type of journalist who doesn't give a shit, who thinks 'I am just getting the story the fastest way I can, the easiest way I can. I am not interested in making society better, or opening it up or creating a new democracy I want the fucking story.' I don't have anything against it because they understood how the system works in Britain in the way I didn't. If I did I wouldn't have wasted my time doing the case, but that isn't the kind of world I want to live in and that is not the kind of journalism that I want to see done.

But the MPs' expenses case has been the defining moment for the Freedom of Information Act in the UK. It gave the Act the most publicity it has ever had and encouraged members of the public to make requests to discover where their money is going. Journalists, at all levels, have continued to scrutinise expenses claimed by officials. The effect the MPs' expenses scandal caused is best summed up by *The Telegraph* (2014): 'Five years on, MPs are still struggling to shake off their expenses legacy. So exercised are they that, in some cases, it remains the topic most likely to get an MP fired up.'

Black Spider Memos

Prince Charles, the heir to the throne, sends letters to the government to lobby them about issues, which may affect his estate or interests. *The Guardian* newspaper, and its journalist Rob Evans, put in FOI requests for the letters in 2005 and the battle to see them released lasted ten years.

The highest court in the land, the Supreme Court, ruled, in 2015, that the letters should be disclosed. Seven judges cleared the way for publication as they said that 27 letters sent by Charles could not be blocked 'without real or adequate explanation' and that the FOI veto cannot 'enable a member of the executive to over-ride a judicial decision' (*Guardian*, 2015).

The Supreme Court was upholding the decision of the Court of Appeal that said the then Attorney General, Dominic Grieve, acted unlawfully when he used the ministerial veto to block the letters' publication. Three judges said that he could not block their disclosure 'merely because he disagrees with the decision' of the Information Tribunal (*Guardian*, 2014a).

The flawed arguments the government tried to use were summed up in Grieve's, now defunct, veto. He says that the public interest in disclosing the information is outweighed by the reasons for non-disclosure because 'it is a matter of the highest importance within our constitutional framework that the Monarch is a politically neutral figure able to engage in confidence with the Government of the day, whatever its political colour' (Attorney General's Office, 2012).

It cost the government more than £250,000 in legal fees to keep the letters blocked from publication (*Guardian*, 2014b), up to the Supreme Court hearing, giving an indication of the desire to keep the information secret. *The Guardian* (2009c) found out that the Prince had directly written to lobby eight ministers over a period of three years. Before the decision that the letters should be published, Evans described the process of trying to access the information.

> It has been worth it. I mean, we haven't got the letters, maybe you could say it isn't worth it because we haven't got the letters, but what it does show, even if we lose at this stage, it just shows how society works really. It shows the lengths they want to go to protect his letters. So I think it has been pretty illuminating already.
>
> (Evans, 2014)

Private emails

Private email accounts were never intended to be used for conducting government business. However, this is what happened at the Department for Education with the Education Secretary Michael Gove. A combination of leaks and skillful FOI use by the *Financial Times'* education correspondent Chris Cook, who has since moved on to the BBC, revealed that the Department for Education were using the private email accounts.

The paper saw email traffic that showed Gove and advisors were conducting government business using their private email addresses. In a subsequent FOI request, the Department of Education says they could not find the emails (*Financial Times*, 2011). To add to the affair, Cook and the *Financial Times* also revealed that Gove's office deleted official correspondence with the media. More than 130 emails were found to be deleted with the Department refusing requests for records of what had been deleted and why (*Financial Times*, 2012).

The email address used by Gove belonged to his wife and was known by officials as the Mrs Blurt account. The Department for Education claimed that the emails, because they were held in private, non-governmental email accounts, did not fall within the scope of the Freedom of Information Act. The Information Commissioner (2012a) issued a DN that says the emails were subject to the Freedom of Information Act as their contents concern government business. The *Financial Times* gave one particular email that was obtained by the paper to the Commissioner when it complained, to prove the practice was happening.

The Commissioner's view was that the case of private email accounts would not have been considered when the Act was formed. He also says that the communications between Gove and five others did not amount to political business because it would create a 'blanket ruling' (ICO, 2012a, p.5).

The emails seen by the *Financial Times* (2011), one from Dominic Cummings, a chief political aide to Gove, say that he 'will not answer any further e-mails to my official DfE account'. After seeing the emails, Cook (2014) says he, and the *Financial Times*, were concerned about causing a mass deletion of public information,

> so we took the decision, which is quite unusual for a journalist, to notify, so we basically asked the ICO do you think this makes sense or not, anonymously. We didn't tell them who it was but we sent them the evidence and they said it was terrible, and terrifying and awful and that they definitely need to take action to sort of secure information. Then as soon as they found out who it was they sort of backed off. I find the whole thing utterly bizarre that they are so terrified of Whitehall and I don't really know why, but they haven't ever been able to do enough, they are a complete paper tiger.

However, Information Commissioner Chris Graham (2014) says that because of the case he now believes officials understand they will still be covered by FOI when using private accounts for public business.

> I have to make a judgment about when I press the nuclear button. It took a long time but we have got there and I think that everyone in government now understands that things don't vanish from the realm of FOI just because you have done it on your smartphone. It's also particularly stupid to do it on your smartphone because, as I think we all now realise, that if you don't have levels of security then lots of people are out there listening. I think the message has got through.

The emails hinted at the wide scale use of private email accounts to try to conduct government business in secret and away from the reach of the Freedom of Information Act. In the DN issued by the Information Commissioner (2012a, p.7), it was noted that the email that was sent could be 'characterised as a significant step in the development of a government communications strategy'.

As reported by the BBC (2012), the decision that private email accounts being used for official business were subject to the Act could mean that private text messages of Ministers may also be subject to the Act.

Iraq war

The UK's decision to go to war in Iraq was a highly controversial one, which split public opinion (YouGov, 2013). The debate over whether or not it was a lawful invasion of Iraq is still ongoing with the Chilcot inquiry. The falling out of the government over the death of Dr David Kelly and the following Hutton Inquiry raised questions over how the government and officials had acted.

As a result of this, there was a natural interest in what had happened behind the scenes. Inevitably, FOI requests were made to probe what had been said at the highest levels. Two main FOI battles have focused on the war in Iraq: one over a copy of the draft dossier which led to the invasion of the country; the other regarding Cabinet minutes relating to the decision to go to war.

Iraq dossier

Leading the way with these requests was Chris Ames, a freelance investigative journalist who was writing for the *New Statesman* when he made his requests for details surrounding the government's 'dodgy dossier' into 'Iraq's weapons of mass destruction'. The dossier was one of the most significant reasons that the government intended to deploy troops in Iraq, as it claimed that nuclear weapons could be deployed in 45 minutes. These claims were eventually rebuked and withdrawn by officials (*BBC News*, 2004).

During the Hutton inquiry into the death of Dr David Kelly, Ames spotted the inquiry mention another draft of the dossier, which had not been disclosed. This came to be known as the William's Draft, created by Foreign Office media boss John Williams (*BBC News*, 2006).

The *New Statesman* (2008) described Ames as using FOI to 'doggedly pursue the evidence that he believed would show that the September dossier was the work not of intelligence experts, but of spin doctors whose intention was to "sex up" the known intelligence'.

Almost five years elapsed between Ames contacting the *New Statesman* and the publication of the William's Draft (*New Statesman*, 2008a). The tribunal criticised a lack of an 'audit trail' to show who had written the dossier in 2002 (*New Statesman*, 2008b). The tribunal and the documents released showed that there were similarities between the draft and the later versions that were produced, the *New Statesman* reported (2008c). This included that a claim about uranium that was not supported by evidence.

This rebutted government claims that there was no involvement of spin-doctors in the creation of the draft, and the final document (*New Statesman*, 2008d). The tribunal, in hearing evidence, which was summarised by the magazine, says:

> Information has been placed before us, which was not before Lord Hutton, which may lead to questions as to whether the William's Draft in fact played a greater part in influencing the drafting of the Dossier than has previously been supposed.
>
> (*New Statesman*, 2008e)

But this was not the full extent of Ames' use of FOI on the Iraq war. As highlighted by the Constitution Unit (2011), he also made requests that recovered emails between Tony Blair and his chief of staff, as well as those that tried to water down the claims in the documents. The Constitution Unit says that the FOI requests from Ames were effective in revealing the information, although the process took four years to complete.

> Ames' work is a clear example of the 'jigsaw effect', a patient piecing together of parts of the process behind the controversial decision to go to war. But it also exposes the limitations of FOI in complex decision-making cases such as these.
>
> (Constitution Unit, 2011)

Iraq Cabinet minutes

Cabinet minutes about the decision to invade Iraq have been subject to the ministerial veto not just once, but twice. The requests concerned the minutes of Cabinet meetings held on 13 and 17 March 2003, around the time that the Cabinet was deciding the legalities of going to war in Iraq.

The initial use of veto for the information, by Jack Straw in 2009, was the first time that it had been used on any FOI case (House of Commons Library, 2009, p.1). This was after the tribunal of Cabinet Office v Information Commissioner and Dr Christopher Lamb (2009) EA/2008/0024; EA/2008/0029 upheld the Commissioner's decision that the minutes of the meetings should be disclosed.

The Lamb tribunal says that sending armed forces to invade another country is a 'momentous' decision (par 79). The tribunal says that the convention of collective responsibility allowed ministers the protection of safe discussions at the highest levels of government. But in this particular case, including the controversial nature of the war, 'the value of disclosure lies in the opportunity it provides for the public to make up its own mind on the effectiveness of the decision-making process in context' (par 82).

However, Straw issued the veto in the House of Commons and says that the Cabinet Office makes the most important decisions and the ability to uphold the collective responsibility was one of the most important matters. He added that the decision of going to war in Iraq had already been looked over with a 'fine-toothed comb' (Guardian, 2009d).

This veto was followed up by Attorney General Dominic Grieve issuing a second veto for the minutes in 2012, after a repeat of the request was made (Guardian, 2012). The Information Commissioner Christopher Graham says that the second veto being issued over the information was disappointing and that the 'significant public interest' in the minutes means that they should be disclosed (ICO, 2012b).

Grieve (2012) says he believed the public interest in disclosing the information was outweighed by the public interest in keeping it a secret. In his statement laid to Parliament, he says the amount of time that had passed, since 2009, was not enough to allow for the damage of disclosure to be reduced, that the issue of Iraq remains a live one and that most of the people involved in the meetings are still in Parliament or active in public life.

Chapter 7 top tips

- Journalists can innovate with the Freedom of Information Act. This includes pushing the boundaries further than ever before.
- Innovating with the Act can mean asking for many different types of information captured by a public authority. One example can be a 'sign in register' at the entrance to a public building.

- Having the backing and support of a media organisation and editors is a benefit for journalists using the Act as it can allow a robust legal challenge against the most stubborn of public authorities.
- When public authorities and officials launch the biggest and most extreme defences against releasing information, this should spur journalists on to reveal the truth.
- Persistence in challenging FOI requests and taking them to the next level can pay off for journalists and eventually get the information published.
- Prominent use of the Freedom of Information Act by journalists can encourage members of the public to send requests and these may touch upon areas that have not been previously considered by the media.

References

Attorney General's Office, 2012. Written ministerial statement: Freedom of Information Act veto of release of Prince Charles letters, 16 October. Available at: www.gov.uk/government/publications/written-ministerial-statement-freedom-of-information-act-veto-of-release-of-prince-charles-letters [Accessed 10 September 2014].

BBC News, 2004. Timeline: The 45-minute claim, 13 October. Available at: http://news.bbc.co.uk/1/hi/uk_politics/3466005.stm [Accessed 23 October 2014].

BBC News, 2005a. McLetchie resigns as Tory leader, 31 October. Available at: http://news.bbc.co.uk/1/hi/scotland/4393622.stm [Accessed 6 October 2014].

BBC News, 2005b. MSP expenses published in detail, 13 December. Available at: http://news.bbc.co.uk/1/hi/scotland/4522478.stm [Accessed 22 October 2014].

BBC News, 2006. Battle over 'secret' Iraq dossier, 8 November. Available at: http://news.bbc.co.uk/1/hi/uk_politics/6130662.stm [Accessed 23 October 2014].

BBC News, 2009. MPs' expenses made public online, 18 June. Available at: http://news.bbc.co.uk/1/hi/uk_politics/8105227.stm [Accessed 21 October 2014].

BBC News, 2012. Freedom of Information to include ministers' private texts, 30 September. Available at: www.bbc.co.uk/news/uk-politics-19775763 [Accessed 15 September 2014].

Brooke, H., 2014. *Interview*. Interviewed by Matt Burgess *[In person]* London: 23 May 2014.

Cabinet Office v Information Commissioner and Dr Christopher Lamb (2009) EA/2008/0024; EA/2008/0029.

Constitution Unit, 2011. FOI and weapons of mass destruction. *UK Freedom of Information Blog*, 13 May. Available at: http://constitution-unit.com/2011/05/13/foi-and-weapons-of-mass-destruction [Accessed 24 October 2014].

Cook, C., 2014. *Interview*. Interviewed by Matt Burgess *[Telephone]* 7 August 2014.

Corporate Officer of the House of Commons v Information Commissioner, Heather Brooke, Ben Leapman and Jonathan Ungoed-Thomas (2008) EWHC 1084.

Daily Express, 2009. U-turn on MP expenses secrecy plans, 19 January. Available at: www.express.co.uk/news/uk/81100/U-turn-on-MP-expenses-secrecy-plans [Accessed 4 October 2014].

Daily Mail, 2012. Former *Daily Telegraph* editor reveals he paid £150,000 for disk containing MPs' expenses information, 10 Jaunary. Available at: www.dailymail.co.uk/news/article-2084826/Former-Daily-Telegraph-editor-reveals-paid-150-000-disk-containing-MPs-expenses-information.html [Accessed 4 October 2014].

Evans, R. 2014. *Interview*. Interviewed by Matt Burgess *[Telephone]* 29 July 2014.

Financial Times, 2011. Gove faces probe over private e-mails, 19 September. Available at: www.ft.com/cms/s/0/cc4b8272-e2c4-11e0-897a-00144feabdc0.html [Accessed 4 October 2014].

Financial Times, 2012. Gove staff destroyed government emails, 2 March. Available at: www.ft.com/cms/s/0/f70db1e0-6458-11e1-b50e-00144feabdc0.html [Accessed 16 September 2014].

Graham, C., 2014. *Interview*. Interviewed by Matt Burgess *[In person]* Wilmslow: 20 May 2014.

Grieve, D., 2012. *Exercise of the Executive Override under Section 53 of the Freedom of Information Act 2000*. Attorney General's Office. Available at: www.gov.uk/government/uploads/system/uploads/attachment_data/file/60528/Statement_of_Reasons-31July2012_0.pdf [Accessed 25 October 2014].

Guardian, 2009a. Telegraph paid £110,000 for MPs' expenses data, 25 September. Available at: www.theguardian.com/media/2009/sep/25/telegraph-paid-11000-mps-expenses [Accessed 4 October 2014].

Guardian, 2009b. What the MPs' expenses scoop tells us about journalists and FoI, 14 May. Available at: www.theguardian.com/media/organgrinder/2009/may/14/freedom-of-information-mps-expenses [Accessed 3 October 2014].

Guardian, 2009c. Prince Charles faces fresh meddling claim over letters to ministers, 16 December. Available at: www.theguardian.com/uk/2009/dec/16/prince-charles-letters-to-ministers [Accessed 4 July 2014].

Guardian, 2009d. Straw vetoes publication of Cabinet Iraq war minutes, 24 February. Available at: www.theguardian.com/politics/2009/feb/24/iraq-freedom-of-information [Accessed 23 October 2014].

Guardian, 2011. Oil and gas spills in North Sea every week, papers reveal, 5 July. Available at: www.theguardian.com/environment/2011/jul/05/oil-gas-spills-north-sea [Accessed 1 August 2014].

Guardian, 2012. Tony Blair's Iraq meetings to remain secret after government veto, 31 July. Available at: www.theguardian.com/politics/2012/jul/31/iraq-invasion-government-documents-secret [Accessed 23 October 2014].

Guardian, 2014a. Prince Charles letters: Attorney General acted unlawfully, say senior judges, 12 March. Available at: www.theguardian.com/uk-news/2014/mar/12/attorney-general-unlawful-prince-charles-letters [Accessed 10 November 2014].

Guardian, 2014b. Ministers spend £250,000 on Prince Charles letters legal row, 28 March. Available at: www.theguardian.com/media/organgrinder/2009/may/14/freedom-of-information-mps-expenses [Accessed 7 August 2014].

Guardian, 2015. Supreme court clears way for release of secret Prince Charles letters, 26 March. Available at: www.theguardian.com/uk-news/2015/mar/26/supreme-court-clears-way-release-secret-prince-charles-letters-black-spider-memos [Accessed 18 April 2015].

House of Commons Library, 2009. *FOI and Ministerial vetoes*. Available at: www.parliament.uk/briefing-papers/SN05007.pdf [Accessed 9 March 2015].

Hutcheon, P., 2014. *Interview*. Interviewed by Matt Burgess *[Telephone]* 4 June 2014.

Independent, 2009a. Probe into expenses leak 'not in public interest', 19 May. Available at: www.independent.co.uk/news/uk/politics/probe-into-expenses-leak-not-in-public-interest-1687473.html [Accessed 1 October 2014].

Independent, 2009b. Brown abandons bid to keep MPs' expenses secret, 22 January. Available at: www.independent.co.uk/news/uk/politics/brown-abandons-bid-to-keep-mps-expenses-secret-1488645.html [Accessed 1 October 2014].

Information Commissioner's Office (ICO), 2012a. *Decision Notice FS50422276*. Available at: https://ico.org.uk/media/action-weve-taken/decision-notices/2012/712854/fs_50422276.pdf [Accessed 9 March 2015].

Information Commissioner's Office (ICO), 2012b. *ICO Statement on Ministerial Veto of ICO Decision over Iraq Cabinet Minutes*, 31 July. Available at: http://web.archive.org/web/20140703174312/http://ico.org.uk/news/latest_news/2012/ico-statement-iraq-cabinet-minutes-ministerial-veto-31072012 [Accessed 9 March 2015].

London Evening Standard, 2011. £42,000 bill for celebrities to motivate London council staff, 1 February. Available at: www.standard.co.uk/news/42000-bill-for-celebrities-to-motivate-london-council-staff-6561905.html [Accessed 5 July 2014].

New Statesman, 2008a. It's official: Blair's government set out to deceive us about Iraq, 21 February. Available at: www.newstatesman.com/politics/2008/02/williams-draft-intelligence [Accessed 23 October 2014].

New Statesman, 2008b. Iraq dossier – watchdog ruling, 24 April. Available at: www.newstatesman.com/politics/2008/04/iraq-dossier-government-ruling [Accessed 23 October 2014].

New Statesman, 2008c. How the war was spun, 31 January. Available at: www.newstatesman.com/uk-politics/2008/01/iraq-draft-uranium [Accessed 23 October 2014].

New Statesman, 2008d. Secret Iraq dossier published, 18 February. Available at: www.newstatesman.com/politics/2008/02/iraq-wmd-dossier-draft [Accessed 23 October 2014].

New Statesman, 2008e. WMD dossier decision 'very soon', Brown says. Available at: www.newstatesman.com/politics/2008/02/draft-iraq-dossier-brown [Accessed 9 March 2015].

Parliamentary Standards Act 2009 (c.13). London: HMSO.

Telegraph, 2008. Police chiefs 'rewarded for failure' by bonuses, 17 February. Available at: www.telegraph.co.uk/news/uknews/1578918/Police-chiefs-rewarded-for-failure-by-bonuses.html [Accessed 29 July 2014].

Telegraph, 2009a. MPs' expenses: Sir Peter Viggers claimed for £1,600 floating duck island, 21 May. Available at: www.telegraph.co.uk/news/newstopics/ mps-expenses/5357568/MPs-expenses-Sir-Peter-Viggers-claimed-for-1600-floating-duck-island.html [Accessed 14 September 2014].

Telegraph, 2009b. MPs' expenses: Full list of MPs investigated by *The Telegraph*, 8 May. Available at: www.telegraph.co.uk/news/newstopics/ mps-expenses/5297606/MPs-expenses-Full-list-of-MPs-investigated-by-the-Telegraph.html [Accessed 14 September 2014].

Telegraph, 2009c. How *The Telegraph* investigation exposed the MPs' expenses scandal day by day, 15 May. Available at: www.telegraph.co.uk/news/newstopics/ mps-expenses/5324582/How-the-Telegraph-investigation-exposed-the-MPs-expenses-scandal-day-by-day.html [Accessed 3 October 2014].

Telegraph, 2009d. MPs' expenses: Information Commissioner performed U-turn over publication, 30 May. Available at: www.telegraph.co.uk/news/newstopics/ mps-expenses/5412674/MPs-expenses-Information-commissioner-performed-U-turn-over-publication.html [Accessed 29 July 2014].

Telegraph, 2010. Trust in politicians halves in wake of MPs' expenses scandal, official figures show, 12 November. Available at: www.telegraph.co.uk/news/ uknews/8127391/Trust-in-politicians-halves-in-wake-of-MPs-expenses-scandal-official-figures-show.html [Accessed 14 September 2014].

Telegraph, 2014. MPs' expenses: A scandal that will not die, 13 April. Available at: www.telegraph.co.uk/news/newstopics/mps-expenses/10761548/MPs-expenses-A-scandal-that-will-not-die.html [Accessed 14 August 2014].

Worthy, B., 2014. *Interview*. Interviewed by Matt Burgess *[In person]* London: 21 May 2014.

Worthy, B. and Bourke, G., 2011. *The Sword and the Shield: The Use of FOI by Parliamentarians and the Impact of FOI on Parliament*. University College London. Available at: www.ucl.ac.uk/constitution-unit/research/foi/foi-and-parliament/sword-and-the-shield.pdf [Accessed 21 October 2014].

YouGov, 2013. *YouGov Survey Results*. YouGov. Available at: http://cdn.yougov. com/cumulus_uploads/document/9p07sppwg8/YG-Archives-Pol-110313-Iraq. pdf [Accessed 20 October 2014].

Know your rights

Timeliness

The delay in responses to requests is the biggest issue for journalists, as it can mean stories are no longer news by the time the authority replies to the request. In the UK, Section 10 of the Freedom of Information Act 2000 means that authorities must respond to requests no later than 20 working days after they are received. It also states that they must reply to requests promptly. Excluding any public holidays, the 20 working day period usually means that requests should come back a month after they have been made.

However, this is not always the case and it is a major frustration for those making requests. It puts journalists off using the Act. Ian Cobain (2014) from *The Guardian* says: 'There's quite a lot of journalists who don't use it, they regard it as too time consuming and unsatisfactory because it doesn't produce ready results.'

Cynthia O'Murchu (2014) from the *Financial Times* says it can be worth informing bosses that it may take some time to produce results. She says: 'But also I think that editors need to understand the amount of time that it takes and to keep them in the loop and then also give it the space.'

This problem is seen around the world. Australian lawyer Peter Timmins (2014) says:

> The problem with FOI as, I guess, a mechanism, is that as you would appreciate most journalists regard time of the essence in seeking access to information and I think all along FOI has been a useful tool to have in the toolkit but most journalists would say that it is slow, it is potentially expensive, there is a lot of scope for getting the run around.

Mark Horvit (2014), representing the USA's National Freedom of Information Coalition, says that requesters are often powerless to delays: 'If they want to delay, if they want to put things off, if they want to put up road blocks the federal government can do it and your options for recourse are fairly limited.' Michael Morisy (2014) from Muckrock in the USA says that it is 'highly discouraging' when authorities take 'two weeks to send you a letter telling you it is going to be months before you hear anything else'.

Back in the UK, in 2013, West Midlands Police considered writing off all requests that it had failed to answer on time. Board members of the Police and Crime Commissioner were told that there was a backlog of 550 FOI requests that had not been answered (*Birmingham Mail*, 2013). The police force blamed the backlog of unanswered requests on staff cuts and an increase in requests, the *Birmingham Mail* reported (2013). Eventually it decided to write to requesters and handle their queries. This is just one example of an authority showing a potential disregard for its FOI obligations.

The Act, in Section 10, states that a request should be answered 'promptly' as well as within the 20 working days. The Upper Tribunal decision of John v ICO and Ofsted (2014) UKUT 444 AAC looked at the meaning of promptly and says it 'is more akin to *without delay*'. This essentially means that it can act upon the request within a time that is reasonably practical. It was considered by the John tribunal that authorities will take time to process requests and they should be allowed to search for information and ensure they are finding all the applicable information held. The John tribunal also says: 'It may be that in some cases it would be appropriate to require a public authority to explain the time that it took to respond to a request' (par 38).

FOI trainer and consultant Paul Gibbons (2014) says delays to requests are often because people within the organisations, not FOI officers, are responsible for providing the information.

> As an FOI officer you're dependent on the people in the departments because you don't have the information at your fingertips, in fact very rarely you have the information at your fingertips. You're reliant on other people who know their subject area and know all the information and obviously they have other jobs to do.
>
> (Gibbons, 2014)

If a request has been with a public authority for 20 working days and they have not responded to the request, this should be followed up, either via phone or email, to see if the authority is able to respond to the request. Laura McInerney says (2014):

> The other thing that I do a lot, with everyone but especially people who aren't used to FOI, is the day before the request is due, I will send a reminder email. Don't send it afterwards because it suggests that you are the sort of person who only follows up after.

Journalist Alex Homer (2014) says that he ensures he has received an acknowledgement for the request and then follows the progress of the request by 'diarying the date the request is due to be returned and on the occasions when it is not returned on time, making sure to chase it up either through email or phone calls'.

Horvit (2014) says that in the USA, people should also badger the authority for responses: 'It usually takes a lot of follow up, consistent phone calls, follow-up emails, pushing to make sure that you are not being ignored or delayed and delayed.'

Proactive authorities will respond before the 20 working day deadline to say they are not able to respond to the request within the statutory time limits. It is possible to complain to the Information Commissioner as soon as the time limit has elapsed. Although it should first be followed up with the public authority to enquire why the information is delayed. The Scottish Information Commissioner, Rosemary Agnew (2014), says she encourages journalists to complain about timeliness straightaway.

Applicant and motive blind

The Freedom of Information Act is intended to be fundamentally applicant and motive blind. This means that the reasons behind a request and who it is made by should not be relevant. The ICO (2007, p.1) says the lack of reference to the identity and motive in FOI and EIR is where the principles are drawn from.

This approach was ratified by the tribunal of S and Information Commissioner v General Register Office (2007) EA/2006/0030. The S tribunal says:

> We wish to emphasise at this point that the Freedom of Information Act is applicant and motive blind. A disclosure under FOIA is a disclosure to the public [i.e. the world at large]. In dealing with a Freedom of Information request there is no provision for the public authority to look at from whom the application has come, the merits of the application or the purpose for which it is to be used.
>
> (par 80)

This means that all requests should be treated equally, but this is not always the case. There are frequent cases of authorities trying to undermine this principle of the Act. These attempts can be part of the overall process of answering requests and the level of interference may differ, but they occasionally have different undertones to them.

Not blind in practice

Despite the principles that the Act is applicant and motive blind, this is only true to a certain extent. The Information Tribunal of K v Information Commissioner (2014) EA/2014/0024 says the principles are a 'misleading oversimplification' and that the principle is only true in a 'limited sense' (par 19). The K tribunal says that as the Act required people to state their real identities, the identities and motives can be revealed for the cost limit Section 12 provisions, as well as assessing whether a request is vexatious. It also says that when fulfilling obligations under Section 16 to provide advice and assistance, it may need to find out what the requester is really after to help them get what they want.

The following circumstances indicate that the Act is not fully applicant and motive blind:

- For any request a name (that should be a real one) is needed under Section 8 of the Act.
- A correspondence address, again needed under Section 8, will often give away the profession or company the requester works in.
- If the information is in the public domain, the authority has to consider if it is reasonably accessible to the particular applicant, which will involve considering their individual circumstances.
- If a request is being treated as vexatious under Section 14, the authority may look at the purpose and motive of the request.

There will always be times where the requester's identity and their motive in making a request are known. When deciding on an exemption to apply, the authority should consider the application of the exemption to the specific information, not the purposes of the requester. Their decision to release, or not release, information should be based on the legal and technical applications of the Act, not the person behind the request.

Meddling

In 2013, Hackney Council accidentally sent a requester 'a briefing note which looked in detail at previous requests made' (*Guardian*, 2014) as well as other research the requester had done, and discussions that had been taken place on blogs. *Trinity Mirror*'s David Higgerson (2014) says this sort of profiling of requesters is not in keeping with the applicant blind principle. He says: 'Second-guessing motives and providing background on how the information might be used is utterly against that principle and runs a serious risk of prejudicing the entire process.'

As in the Hackney Council case, if some authorities are profiling those who are making requests, it is not surprising that journalists feel they may be treated differently to other requesters by FOI staff. Journalist Matt Davis (2014) says there may be cases where it does happen:

> I think that is probably true but only in a very limited number of cases to be honest with you. I don't think it is widespread I think people on the other side, the Freedom of Information side, have got wise to that.

The Met's high risk list

The Metropolitan Police, during 2010, kept a list of disclosures that came from journalists and other requesters who were on a 'high risk' register. In these lists, the police force includes requests that may have 'potential media interest'. Internal documents, which were released following an FOI request made through WhatDoTheyKnow.com, say that 'you MUST obtain approval from DPA/Press Liaison and / MPS ACPO portfolio lead before release if this request is from a journalist or identified as high risk' (WhatDoTheyKnow, 2010a).

The correspondence lists requests about surveillance, the royal household, witness protection, and many other sets of information considered high risk to the force (WhatDoTheyKnow, 2010b).

FOI trainer Tim Turner (2010) says, having worked for both public authorities that disclose who the requester is to their colleagues and those that do not, the latter is better for answering requests.

> It is so much of a distraction that I fundamentally disapprove of the idea of letting your colleagues know who the requester is. One thing I still think is a reasonable idea is that when the request is done and the response is ready I would still give that to the PR team. I think those organizations who profile their applicants who have risk registers, as someone who thinks FOI is a good thing and someone who thinks data protection is a good thing, I am appalled, I think it is a terrible idea.
>
> (Turner, 2014)

Press officers/cooperation

As outlined above, the Act is not fully applicant and motive blind. This can lead to press officers becoming involved in the FOI procedure, which for journalists can be a positive and a negative influence. It may lead to fears that requests are not being treated equally and that the influence of press officers could stop some information being disclosed.

FOI can add a new element to the relationship, although this does not necessarily have to be negative. There are times where press officers will help journalists get around the formality of the FOI process by treating requests for information as business as usual situations. Where this happens it can reduce the wait for information, and circumvent bureaucracy.

However, this may not always work in practice. Rosenbaum (2014) says:

> It may be the case that some of the information obtained by FOI requests could, in theory, be sought from and provided by press offices of the public authority in question. However, press offices are working to the authority's own remit and under pressure. Questions are not always answered fully nor with precise detail in which they have to be in response to FOI requests.

In many ways, it should be anticipated that a request from a journalist will be sent to a press office before information is disclosed. Scottish journalist Rob Edwards (2014) says:

> As a journalist you kind of expect that. I know that every time I make a request to the Scottish government it straight away gets copied to the press office. I'm pretty certain that happens in other places, so you kind of accept that.

Although, he did add: 'I'm not unrelaxed about that.'

FOI Officer Kit Good (2014) says that FOI officers and press officers cooperating can be 'beneficial' when journalists are making requests, as it allows the authority to come up with a response to help the journalist at the same time as the information has been sent out. Good says he has not experienced press officers trying to alter the information that is being sent out.

> All the press professionals I have ever worked with in different organisations say they are quite used to having this, the information that is going to be out there and this is the way, you'll have to have comments on it that way, rather than the sense of press officers manipulating information, most press officers they might look at some of the phrasing but they know that they can't alter the content of any communication there.

Matt Davis (2014) says that authorities knowing he is a journalist can often mean that a more complete response comes from the request. Speaking about the Driver and Vehicle Licensing Agency:

> They know that I am a journalist and what I will quite often get is I will get a response from the Freedom of Information team and a prepared response from the press office as well, and not a nasty response from the press office, but a sort of an explanation from the press office and an invitation to ring them up to discuss it further.

Prolific American requester Jason Leopold (2014) says that there can be times where his reputation for making requests does result in some differences to how he is treated. 'I think that the government is well aware that I sue, that I litigate, that I am not going to wait in some instances. I have noticed that they pay closer attention.'

Where there is any suspicion that an authority's press office, or any person, has meddled with an FOI response, to change what has been provided, a complaint should be made to the ICO as soon as possible. Requests can also be made for information about how the original response was handled.

Redacting

Under Section 12 of the Act, a public authority does not have to answer a request that exceeds the appropriate cost limit. The Freedom of Information and Data Protection (Appropriate Limit and Fees) Regulations 2004 set out what the appropriate limit is and what the authority can include in its estimation of the cost of complying with the request.

The Fees Regulations say the appropriate limit for government authorities is £600 (reg 3), or 24 staff hours at the equivalent of £25 per hour (reg 4). For other authorities it is £450 (reg 3), which equals 18 staff hours at £25 per hour (reg 4). The flat hourly rate does not alter depending on which member of staff is answering it, or how much they are paid. It is purely a general figure to assist authorities in their calculations.

Redaction of documents cannot be included in cost estimates and should be appealed if an authority tries to claim that it does count. The tribunal of Chief Constable of South Yorkshire Police v Information Commissioner (2009) EA/2009/0029 can be cited. The only four things that can be included in estimating costs are:

- working out whether it holds the information;
- locating the information or a document that may contain the information;
- retrieving the information or a document that may contain the information;
- extracting the information from a document containing it.

(Fees Regulations, 2004, reg 4)

Public Interest Test

Whenever a public authority wishes to use a qualified exemption, it has to conduct a PIT. The test requires the public authority to balance the interests of withholding the information against the interests of disclosing it. The Freedom of Information Act itself does not define what the public interest is. The Information Tribunal in the case of Guardian Newspapers Ltd and Heather Brooke v Information Commissioner and British Broadcasting Corporation (2007) EA/2006/0011; 0013 relied on a previous interpretation of what the public interest can mean (from outside of the Freedom of Information Act) and is taken from British Steel Corp v Granada Television Ltd (1981) AC 1096 (at 1168): 'There is a wide difference between what is interesting to the public and what it is in the public interest to make known.'

An authority, when refusing a request using a qualified exemption, must under Section 17 ensure that it 'state(s) the reasons' for using the exemption and also that 'in all circumstances' the public interest in disclosure is outweighed by the public interest in using the exemption. The ICO says general factors that will always boost the public interest in disclosure are:

- transparency;
- accountability;
- promoting public understanding;
- safeguarding the democratic process;
- good decision-making by public bodies;
- upholding standards of integrity;
- ensuring justice and fair treatment;
- securing the best use of public resources;
- ensuring fair commercial competition;
- suspicion of wrongdoing;
- if information in the public domain is wrong.

(ICO, 2013, pp.5–15)

There are different public interest levels for 'prejudice' and 'class-based' exemptions (explained in Chapter 4). For prejudice-based exemptions, the Commissioner (2013, p.10) says there will always be some inherent public interest in maintaining the exemption. A major disadvantage for journalists when making requests that involve a judgment of the PIT is that when conducting one, the public authority is granted an extension to the amount of time it has to respond to the request. Section 10(3) of the Act allows for a 'reasonable' time extension to conduct a PIT.

However, there is no statutory time period for this to be completed in, which in reality means an indefinite amount of time can be taken. There are no punishments or repercussions for an authority dragging out the time it takes to consider the public interest. The authority can take as long as it needs to complete the PIT but Section 10(3) makes it clear that the authority must tell the requester if it is going to rely on a qualified exemption within the initial 20 working days.

The Times investigations editor Dominic Kennedy (2014) says that he always considers the public interest when making a request to an authority and puts his reasons for why disclosure should happen in the initial request, even though there is no obligation to do so.

I always put in some public interest arguments, there's no need to do that at all but it kind of starts you off with a public interest argument that they are going to have to knock down if they are doing a balancing exercise.

Including public interest arguments in a request can help to hone the request, the reasons why it is being made and provide a foundation for any further challenge in the FOI process, such as an internal review or complaint to the Commissioner. The tribunal of Christopher Martin Hogan and Oxford City Council v Information Commissioner (2006) EA/2005/0026; 0030 says that the focus of the public interest arguments for maintaining the exemption, put forward by authorities, should relate to the exemption at issue.

Considering the wider implications of the release of information will strengthen the PIT argument. This is a view that is shared by Paul Gibbons (2014). He says it would be 'pointless' for a public authority to conduct a PIT if they were not intending to withhold the information. He also says that often authorities do not think very hard about the arguments in favour of disclosure. Gibbons' advice for writing a strong public interest argument involves considering reasoning that is wider than just general points, and trying to be as specific as possible to the requests' circumstances.

> If you can find some way of demonstrating that disclosure would benefit society as a whole rather than just your news story then that is going to help. Is there a human rights angle? Is it better if the organisation discloses this information? Will it help people to avoid injustice, or a breach of their privacy? Will it expose breaches of privacy? If you can demonstrate there is a much wider public interest than just this is an interesting story, then that's really going to help argue your case in an FOI case where you're arguing against the public interest.
>
> (Gibbons, 2014)

If information that would be disclosed is inaccurate, this does not diminish the public interest in releasing it. In Home Office v Information Commissioner (2008) EA/2008/0027, the tribunal was summed up as saying that if the information is inaccurate, it is irrelevant because the Act gives a right to information. The Ministry of Justice (2012) says the balancing of the public interest will change over time and with decisions from the courts and tribunals.

Keyword requests

A request that has been made based around a single keyword is a valid request. By their very nature, a lot of requests will require an authority to search for information using keywords. A request is allowed to be specifically based around a keyword that the authority is due to search, as long as there is enough information provided to allow the authority to identify and locate the information.

Chris Cook was at the *Financial Times* when he made the request regarding former Education Secretary Michael Gove's use of private email accounts for public business (see Chapter 7 for more). Although the request for the search word of 'Gove' was refined, the Cabinet Office contested that this was not a valid request for information as it could not identify what was being asked for specifically. In this case, the Commissioner says that even though he had not specifically identified the information by name, it does not mean that it is unidentifiable (ICO, 2013, p.7).

The Commissioner (2013, p.8) also says: 'The idea of a requirement of prior knowledge that the relevant information exists is itself contrary to the very purpose of the legislation, let alone prior knowledge as to what it comprises.' It was concluded that, because Cook had asked for information that could be identified from the date, the subject and the location, that his request was a valid one. 'While public authorities might find such requests irritating, the FOIA does not legislate against so-called "fishing expeditions"', the Commissioner (2013, p.8) reiterated to the Cabinet Office.

How a keyword is likely to be used should be considered when you are making a request for information around a specific keyword. For example, a search for correspondence about *The Guardian* newspaper could yield a large number of results. A search could flag up all direct mentions of the newspaper's name, as well as the URL www.theguardian.com, and any mentions of the word 'guardian'. Therefore further details should be included, such as a date frame, a sub-category, i.e. *The Guardian*'s coverage of the specific issue, or the name of a specific department that has information relating to *The Guardian*.

Advice and assistance

Public authorities are required to provide advice and assistance, as set out in Section 16 of the Act. Requests do not have to be sent to receive advice from a public authority – Section 16(1) states it is possible for anyone to be provided with guidance if they propose to make a request. Providing advice and assistance under Section 16 will mean that an authority complies with the Section 45 Code of Practice. As the need to provide advice and assistance is captured in the Act, it is possible for the Commissioner to issue a DN or an EN requiring parties to comply with their duties.

The Code of Practice, which was issued in 2004 shortly before the Act came into force, covers five main areas (although it is due to be updated). One of these details the Section 16 obligations. The Code of Practice says that public authorities should be flexible in offering help and should do so in a way that is most appropriate to circumstances of the requester (MoJ, 2004).

The ICO (2008, pp.2–3), in guidance for authorities, lays out other important duties of advice and assistance. The need to provide advice and assistance, the Information Commissioner says, is 'extensive' and potentially applies to most of the request stages (ICO, 2008, p.2), as follows:

- Contact: early contact and maintaining a dialogue throughout the request.
- Record: all communications on the handling and clarification should be recorded.
- Format: if it is not possible to give the requester the information in the format they have specified for it, then it should be discussed whether it is possible to give it to the requester in another way.
- Rejection: the authority should be prepared to give help to those who have had requests turned down.

Proposing to make requests

If you are planning on making a request, you can ask the authority to provide help in formulating it. FOI officer Lynn Wyeth (2014) says:

> I would say, pick the phone up, discuss it with people. We have a duty under Section 16 to advise and assist and an FOI officer will happily do that. We don't want to be looking for information that you want and then you come back and say 'I didn't want that, I want this now'.

Martin Stable (2014) from the *Financial Times* also recommends proactively speaking to FOI officers: 'I think that one of the things that I have taught people who have sought my advice on this is, the FOI officers in a public authority are usually your best friend.'

Additionally, authorities should publish their procedures for dealing with requests for information, although this is often not carried out. This should include an email address or system to which applicants may direct requests, in addition to a telephone number and, where possible, details of a named individual who can provide assistance (MoJ, 2004).

Clarifying a request

Under Section 8 of the Act, a request must describe the information to a level that can allow the authority to locate what is being asked for. The Code of Practice says that authorities can ask for more detail if it is needed to enable them to locate information. A non-exhaustive list of types of assistance that they may provide is written in the code as follows:

- An outline of the information that might meet the terms of the request.
- Providing access to detailed catalogues and indexes to help the requester understand what is held.
- A general response to the request setting out further options for information.

(MoJ, 2004, p.7)

Fees

For the government's review of the Act, the Campaign for Freedom of Information (2012) says that there should be a requirement for authorities to state under Section 16 how they exceeded the cost estimate when the limits have been exceeded. The Code of Practice says that the authority should consider providing a breakdown of what information could be provided within the cost limits. It also says that the authority should consider advising applicants how they could reword their request to ensure clarity (MoJ, 2004). There is more on this is Chapter 4.

Privatisation and outsourcing

Private companies are increasingly holding a large stake in the UK's public services, under contracts to run services. Yet, they are not covered by FOI laws. The four biggest companies are G4S, Serco, Atos and Capita, which combined earn £4 billion of public money through government contracts (*Guardian*, 2013). Yet, despite receiving vast quantities of public money, these companies are not included in the scope of the Freedom of Information Act. They cannot be asked basic questions about their work and do not have to provide an answer by law.

Many private providers already have provisions to help authorities comply with the Act built into their contracts, which were created when the tendering process was completed. These often mean that they will have to help the authority comply with a request that has come to them, potentially by providing the requested information. The authority would then consider whether the information is exempt under any of the provisions of the Act.

In any case, the requests should be made to the public authority, who will then, in theory, ask the private service to provide it with the information. This, as highlighted by Brooke (2006, p.170), has been an ongoing problem: 'Until these companies are added to the FOIA, the only way to find out about their work is to make an FOI request to the relevant public authority that has contracted out its services.'

Chapter 8 top tips

- The authority is obliged to reply to a request promptly and within 20 working days of it being received.
- Delays with the Act can be rife, which means it is important to do as much research that may benefit the request before it is sent.
- The Act is fundamentally applicant and motive blind and there are very limited circumstances when the authority should try and clarify who is making the request and their reason for doing so.
- It is possible to complain to the Information Commissioner about a late response without asking for an internal review. Although the request should be chased up with the authority prior to this.
- Authorities cannot include the time that they have spent thinking about applying an exemption to a request, or redacting information for a response, into their calculations of the Section 12 cost estimates.
- Under the Section 45 Code of Practice, it is good practice for an authority to give a breakdown of how they reached the cost limits when they apply Section 12.
- When conducing a PIT, the authority must say why it has refused the request and to do so the public interest must be outweighed by maintaining the exemption in all the circumstances of the request.
- There are general areas such as promoting transparency and allowing a further understanding of issues that will always be the public interest to disclose information but the more specific reasons that can be given will increase the chances of the information being disclosed.
- An authority has a duty under Section 16 of the Act to provide advice and assistance to the requester. The Information Commissioner says this duty can be extensive and apply to all stages of a request.

References

Agnew, R., 2014. *Interview*. Interviewed by Matt Burgess *[Telephone]* 20 June 2014.

Birmingham Mail, 2013. Police ditch plans to write off backlog of Freedom of Information requests, 18 November. Available at: www.birminghammail.co.uk/news/local-news/police-ditch-plans-write-backlog-6312834   [Accessed 10 September 2014].

British Steel Corp v Granada Television Ltd (1981) AC 1096.

Brooke, H., 2006. *Your Right to Know: A Citizen's Guide to the Freedom of Information Act*. London: Pluto Press.

Campaign for Freedom of Information, 2012. *Written Evidence by Campaign for Freedom of Information.* Available at: www.publications.parliament.uk/pa/cm201213/cmselect/cmjust/96/96we19.htm [Accessed 10 June 2014].

Chief Constable of South Yorkshire Police v Information Commissioner (2009) EA/2009/0029.

Christopher Martin Hogan and Oxford City Council v Information Commissioner (2006) EA/2005/0026; 0030.

Cobain, I., 2014. *Interview.* Interviewed by Matt Burgess *[Telephone]* 2 June 2014.

Davis, M., 2014. *Interview.* Interviewed by Matt Burgess *[Telephone]* 21 May 2014.

Edwards, R., 2014. *Interview.* Interviewed by Matt Burgess *[Telephone]* 14 May 2014.

Freedom of Information Act 2000 (c.36). London: HMSO.

Freedom of Information and Data Protection (Appropriate Limit and Fees) Regulations 2004 SI 3244. London: HMSO.

Gibbons, P., 2014. *Interview.* Interviewed by Matt Burgess *[In person]* London: 22 May 2014.

Good, K., 2014. *Interview.* Interviewed by Matt Burgess *[Telephone]* 11 June 2014.

Guardian, 2013. UK's biggest outsourcing firms agree to more public scrutiny, 20 November. Available at: www.theguardian.com/business/2013/nov/20/uk-outsourcing-firms-public-scrutiny [Accessed 8 August 2014].

Guardian, 2014. Hackney council is not alone in its reluctance to embrace the spirit of FOI, 30 April. Available at: www.theguardian.com/local-government-network/2014/apr/30/freedom-information-council-foi-public-right-know [Accessed 26 October 2014].

Guardian Newspapers Ltd and Heather Brooke v Information Commissioner and British Broadcasting Corporation (2007) EA/2006/0011; 0013.

Higgerson, D., 2014. FOI: The council which does research on people making FOI requests. *David Higgerson*, 26 April. Available at: http://davidhiggerson.wordpress.com/2014/04/26/foi-the-council-which-does-research-on-people-making-foi-requests/#more-5176 [Accessed 15 October 2014].

Home Office v Information Commissioner (2008) EA/2008/0027.

Homer, A., 2014. *Interview.* Interviewed by Matt Burgess *[Email]* 29 August 2014.

Horvit, M., 2014. *Interview.* Interviewed by Matt Burgess *[Telephone]* 27 May 2014.

Information Commissioner's Office (ICO), 2007. *Freedom of Information Good Practice Guidance No 6.* Available at: http://ico.org.uk/for_organisations/guidance_index/~/media/documents/library/Freedom_of_Information/Detailed_specialist_guides/MOTIVE_BLIND_V1.ashx [Accessed 13 June 2014].

Information Commissioner's Office (ICO), 2008. *Good Practice in Providing Advice and Assistance.* Available at: http://ico.org.uk/for_organisations/guidance_index/~/media/documents/library/Freedom_of_Information/Detailed_specialist_guides/good_practice_advice_assistance.ashx [Accessed 20 June 2014].

Information Commissioner's Office (ICO), 2013. *The Public Interest Test.* Available at: http://ico.org.uk/for_organisations/guidance_index/~/media/documents/library/Freedom_of_Information/Detailed_specialist_guides/the_public_interest_test.ashx [Accessed 15 June 2014].

John v ICO and Ofsted (2014) UKUT 444 AAC.

K v Information Commissioner (2014) EA/2014/0024.

Kennedy, D., 2014. *Interview*. Interviewed by Matt Burgess *[Telephone]* 28 May 2014.

Leopold, J., 2014. *Interview*. Interviewed by Matt Burgess *[Telephone]* 28 May 2014.

McInerney, L., 2014. *Interview*. Interviewed by Matt Burgess *[In person]* London: 12 June 2014.

Ministry of Justice (MoJ), 2004. *Secretary of State for Constitutional Affairs' Code of Practice on the Discharge of Public Authorities' Functions under Part I of the Freedom of Information Act 2000*. Available at: www.justice.gov.uk/downloads/information-access-rights/foi/foi-section45-code-of-practice.pdf [Accessed 17 September 2014].

Ministry of Justice (MoJ), 2012. *Public Interest Test*. Available at: www.justice.gov.uk/information-access-rights/foi-guidance-for-practitioners/exemptions-guidance/foi-exemptions-public-interest [Accessed 6 September 2014].

Morisy, M., 2014. 2014. *Interview*. Interviewed by Matt Burgess *[Telephone]* 22 May 2014.

O'Murchu, C., 2014. *Interview*. Interviewed by Matt Burgess *[Telephone]* 28 May 2014.

Rosenbaum, M., 2014. *Interview*. Interviewed by Matt Burgess *[In person]* London: 30 May 2014.

S and Information Commissioner v General Register Office (2007) EA/2006/0030.

Stable, M., 2014. *Interview*. Interviewed by Matt Burgess *[Telephone]* 9 May 2014.

Timmins, P., 2014. *Interview*. Interviewed by Matt Burgess *[Telephone]* 30 May 2014.

Turner, T., 2014. *Interview*. Interviewed by Matt Burgess *[Telephone]* 19 May 2014.

WhatDoTheyKnow, 2010a. *High Profile List: DAVISON HP Redacted Advice Note*. Available at: www.whatdotheyknow.com/request/29145/response/76267/attach/html/3/DAVISON%20HP%20Redacted%20Advice%20Note.doc.pdf.html [Accessed 26 October 2014].

WhatDoTheyKnow, 2010b. *High Profile List*. Available at: www.whatdotheyknow.com/request/high_profile_list#incoming-76267 [Accessed 26 October 2014].

Wyeth, L., 2014. *Interview*. Interviewed by Matt Burgess *[Telephone]* 10 July 2014.

Chapter 9

Appeals

As well as establishing the right for anyone to ask for any information, the Freedom of Information Act allows requesters to complain when they do not get that information, or any response at all. Appealing against FOI responses can go from the original authority, all the way up to the European Courts. The more complex, the more legally challenging and politically sensitive a request is, the longer the process is likely to be dragged out.

The rights of complaint are set out in Sections 50–56 of the Freedom of Information Act 2000. The first step of any complaint about a request should, almost always, be asking for an internal review with the authority from which the information was requested. This can then be escalated to the ICO, which will issue a decision on the complaint. It may also issue a notice for the authority to send it the information or to comply with the obligations of the Act. Beyond the Commissioner lies two levels of Information Tribunal and, higher still, the High Court and the Supreme Court.

All of the complaint stages are plagued with levels of delay that can drag out the FOI process and leave requesters waiting years for answers. The prime example of this is *The Guardian*'s battle to release lobbying letters Prince Charles sent to government ministers, which has been ongoing for more than nine years, almost the entire duration of the existence of the Act itself. The case has been rebuffed through the UK's legal system where the government lost the case in the Supreme Court and was told to publish the letters sent by the Prince (*Guardian*, 2015).

The Campaign for Freedom of Information (2014) says there needs to be 'better sanctions against unjustified delay' with the FOI process and that the Act is 'too forgiving' of delays. Despite delays, American journalist and, according to the FBI, FOI 'terrorist' Jason Leopold (2014) says that reporters need to think how they will use newly released documents, which are not current, in a newsworthy way. 'Your job as a journalist is to try and figure out how to make it new', Leopold (2014) says after reflecting on the fact that delays can be much longer in the USA.

Delays are a common feature around the world with FOI laws. Investigative journalist Dean Beeby (2014) in Canada also says that in the country, departments and agencies can claim long extensions beyond the 30-day initial response period set out in the legislation. There really is no check on the amount of extra time that can be claimed, so that some requests can take years (literally) to respond to.

Complaints that are made to the Information Commissioner help the regulator to assess which authorities are performing their FOI obligations well and which are not.

They do now put delinquent authorities on a monitoring programme for three months, with a view, under the threat of enforcement notices, if they don't improve, some of them I think have been, may have been given a lot of leeway, in terms of non-compliance. I think we would like to see the Commissioner using his enforcement powers, the enforcement notice powers, which are very rarely used, more readily to deal with that.

(Campaign for Freedom of Information, 2014)

However, Information Commissioner Christopher Graham (2014) alluded to preferring a non-public approach to dealing with authorities that do not respond to requests in time.

But there's no suggestion of us not being able to throw its weight around when it needs to and I get access to very senior people when I need to. So before Christmas [2013], when the Cabinet Office were back in the sin-bin, I wrote to the Permanent Secretary Richard Heaton and the Cabinet Secretary Sir Jeremy Heywood and I got in to see them in early January and we discussed a ratification programme with Richard Heaton and I had a very serious talk with the Cabinet Secretary about a whole range of issues. So the Information Commissioner tends to get access to the key people.

Internal review

The first level of complaint over a refused request should be asking for an internal review from the authority with which the request was made. Internal reviews should be made in writing to the authority and the grounds for requesting one should be included, as doing so can highlight the ways in which the request has not been answered properly.

There is no legal obligation for a public authority to have an internal complaints system that looks at FOI requests. However, the ICO recommends that authorities do, so they are able to conform to the Act's Section 45 Code of Practice (ICO, 2012, p.9). In reality, public authorities without internal review systems are likely to be small authorities that rarely receive requests.

The process of an internal review will typically involve a second member of staff looking at the original request and the authority's response to come to a decision. A training document published by the Commissioner says that an internal review should:

- be conducted by someone more senior than the person who dealt with the original request;
- be completed in 20 working days, although 40 working days should be the very most;
- be a thorough reconsideration;
- provide information immediately if information needs to be disclosed;
- fully explain why the original response is being upheld, if that is the outcome.

(ICO, nda)

Writing to an authority to ask for an internal review should be done within two months of the refusal, the Commissioner (ndb) says. Jon Baines (2014), who handled complaints for a local authority, says that often an initial response may be cautious and a second pair of eyes looking at the request may see it differently.

> When I do internal reviews, I will often overturn the decision on the first instance because we are living in the real world and a lot of public authorities get hundreds or thousands of requests a year and with the greatest of respect to people dealing with them in the first instance they may not have the time or the resources to fully apply their mind to the facts.
>
> (Baines, 2014)

With no statutory time pressure for carrying out a review, authorities can drag their heels and hope that by the time they respond the issue may not make the news. The Campaign for Freedom of Information (2013) has been consistently vocal in saying that delays to the complaints process should be reduced and that the Commissioner should take more action when they do occur.

Rob Edwards (2014), a Scottish environment journalist, says he believes that some authorities have purposefully used the internal review stage to delay sending him information as 'the longer they can delay things the older the story gets and the less likely I am to be able to get it in a paper'.

The House of Commons Justice Committee (2012, p.42) recommended that internal reviews should have a statutory time limit of 20 working days. But the government dismissed this view, saying that where an authority is taking an 'unreasonable' time to conduct an internal review, then a complaint should be made to the ICO which can 'order the completion' of the review (MoJ, 2012, p.13). The government failed to say how long 'unreasonable' would be. However, it says that the Government may amend the Section 45 Code of Practice so that internal reviews should be completed within 20 working days (MoJ, 2012, p.14).

Late reply complaint

As made clear by Section 10 of the Act, public authorities should reply to FOI requests within 20 working days, unless they are applying a PIT to a qualified exemption. However, this does not stop authorities from flouting their obligations to answer within 20 working days. And there is no punishment, nor incentive, to make them answer on time. There is no need for an internal review to be conducted before a complaint about timeliness is made. When an authority takes an excessive amount of time to respond to a request, a complaint should be made to the Information Commissioner. This can be done using the complaint form on the Commissioner's website.

The Ministry of Justice, which is responsible for Freedom of Information policy, publishes quarterly statistics on central government's FOI performance (MoJ, 2013a), which indicates to the Information Commissioner which authorities are performing poorly. As no official statistics are centrally recorded for other types of public authorities, the volume of complaints to the Commissioner will expose authorities that are failing to fulfill their FOI responsibilities.

A small number of authorities do publish their own statistics, although they are not required to do so. For example, Kent County Council keeps an updated log of its request numbers and performance online. It shows that between the Act coming into force in 2005 and the end of 2013, the council received 11,252 requests. Over this time, the authority's performance in responding to requests within the statutory time period has ranged from a low of 67 per cent up to a high of 95 per cent of all requests answered in time, in 2013 (Kent County Council, 2014).

Times journalist Jules Mattsson (2014) says that requesters should be more aware and more willing to complain when a request is overdue. He also warned that it will often take a month for the Commissioner to tell the authority to respond. It is also possible to complain about how long the authority took to respond to a Freedom of Information request even if they have already provided the information.

Information notice

When a public authority is being difficult and not providing information as part of the Information Commissioner's investigations into complaints, or if the Commissioner wants information to see if the authority is fulfilling its FOI obligations, the Office can issue an Information Notice (IN) under Section 51(1) of the Act. The notice will tell the authority to provide the Commissioner with information. The authority has to do this within the timescales set out by the notice (s.51(1)).

An authority can appeal an IN (s.51(3)) and does not have to stump up the information if they are intending to appeal the notice (s.51(4)). If an authority fails to comply with the Commissioner's IN then the regulator has the power, under Section 54, to write to the High Court in England, or the Court of Session in Scotland. The court may then investigate the matter and deal with the authority as if it has committed contempt of court (s.54(3)).

If the authority refuses to comply with its duties as part of the Act, if it is being obtuse, refusing to provide information and the Commissioner believes they are doing this on purpose, the regulator can act on this. Under Schedule 3 of the Act, with a warrant, the Commissioner or any of the Office's staff can enter and search a premises, inspect and seize any documents, and inspect and test any equipment found which may contain information held by the authority.

Enforcement notice

An Enforcement Notice (EN) is the bigger, scarier, but lesser spotted older sibling of an IN. When the Commissioner believes that the public authority has failed to comply with a request, he/she may instruct them to take action to comply with the Act (s.52(1)). The ICO (2014a) says that in practice ENs will be issued when there is a 'systemic or repeated non-compliance' with the Act.

As with an IN, the authority has the ability to appeal the EN being issued through the legal system. This right is laid out in Section 57 of the Act. If the public authority does not comply with the EN notice issued against it, the case may progress to being treated as an instance of contempt of court, as allowed by Section 54.

A government minister is able to give the Commissioner a certificate, under Section 54 of the Act, saying they have formed a reasonable opinion that there was no failure to provide the information and therefore the EN will not be complied with.

As highlighted above, these powers are very rarely used by the ICO. This was echoed by Heather Brooke (2014), who says the Commissioner 'doesn't really have any real power on FOI. He can't levy fines, all he can do is make a decision, which people can appeal, or issue a slap on the wrist, which is effectively what he does'.

Decision Notices

If a requester is not satisfied with the response of an internal review, they are able to make a complaint to the ICO. If it is a valid complaint, the ICO will then have to issue a Decision Notice (DN). The complexity of the request, and the authority's willingness to be cooperative, will affect the time it takes for the Commissioner to resolve the case. Guidance issued to authorities, from the ICO (2011, p.1), states that the Office endeavors to resolve cases within six months of receiving them. This means that after the initial 20 working day period the authority had to respond to the request, and if the internal review was handled promptly, that by the time a DN has been issued it may be more than eight months after the initial request was made.

Making a complaint to the Commissioner can be done using the complaint form 'Accessing Official Information', which is on the ICO website (it can also be done by sending the following in an email). When registering a complaint, the requester must provide personal details, all correspondence with the authority, including their responses to the request and internal review, and details of the case (ICO, ndc). Public authorities are told that when the Commissioner receives a complaint about a request, they will have to reconsider the case and provide a submission. This includes why the exemption applies and, in the case of qualified exemptions, why the public interest favours withholding the information (ICO, 2011).

The guidance from the Commissioner also makes it clear that the authority can still speak to the requester after a complaint has been made, which may increase the chance of the case being resolved informally (ICO, 2011, p.3). The 2013/14 annual report and financial statements of the ICO (2014b, p.16) show that 19 per cent of all complaints that were made to the Office were resolved informally. This is indicative of the Commissioner's willingness to try to resolve cases with as little official paperwork as possible, although a cynical view would be that it means it does not have to send as many DNs to authorities.

Heather Brooke (2014) says that this informal approach can mean that requesters do not find out as much of the decision-making process as they should be able to. 'There's even now a process where they do a secret arbitration between the parties and a lot of times they will come to a settlement, and you will never have the decision made public.'

Requesters can, under Section 50, ask for a DN even if the complaint is resolved informally. Under the legislation, the Commissioner must issue a DN for a valid complaint, unless it is withdrawn, frivolous or vexatious. A decision must be made, by the Commissioner's office, unless any of the following reasons apply:

- Internal complaints procedures have not been exhausted (s.50(2)(a)).
- The complaint has come after an 'undue delay' (s.50(2)(b)).

- The application is frivolous or vexatious (s.50(2)(c)).
- The application has been withdrawn or abandoned (s.50(2)(d)).

Complaints can also be made directly to the Commissioner before an internal review takes place, although the Commissioner will only consider exceptional cases. If it is found that the public authority has not handled the request properly, or not provided the information when it should have done, the Commissioner can tell it to do so (s.50(4)). Once a DN has been issued, it is not possible for the Commissioner to withdraw or amend it (ICO, 2011, p.5).

Where an authority does not follow a DN, it could lead to the Information Commissioner writing to the High Court to have the issue dealt with as a contempt of court (s.54(3)). Under Section 53 of the Act, a government minister, or the Attorney General, is able to issue a certificate saying they have formed an opinion, on reasonable grounds, that there was no failing in the authority's responsibilities under the Act.

Tribunals

When a requester or public authority does not agree with the Information Commissioner's DN, it is possible for either to appeal the case to the Information Tribunal. Where a DN has been issued, the requester or the public authority can escalate the issue to the Information Tribunal (s.57(1)). A public authority that has had an EN or IN issued against it also has the right to appeal, as set out in Section 57(2). The tribunal's powers mean it can allow the appeal, substitute a notice that has been issued by the Commissioner or dismiss the appeal (s.57).

The two tribunals

- First-Tier Tribunal – deals with complaints that have been escalated from an appeal against a DN issued by the Commissioner or an appeal from a public authority against an EN or an IN.
- Upper Tribunal – deals with complaints from the first tier tribunal. However, it only accepts arguments that are based on legal issues. The Upper Tribunal's decisions set binding precedents.

(Information Tribunal, 2010, p.10)

Any appeal for a case to be heard in a tribunal should be made within 28 days of the Commissioner's DN (MoJ, 2013b). Appeals may only consider questions that are relevant to the Act and if the case is particularly complex it may automatically be transferred to the upper level. The tribunal process can be lengthy. Information lawyer Robin Hopkins (2014) says that although the tribunal is trying to make the process quicker, in most cases two years pass between the original request and the tribunal's decision. Direction hearings will be held before the tribunals can take place.

Guidance from the Ministry of Justice states that when applying for an appeal to the tribunal, the details that will need to be provided are the grounds of appeal, expected outcome, information about the DN and all supporting documents. It emphasises that one of the most important parts of the appeal process is making the arguments as to why the decision may be wrong (HM Courts & Tribunals Service, 2014).

Tribunals will conduct their proceedings in an oral or paper hearing. A requester can state a preference but it is ultimately the tribunal's decision (Information Tribunal, 2010, p.3). Hopkins (2014) says the tribunal, while already being more informal than other court proceedings, has been trying to improve upon this further.

> I think the tribunal management have done a lot to make it as fast as possible, there's also been a big shift in trying to make it as user friendly as possible and that means informality of case management notes, allowing requesters quite a lot of flexibility in terms of their participation in the hearings and trying to make it a process that is not terrifying and not overly legalistic for them.

In cases where the public authority is opposed to the decision of the Commissioner, at any tribunal stage, the Commissioner is likely to have a lawyer on the side of the requester. The requester can act as a second respondent.

The tribunals allow individuals to represent themselves in their appeals – in fact, the Information Tribunal (2010, p.8) says that in around 60 per cent of cases, the appeal is started by the requester and in the majority of these cases they will represent themselves. The Information Tribunal says (2010, p.10) all parties pay for their own legal costs, and the result of the tribunal's decision does not affect this. Tribunals may become harder for applicants as the government has said it will consider making users contribute towards the costs of the tribunals (MoJ, 2012, p.11).

Tribunal advice

Robin Hopkins, information lawyer for 11KBW, gave the following pieces of general advice for those who may go to the tribunal stage, which have been collated into Dos and Don'ts.

Do

- Try to have an input into the case, as the cases in which requesters get the opportunity to participle are the most rounded.
- Focus on the issues the tribunal has to decide upon in the particular case.
- Focus on the information that has been asked for, what was going on at the time of the request, what the public interest issues are, why the information would help and why the harm is not as serious as the public authority says it is. The 'best' requesters in tribunals have done their homework regarding the relevant FOI principles.
- If there are closed sessions, where the requester has to leave the room, ask for as full a summary of what happened as possible, work out before if there are any questions you wish to ask despite not being present.
- Be prepared to explain background issues.

The type of questions Hopkins says should be considered by a requester are: 'Here is a scenario or a public interest difficulty that I as a member of the public might want to understand, where am I to look for information on that, if not the information I have asked?'

Don't

- Feel constrained by not being a lawyer or by the process of the tribunal.
- Verbally attack the public authority's witnesses because of frustration or time the request has been ongoing for.
- Focus on events after the DN has been issued, as it is rare that after these will be considered.
- Focus on background information that may be irrelevant.

(Hopkins, 2014)

Higher Courts

If the decision of an Upper Tribunal, which can only be based on the law, is brought into question, then an appeal can be made. Any appeal above the Upper Tribunal has to be made to the High Court. Proceedings can progress all the way to the European courts.

Destruction of information

There is only one criminal offence that it is possible to commit under the Freedom of Information Act. This relates to altering records to prevent disclosure. Under Section 77(1), it is an offence if a person 'alters, defaces, blocks, erases, destroys or conceals' information to prevent disclosure by a received request. If the Commissioner finds a public authority, or individual, has done this, they will be liable to a summary conviction or a fine (s.77(3)).

However, it is currently incredibly difficult, if not impossible, for anyone to be prosecuted for tampering with information, due to the requirement for prosecution to take place within six months of the offence being committed. The government says it will change the time frame to six months after the Commissioner becomes aware of the offence (MoJ, 2012, p.15).

When to complain

Deciding when to request an internal review or when to complain to the Commissioner comes down to a balance of judgement. Primarily, the considerations for whether to complain about the application of an exemption should be based upon previous case law, public interest and an authority's obligations under the Act. Complaints to the ICO about the timeliness of a response to a request should be made after the 20 working day period has passed and the authority has been chased for a response but still not provided one.

Paul Gibbons (2014), who has been working within FOI for ten years, says that requesters and journalists do not complain enough. He says people should ask for internal reviews and make Section 50 complaints to the ICO more often.

> It really used to frustrate me that sometimes I would have to withhold something, I was referring before to that sometimes you do come under political pressure, and sometimes you are forced to not send something out that you think should have gone out, and you're waiting for somebody to appeal because you know if it is appealed it will be overturned. But nobody ever comes back. That's the first thing, I think journalists if they don't like the decision they should definitely appeal it. That's how the law develops.

Scottish journalist Rob Edwards (2013), who frequently uses the Freedom of Information Act and EIR regulations to cover the environmental sector, said in a talk to students at the Strathclyde University that journalists should always ask for an internal review. He said that with some authorities it prompts a thorough review and can also cause the release of more information.

Journalist Matt Davis (2014) says that getting the judgement correct about when to appeal can be difficult. He says that the most interesting cases to challenge are the ones that involve the balancing of the PIT and also in cases where it will be possible to use the result on other requests.

> I will appeal if I think a), they have got something obviously wrong, or b), where they have given me information in the past to a question but then for some reason they have decided this year they are not going to give it to me because they then have decided that they have changed their mind to whether that information should be released or not.

The ICO's (2014b, p.16) statistics for the 2013/14 financial year show that the Office issued 1,261 DNs relating to FOI or EIR requests and 39 per cent of these were either completely or partially upheld. These figures show that there is a decent chance of a complaint to the Commissioner being upheld and that the ICO is willing to make decisions against public authorities. The ICO even made decisions against itself, fully or partially upholding 18 internal reviews it conducted over the financial year (ICO, 2014b, p.35).

York Press news editor Gavin Aitchison (2014) says it is important to fight requests when you feel that you are right, as well as knowing the legislation.

> The main advice is largely on attitude, in that mainly don't take no for an answer if you believe that you're entitled to the information that you're after. I think not to just be dismissed with a brushing off response from an authority.

However, the figures in the ICO's report (2014b, p.16) show that 37 per cent of all complaints that are made to the Commissioner are made 'too early' and before an internal review has been completed by the authority. This highlights the importance of using the internal review process.

Resources for complaints

The general principles that apply to FOI exemptions, and the case law that backs them up or says what a public authority cannot do, are laid out in the Exemptions and Know Your Rights chapters in this book (Chapters 4 and 8). But as every FOI case is different, decisions to complain need to be based on the facts of each individual one. In particular those that rely upon the balancing of the PIT can vary greatly depending on when the request was made and evolving circumstances based on world events. Additionally, the law is constantly developing with new decisions and precedents being set by the Commissioner, tribunals and courts. The following sources can be used for information to support appeals:

- Legislation
  The Freedom of Information Act's legislation itself, as published at www.legislation.gov.uk/ukpga/2000/36/contents.
- Asking the Commissioner
  The ICO provides a telephone helpline for requesters to make enquiries. The helpline can be contacted on 0303 123 1113 (local rate) or 01625 545 745 (national rate) during weekday office hours. It is also possible to email the ICO at casework@ico.org.uk.
- Commissioner's guidance
  The ICO produces detailed guidance for public authorities on all of the key FOI and EIR exemptions and exceptions. It also provides guidance for the best practice on issues such as how the authority should reply to a request. This guidance has been used throughout this book to help provide an informed opinion of the key issues that relate to the main sticking points of the Freedom of Information Act. The most recent guidance, which is available at the time of access, has been used. The guidance can be found at https://ico.org.uk/for-organisations/guidance-index/freedom-of-information-and-environmental-information-regulations.
- DNs
  DNs that have been issued by the ICO can be found on the regulator's website. They can be found in the 'Enforcement' section of the website or directly at http://search.ico.org.uk/ico/search/decisionnotice. It is possible to search DNs by keywords, a reference number, the sector the public authority is in, the authority's name, the section of the Act, date and what the ICO's decision was. The ability to search for complaints that have been upheld gives the requester the ability to see cases where the authority has applied a specific section in the wrong way.
- Tribunal decisions
  All First-Tier Tribunal decisions are stored on the Information Tribunal's website. The tribunal system for information law covers Data Protection, EIR, FOI, Human Rights Act, and Privacy & Electronic Communication Regulations among others. For Freedom of Information cases, the website allows you to search within a subject, such as 'Request for Information' or the exemption types. Within this, it is possible to search a subsection, i.e. a specific exemption. It also allows the search of an appeal, a party to the case and the date of the case. Unlike the ICO's DN search, it is not possible to search by whether

the appeal was dismissed, struck out or upheld. Search for First-Tier Tribunal decisions at www.informationtribunal.gov.uk/Public/search. aspx. Upper Tribunal decisions and higher can be found on the website of the British and Irish Legal Information Institute at www.bailii.org.

• WhatDoTheyKnow

The website, which is run by charity mySociety, allows anyone to make FOI requests online, publishes them and the responses. At the time of writing, the website, which launched in 2008, has an archive of more than 235,000 requests that cover more than 15,500 public authorities (WhatDoTheyKnow, 2014). This has now swelled to more than 250,000. The website allows users to search for successful requests, unsuccessful requests, unresolved requests and internal reviews. The advanced search feature allows you to search fields such as tags that have been included on the website, the type of files that are attached to responses and more. The website can be accessed at http:// WhatDoTheyKnow.com.

Chapter 9 top tips

• Initial complaints about an FOI response should be made with the original authority, who can be asked to complete an internal review of the request.

• When an authority has failed to respond to a request within 20 working days, a complaint can be made straight to the ICO.

• It is possible to challenge an FOI response all the way though the legal system up to the European Courts.

• There are no time limits on how long a public authority has to conduct a PIT but the ICO has issued guidelines that say it should not take more than an extra 20 working days, and only in exceptional circumstances should it take an extra 40 working days.

• If an authority upholds its original decision at the internal review stage, it is possible to complain to the ICO under Section 50 of the Act. If the complaint is a valid one, the Commissioner will investigate and issue a DN.

• A DN can tell the authority to disclose the information, uphold its original position or say that the complaint was not a valid one.

• If the authority, or the requester, disagrees with the DN, it is able to apply, within 28 days, to the First-Tier Tribunal for the case to be re-assessed there.

• For cases that progress to the Upper Tribunal, this can only be done where a point of law is in contention.

References

Aitchison, G., 2014. *Interview*. Interviewed by Matt Burgess *[Telephone]* 12 May 2014.

Baines, J., 2014. *Interview*. Interviewed by Matt Burgess *[Telephone]* 22 May 2014.

Beeby, D., 2014. *Interview*. Interviewed by Matt Burgess *[Email]* 4 November 2014.

Brooke, H., 2014. *Interview*. Interviewed by Matt Burgess *[In person]* London: 23 May 2014.

Campaign for Freedom of Information, 2013. *Information Commissioner Should Clamp Down on Excessive FOI Delays*, 25 April 2013. Available at: www.cfoi. org.uk/foi250413pr.html [Accessed 4 September 2014].

Campaign for Freedom of Information, 2014. *Interview*. Interviewed by Matt Burgess *[In person]* London: 19 May 2013.

Davis, M., 2014. *Interview*. Interviewed by Matt Burgess *[Telephone]* 21 May 2014.

Edwards, R., 2013. 16 tips for using freedom of information law in the UK, 30 April. Available at: www.robedwards.com/2013/04/exercising-your-right-to-know-.html [Accessed 4 August 2014].

Edwards, R., 2014. *Interview*. Interviewed by Matt Burgess *[Telephone]* 14 May 2014.

Freedom of Information Act 2000 (c.36). London: HMSO.

Gibbons, P., 2014. *Interview*. Interviewed by Matt Burgess *[In person]* London: 22 May 2014.

Graham, C., 2014. *Interview*. Interviewed by Matt Burgess *[In person]* Wilmslow: 20 May 2014.

Guardian, 2015. Supreme court clears way for release of secret Prince Charles letters, 26 March. Available at: www.theguardian.com/uk-news/2015/mar/26/supreme-court-clears-way-release-secret-prince-charles-letters-black-spider-memos [Accessed 18 April 2015].

HM Courts & Tribunals Service, 2014. *Guide to Completing the Notice of Appeal*. Available at: http://hmctsformfinder.justice.gov.uk/courtfinder/forms/t097-eng. pdf [Accessed 5 September 2014].

Hopkins, R., 2014. *Interview*. Interviewed by Matt Burgess *[Telephone]* 6 June 2014.

House of Commons Justice Committee, 2012. *Post Legislative Scrutiny of the Freedom of Information Act 2000*. Available at: www.publications.parliament. uk/pa/cm201213/cmselect/cmjust/96/96.pdf [Accessed 17 July 2014].

Information Commissioner's Office (ICO), 2011. *How we Deal with Complaints*. Available at: http://ico.org.uk/~/media/documents/library/Corporate/Practical_application/complaints_guide_for_public_authorities.ashx [Accessed 14 June 2014].

Information Commissioner's Office (ICO), 2012. *Refusing a Request: Writing a Refusal Notice*. Available at: http://ico.org.uk/for_organisations/guidance_index/~/media/documents/library/Freedom_of_Information/Detailed_specialist_guides/refusing_a_request_writing_a_refusal_notice_foi.pdf [Accessed 10 June 2014].

Information Commissioner's Office (ICO), 2014a. *Enforcement Notices*. Available at: http://ico.org.uk/enforcement/notices [Accessed 26 September 2014].

Information Commissioner's Office (ICO), 2014b. *Information Commissioner's Annual Report and Financial Statements 2013/14.* Available at: https://ico.org.uk/media/about-the-ico/documents/1042191/annual-report-2013-14.pdf [Accessed 8 March 2015].

Information Commissioner's Office (ICO), nda. *Freedom of Information: Internal Reviews.* Available at: http://web.archive.org/web/20140803222508/http://ico.org.uk/news/events/~/media/documents/library/Freedom_of_Information/Practical_application/FREEDOM_OF_INFORMATION_INTERNAL_REVIEWS.ashx [Accessed 8 March 2015].

Information Commissioner's Office (ICO), ndb. *How to Access Information from a Public Body.* Available at: http://ico.org.uk/for_the_public/official_information [Accessed 6 September 2014].

Information Commissioner's Office (ICO), ndc. *Report a Concern about Accessing Information from a Public Body.* Available at: https://ico.org.uk/media/report-a-concern/forms/1477/access-official-information-form.pdf [Accessed 8 March 2015].

Information Tribunal, 2010. *Guidance Notes for Individuals Representing Themselves in Freedom of Information Appeals in the General Regulator Chamber of the First-tier Tribunal.* Available at: www.informationtribunal.gov.uk/Documents/6_Guidance_IndividualsRepThemselves_Nov10.pdf [Accessed 8 September 2014].

Kent County Council, 2014. *Requests for Information Falling under the Scope of the Freedom of Information Act 2000 or Environmental Information Regulations 2004 or Data Protection Act 1998.* Available at: www.kent.gov.uk/__data/assets/pdf_file/0005/5288/Requests-for-information-year-by-year-comparison-statistics.pdf [Accessed 26 September 2014].

Leopold, J., 2014. *Interview.* Interviewed by Matt Burgess *[Telephone]* 28 May 2014.

Mattsson, J., 2014. *Interview.* Interviewed by Matt Burgess *[Telephone]* 23 June 2014.

Ministry of Justice (MoJ), 2012. Government response to the Justice Committee's report: Post-legislative scrutiny of the Freedom of Information Act (Cm 8505). London: HMSO.

Ministry of Justice (MoJ), 2013a. *Government FOI Statistics.* Available at: www.gov.uk/government/collections/government-foi-statistics [Accessed 4 September 2014].

Ministry of Justice (MoJ), 2013b. *Making an Appeal.* Available at: www.justice.gov.uk/tribunals/general-regulatory-chamber/making-an-appeal [Accessed 5 September 2014].

WhatDoTheyKnow, 2014. *Homepage.* Available at: www.whatdotheyknow.com [Accessed 1 November 2014].

Chapter 10

Journalistic considerations

Monitoring requests

Once an FOI request has been sent, there is a tendency for journalists to forget they were made or neglect to chase them up or use the results. It is times like these when authorities are able to get away with not responding to requests on time, properly or at all, as they know they might not be challenged on them. Every journalist making requests should keep track of them – it is not a time-consuming job once set up but monitoring what has been sent and when a reply may be expected can help in the overall story.

There are two simple ways to monitor FOI requests. If you are not making many requests, and they are standalone, single requests, it is possible to put a reminder in a calendar or diary system. Marking down when the 20 working day deadline is up will mean it is easy to see when the response is due.

If you are making multiple requests to authorities for the same information, what are often called round robin requests (see Chapter 6), you can use a spreadsheet for keeping track of requests. This can also be updated for internal reviews, complaints to the Commissioner and any delays that may occur.

Some fields that you may consider including in a spreadsheet are:

- Name of the authority.
- Authority's email.
- Details of the request.
- The date the request was sent, and when the reply should be received.
- If the authority has acknowledged the request.
- If a reply has been received.
- If the request has been clarified.
- If there is a PIT being conducted.
- Any exemptions relied upon by the authority.
- If an internal review needs to be conducted.

- If a complaint to the Information Commissioner needs to be made.
- When the request for an internal review or complaint was made.

In a spreadsheet, it may be advantageous to use different tabs for different larger requests. It is also worth keeping requests for information in separate email folders, and, if possible, using tags to distinguish whether the results have been entered into a collating system. It means that all the requests on a specific subject can be stored in the same place and returned to when they need to be processed. Transferring them all into one specific folder decreases the likelihood of an email being missed and helps to keep track of the number of FOI responses that have been received. It is also possible to record requests and the responses to them in one larger spreadsheet.

Collating

As well as monitoring when requests are made and received, it is also wise to create databases, with the information provided when requests are replied to. In particular this is useful for round robin requests, where information will come in from multiple authorities and may need to be compared. This will mean, if asking for data, putting this all into a form that you can analyse and reuse as it is given by the authority. It can be as simple as creating a spreadsheet that allows the information requested to be easily entered and manipulated.

Example

Online journalist, author and lecturer Paul Bradshaw (2014), alongside a group of volunteers, conducted a large FOI-initiated investigation into local councils' spending on the 2012 London Olympic torch parade. For this story, all the spending data provided by the council was entered into a spreadsheet which detailed each category of spending. In order to ensure that stand-out data was not missed, and to enable using the data in as many different forms as possible, the team separated data out.

> As it was being entered we also had a column for people to put a particular item of spending if it was newsworthy so again aside from the main story, were there any other stories buried inside this data and there were lots of individual items of spending which raised questions, more than we could cover ourselves.

> (Bradshaw, 2014)

Reading

It may sound obvious, but it is crucially important to closely read responses. A response may contain buried details which are not clearly indicated by the authority. It may be possible that they have tried to cloak information that may be embarrassing or revealing in the midst of a mass of information.

Although FOI officer Kit Good (2014) says that the majority 'of the stuff that we hold is very vague correspondence, minutes and procedural documents and stuff like that', this does not stop journalists thinking, or believing, that there is a golden bullet hidden in the information that the authority has released. There is every right to go looking for it, sometimes it is found and, the majority of others, it is elusive. Finding it may be difficult if it is hidden within a mass of information.

FOI professional Bilal Ghafoor (2014) says that the responses to requests do need to be read thoroughly in order to make the most of the information provided – otherwise the crucial piece of information, if there is one, may be missed.

> I have had so many cases in the past where we have had to go off to the press office, the media office or whatever it was called in that organisation, and say this information is about to go out, this shit is about to hit the fan, reactive lines have all been prepared and everyone is sitting there, senior people have been briefed on it and nothing happened because nobody read the answer. Read the answer.
>
> (Ghafoor, 2014)

Ghafoor continued that when a request does come back with 'an attachment with 200 pages to read, it suddenly becomes a pain', and that many cases show that the request may not have been specific enough to draw out the desired piece of information.

This is even the case when the authority does not provide the requester with what they have asked for. FOI trainer Paul Gibbons (2014) says that if you do not get the information you requested then you should carefully read what the authority has said as it will help you to understand if they have refused it properly and allow you to learn the reasons behind refusals, thus improving the next request that you make.

The most important parts are the exemption(s) that the authority has applied to the information, the reasons why the exemptions apply and any PIT that has been conducted. Ghafoor (2014) also recounted one case in which a former colleague was forced to bury some information from the requester in a large amount of other information that was disclosed.

> I must confess there was a case where, I can't go into any specifics and the only reason I even mention it is because I don't work for this

organisation any more, where some information was asked for, there was no way of withholding it and it was incredibly sensitive information. In order to give context to it the organisation simply printed off 20,000 pages worth of other stuff in and around it. The information was buried in the middle. There would be no way anyone could read it. I remember it because we had to send it by courier and it was a few hundred quid to send the bloody thing.

(Ghafoor, 2014)

Reusing FOI responses

Many FOI responses come with a disclaimer. This usually states that the information cannot be reused as it would infringe on copyright laws that are afforded to the creator, in this case the public authority, of the information. While these statements are generally reflective of the ability to use, or reuse, the information, it is very unlikely that an authority would take action against its publication in a story. In most cases the information that will be provided by the public authority will be facts. There is no copyright in news, facts or information (Dodd and Hanna, 2014, p.350).

This is supplemented by an exception to the Copyright, Designs and Patents Act 1988 which allows for the use of copyrighted material for criticism, review and news reporting (s.30 of the Act). This allows for any copyrighted material, other than photos, to be published as long as the source is acknowledged, where practicable, and can be defended by fair dealing principles. The defence of fair dealing and if it can apply to FOI requests being reused will depend on the substantial use of the information. This is because 'there is no statutory definition of fair dealing – it will always be a matter of fact, degree and impression in each case' (Intellectual Property Office, 2014). As Gray *et al.* (2012, p.122) say in the *Data Journalism Handbook*:

> While you should always clear all of this with your legal team, as a rule of thumb: if it is published by the government, you should never ask for forgiveness nor permission; if it is published by an organisation that doesn't make money selling data, you shouldn't have to worry too much; if it is published by an organization that does make money from selling data, then you should definitely ask for permission.

Defamation from FOI

It is widely believed that using information provided in response to an FOI request removes the possibility that defamation can be caused from publication. This is untrue, although it is unlikely to be acted upon. Section 79 of the Freedom of Information Act 2000 legislation covers defamation as follows:

Where any information communicated by a public authority to a person ('the applicant') under Section 1 was supplied to the public authority by a third person, the publication to the applicant of any defamatory matter contained in the information shall be privileged unless the publication is shown to have been made with malice.

This gives the public authority protection from a defamation suit for information that they have published. As the Ministry of Justice (2008) states, the information is only privileged if it is provided to the pubic authority by a third party. If the public authority creates the information itself, it will not have a privileged protection from being classed as defamatory.

It does not provide the journalist with protection for further publishing the information in a resulting story. The strengthening of the defamation protections, as part of the Defamation Act 2013 Section 1, now means that a statement is not defamatory unless its publication has caused, or is likely to cause, serious harm to the reputation of the claimant. Further protections are offered in Section 4 of the Defamation Act, if the story was published on a matter of public interest, which many FOI stories are.

Waiting for all responses

There are more than 400 town, city and borough councils, more than 40 police forces and hundreds of NHS trusts, all of which are subject to the Act. As covered in Chapter 6, journalists may make 'round robin' requests to all of a certain type of public authority.

Although authorities should reply to an FOI request 'promptly' and within 20 working days at the very most (under Section 10), this will often not be the case. The more authorities targeted by a request, the higher the chance that there will be delays on receiving the desired information in its entirety, as there is a risk that authorities may reply late. This may lead to having to rely on incomplete datasets, perhaps to predict what the bigger picture, and overall figures, may be. This leads to lines in stories, such as:

> A total of 27 forces provided responses on the use of Tasers against children during 2010, 2011 and 2012. But the true figure of Taser use on young children is likely to be much higher.
>
> (*Daily Mail*, 2013a)

> Analysis of detailed statistics from 23 forces across England, Wales and Scotland...
>
> (*BBC News*, 2012)

> Extrapolating the figures from 61 NHS trusts...
>
> (*Telegraph*, 2013)

The BBC's FOI expert, Martin Rosenbaum (2014), says the issue of waiting for responses can provide a challenge for journalists who are running stories from mass FOI requests.

It might be influenced by you having responses from the big authorities that are important, if you are talking about police you would want to know you have got a reply from the Met and Police Scotland, which are by far the two biggest forces. So you would also want to think, the people who have replied, are they likely to be different in some way to the people who haven't replied? Is there a reason why some people are being slow? So the first practical thing is how many do you need before you go with a story.

Rosenbaum continued that there needs to be a fair comparison between the authorities being examined.

Adding context

Once a response has been received and the data collated and analysed, the story may start to become apparent. But the fact that the information may not have been revealed without the FOI request, and the information is newsworthy, does not mean that it will make a strong story regardless of what has been handed out. *Washington Post* journalist James Grimaldi (2014) says:

I think a lot of people have a misconception that the actual documents that come back from an FOIA request are the beginning and ending of the story, and most of the time it's surely adding some context or interesting facts or helping to build a bigger picture.

As with any story, whether it is written, produced or recorded, there needs to be some combination of background, context, analysis, comment and more to turn it into a piece of journalism. This is no different when writing around an FOI response. Former Scottish Information Commissioner Kevin Dunion (2014) says: 'The best stories that I see is where journalists have generally added value, usually that means corroborating information from a variety of sources in a way that hasn't been done before.' While Scottish-based journalist Rob Edwards (2014) says it is 'just another tool through which we get information' in a similar way to interviewing.

Tim Turner (2014) says sometimes this does not happen and can be akin to re-writing a press release:

You get the story and you get the press release and they are effectively the same thing. There are people who do that with FOI requests they take the figures from the FOI request, they don't analyse them, they don't get an interesting expert on that topic.

Online journalist and lecturer Paul Bradshaw (2014) shares the same view that the journalist should try to avoid writing a story that just repeats the contents of the FOI response.

> You want to be adding to that response with some quotes, you want some colour, you might want to go and visit some of the places that play a role in that, speak to the people who analysed the data or who have researched similar things. That's what makes it into the story rather than just an academic report.

For complex data stories Kathryn Torney (2014) says she often speaks to the experts from the authority: 'If in doubt, ask someone who will know or speak to the statisticians directly. Be honest about any limitations in the data – be clear about any calculations you have carried out and why you have done this.' The ability to add context to a story makes it worth the paper, or pixels, that it is written on.

Example

The brazen *Daily Mail* (2013b) headline says: 'BBC blows £220,000 of license fee payers' money on training staff how to use an iPhone.' According to the paper, and the FOI request the story was based on, the corporation spent £300 per staff member on training how to use an iPhone. However, when you add the full context into the story, the picture changes quite dramatically.

In a blog post on its website, the organisation hit back:

> No-one needs training on how to use a phone, text or even to use many apps that are designed to be intuitive and which most of us now deploy without a moment's thought. But to know how to capture audio, video and stills of sufficient quality to share with millions; to edit that material; to learn how to deploy specially designed apps to allow this rich content to be filed from remote locations ...'
> (Wray, 2014)

It continued that, when put in context, reporting from iPhones and new technology significantly reduced the costs in comparison with methods previously used for broadcasting (Wray, 2014). The context and details behind the story completely change how valid the article should be treated.

Human angle

Almost any story is improved by making it one that the audience can understand because it relates to their own lives. A story based on figures from an FOI request can be a story in its own right if the figures are revealing or shocking. But any figures can be enhanced by providing a human example of what the figures show.

For example, a story about a street that has had the most pothole repairs will be a better read if it is accompanied with the views of the people who live on the street, and pictures of the patched-up road. In these cases the FOI request provides the detailed facts and the reporting around the other relevant issues increases the worth of the story.

Matt Davis (2014) says he often makes requests based on what he thinks the story will be. But then, when the information comes back there is more work to be done to add value to a story. Speaking on an example of assaults occuring surrounding alcohol intake, he says:

> You get the information back, if it proves your theory you are away, and you can embellish your story with some sort of human example of somebody who has been attacked at night and you have got a great story.
>
> (Davis, 2014)

'NHS horror: heart-attack victims forced to wait FOUR hours for ambulances'

The story from the *Daily Express* (2014) uses figures that have come from an FOI request to show that the number of patients waiting for ambulances had increased from previous years. But this isn't the focus of the story – more has been included to lure the reader away from the numbers.

The story of the 81-year-old grandmother who had to wait for four hours to be taken home, after a post-heart attack check-up, by a pre-booked ambulance adds to the overall impact of the story. The angle of the human impact shows how the statistics affect people and their lives, rather than just being a number. The original story may have been from the FOI request with the human element added in, or the FOI statistics obtained to support the story. Either way, combining both elements made the story stronger.

The response is wrong

Even in cases where the response may not be defamatory, an answer to an FOI request may be incorrect. Although there are limited examples of this, it does happen and is something that should be watched out for. As the BBC's FOI expert Martin Rosenbaum (2014) says:

> The whole point of this is you want to get information that is true and accurate and fair and is telling people stuff that is right and if you are not comparing places on the right basis then you are not advancing human knowledge.

In October 2013, Wakefield Council was forced to apologise after sending out an incorrect response. It stated that it was not responsible for the running of a welfare centre that was due to be outsourced but had not been completed. The local paper the *Hemsworth and South Elmsall Express* (2013) reported that local residents were angry about the incorrect change in responsibilities. This shows that journalists should not take the accuracy of FOI responses for granted and should critically look at the figures provided to assess whether they sound realistic or could be down to human error. When looking at data-based requests, and in particular searches of databases, care should be taken to ensure that the figures that are presented are accurate. This means that they are examined and analysed in the same way that information from any other source would be.

The danger of search

Economist, author and journalist Tim Harford demonstrated a potential problem with producing FOI stories based on statistics from a search result. The story, which his radio show critiqued, was about the number of children under the age of 18 that had been to Accident and Emergency Departments in relation to incidents involving alcohol. The results showed that in some circumstances more than 300 under-11s had been taken to A&E.

However, Harford's team looked at the original request that was sent. The phrasing of the request used 'alcohol-related condition', which, as Harford pointed out, is very different to being drunk. The show went on to speak to one hospital trust, NHS Grampian. From speaking to the authorities it found that a search of its databases included notes added to medical files. 'They add some descriptive phrases in what's called a free text field, or notes ... They simply search that free text field for words such as "drunk", "been drinking" or "intoxicated"', the show says. The result would bring up cases in which children went to a hospital with an injury, and were accompanied by a drunk adult, and more detailed notes added by staff members would increase the chance of details of drunkenness anywhere being swept up by an FOI-related search, and make the data provided inaccurate.

(Harford, 2013)

Chapter 10 top tips

- When making requests it is important to note the date that they were sent on and mark when a reply is expected to be received.
- Requests and their responses can be collated and monitored in spreadsheets that allow the stage of the request to be followed.
- It is crucial to thoroughly read FOI responses as information may be buried deep in the document. Also, by reading the response you will learn how the Act works.
- FOI responses do not hold any inherent protection from defamatory action. However, the strengthened Defamation Act may be likely to offer protection should any issues arise.
- Try to add a human angle or case study to an FOI story to increase its worth.
- Be cautious with the accuracy of requests that prompt a search result from an authority, they may be unintentionally misleading.

References

BBC News, 2012. Arrest warrants: Police hunt more than 30,000 suspects, 22 March. Available at: www.bbc.co.uk/news/uk-17179003 [Accessed 13 September 2014].

Bradshaw, P., 2014. *Interview*. Interviewed by Matt Burgess *[Telephone]* 19 May 2014.

Copyright, Designs and Patents Act 1988 (c.48). London: HMSO.

Daily Express, 2014. NHS horror: Heart-attack victims forced to wait FOUR hours for ambulances, 18 August. Available at: www.express.co.uk/news/uk/500868/NHS-ambulance-scandal-as-heart-attack-victims-forced-to-wait-up-to-four-hours [Accessed 26 October 2014].

Daily Mail, 2013a. Police shot children as young as 12 with 50,000-volt Taser linked to causing fatal heart attacks, 2 June. Available at: www.dailymail.co.uk/news/article-2334750/Police-shot-children-young-12-50-000-volt-Taser-linked-causing-fatal-heart-attacks.html [Accessed 13 September 2014].

Daily Mail, 2013b. BBC blows £220,000 of licence fee payers' money on training staff how to use an iPhone: Nearly 800 employees sent on course that costs £300 per person, 13 October. Available at: www.dailymail.co.uk/news/article-2790700/bbc-blows-220-000-licence-fee-payers-money-training-staff-use-iphone-nearly-800-employees-sent-course-costs-300-person.html [Accessed 26 October 2014].

Davis, M., 2014. *Interview*. Interviewed by Matt Burgess *[Telephone]* 21 May 2014.

Defamation Act 2013 (c.26). London: HMSO.

Dodd, M. and Hanna, M., 2014. *McNae's Essential Law for Journalists*. 22nd edn. Oxford: Oxford University Press.

Dunion, K., 2014. *Interview*. Interviewed by Matt Burgess *[Telephone]* 23 May 2014.

Edwards, R., 2014. *Interview*. Interviewed by Matt Burgess *[Telephone]* 14 May 2014.

Freedom of Information Act 2000 (c.36). London: HMSO.

Ghafoor, B., 2014. *Interview*. Interviewed by Matt Burgess *[In person]* London: 31 May 2014.

Gibbons, P., 2014. *Interview*. Interviewed by Matt Burgess *[In person]* London: 22 May 2014.

Good, K., 2014. *Interview*. Interviewed by Matt Burgess *[Telephone]* 11 June 2014.

Gray, G., Bounegru, B. and Chambers, C. (eds), 2012. *The Data Journalism Handbook*. Cambridge: O'Reilly.

Grimaldi, J., 2014. *Interview*. Interviewed by Matt Burgess *[Telephone]* 27 May 2014.

Harford, T., 2013. *An Army of Drunk Children?* BBC Radio 4, 4 October 2013. Available at: www.bbc.co.uk/programmes/b03bsb9y [Accessed 26 October 2014].

Hemsworth and South Elmsall Express, 2013. FoI request was incorrect, 14 October. Available at: www.hemsworthandsouthelmsallexpress.co.uk/news/local-news/foi-request-was-incorrect-1-6145924 [Accessed 15 September 2014].

Intellectual Property Office, 2014. *Exceptions to Copyright*. Available at: www.gov.uk/exceptions-to-copyright#criticism-review-and-reporting-current-events [Accessed 26 October 2014].

Ministry of Justice (MoJ), 2008. *Exemptions Guidance Section 44 – Prohibitions on Disclosure*. Available at: www.justice.gov.uk/downloads/information-access-rights/foi/foi-exemption-s44.pdf [Accessed 13 September 2014].

Rosenbaum, M., 2014. *Interview*. Interviewed by Matt Burgess *[In person]* London: 30 May 2014.

Telegraph, 2013. Shortage of 20,000 nurses in NHS, report warns, 12 November. Available at: www.telegraph.co.uk/health/healthnews/10441408/Shortage-of-20000-nurses-in-NHS-report-warns.html [Accessed 13 September 2014].

Torney, K., 2014. *Interview*. Interviewed by Matt Burgess *[Email]* 16 June 2014.

Turner, T., 2014. *Interview*. Interviewed by Matt Burgess *[Telephone]* 19 May 2014.

Wray, M., 2014. The smartphone revolution and why training matters. *BBC College of Journalism*, 14 October. Available at: http://foia.blogspot.co.uk/2006/01/2005-media-figures-figures-below-are.html [Accessed 26 October 2014].

FOI around the world

There are at least 100 Freedom of Information Acts in existence around the world, in different shapes and sizes. Some allow journalists and citizens alike significant access to information, while others are often not worth the paper that they are written on. Paraguay was the 100th country to pass an FOI law. There is a history behind FOI laws around the world that dates back to 1766 in Sweden, although it must be noted that it took 200 years until the next law was put in place (*Guardian*, 2014a).

They are not always called Freedom of Information Acts but vary between Right to Know and open access laws, and some countries have localised Acts for states and counties. Former Scottish Information Commissioner, Kevin Dunion (2014), says that some of the strongest Acts for requesters are the most modern.

> I think what we are seeing is that there is a number of countries who were in the vanguard of implementing Freedom of Information laws who have got stuck or who have gone backwards. And there are a whole bunch of new countries coming onto the scene who have got much more modern and much better integrated information laws that are anticipating the future or are at least dealing with the complexities of the present.

In this chapter, Acts from around the world are examined with advice from journalists who have pushed the boundaries using the laws.

Case study: Legal Leaks

Organisation Legal Leaks is a network of journalists who are using access to information laws in their own countries, as well as other countries. While almost all FOI regimes around the world allow for anyone to make requests (a notable exception is Canada), Legal Leaks says there is one large barrier. 'In practice, however, a major obstacle to the transnational exercise of the right of access to information is that requests normally have to be submitted in the official language(s) of the country' (Legal Leaks, 2014, p.36).

The organisation's aim is to put journalists who want to make requests in other countries in touch with those who speak and work in them. The Legal Leaks Toolkit provides more advice for journalists who want to make requests to other countries and more.

(Legal Leaks, 2014)

Scotland

The Freedom of Information Act in Scotland was implemented at the same time as the one in the rest of the UK. However, it was passed into law in 2002, compared with the UK's 2000, which gave public authorities less time to prepare for the impact it would have upon them. The Scottish Act applies to public bodies in the country and is overseen by a separate Scottish Information Commissioner.

That Act in Scotland has many elements that make it stronger and more likely for requesters to receive the information that they are asking for. These differences vary from the cost limits and other technical parts of the Act such as the balancing of the PIT to the attitude and enforcement of the Scottish Information Commissioner. The exemptions in the Scottish Act are incredibly similar to those in the UK Act, so are not covered here.

Main differences

Much of the Freedom of Information Act in the UK and in Scotland is the same, but there are some fundamental differences that favour the requester and access to information in Scotland. The main differences of the two Acts are outlined below.

Cost limits

As with the UK Act, there are limits on what can be disclosed without costing public bodies too much money. In the UK, the upper limits for estimated costs, above which a request can be refused, are £600 for central government and £450 for other public authorities. In Scotland the figure is also £600 but this applies to all authorities, as set out in the Freedom of Information (Fees for Required Disclosure) (Scotland) Regulations 2004. In working out this estimate, Scottish authorities cannot calculate an hourly rate to locate, retrieve or provide information at more than £15 per hour (reg 3). In the UK and the hourly rate is calculated at £25.

A direct result of this, Callum Liddle (2014), who has previously worked for the ICO but is now a PhD candidate looking at FOI in Scotland, says:

> The practical consequences of that is that you are more likely to have information disclosed from a Scottish public authority and you are also more likely to receive more information or information in whole from a Scottish public authority than you otherwise would under the UK regime.

Aggregation

The Scottish Act also allows related requests to be made within a short time frame without the cost of these being aggregated, although the Scottish Information Commissioner's Office (SICO) says that there are as yet unimplemented provisions for regulations to allow aggregation to take place (SICO, 2005, p.16). However, in the UK requests can be aggregated under Section 12 of the Freedom of Information Act 2000 when two or more requests, for the same or similar information, are received within a period of 60 working days.

Public Interest Test

When applying the PIT for a qualified exemption, like the UK, an authority must prove that the public interest in withholding information outweighs that of disclosing it, if they want to rely on the exemption. However, in Scotland the authority has to come up with the reasoning within the time limit of 20 working days (SICO, 2005, p.3). There is no extension available to Scottish public authorities.

Internal review

The Freedom of Information (Scotland) Act 2002 imposes a timescale for the public authority's requirement to conduct an internal review. An internal review must be completed no later than 20 working days after it was requested (s.21). An indefinite amount of time can be taken in the rest of the UK.

Appeals

The tribunal stage of appeals does not exist in Scotland. This was left out of the Act as officials felt it added an extra unnecessary tier to the complaint system (SICO, 2005, p.5). Instead, appeals can be made to the Scottish Information Commissioner, and then the Court of Session for further appeals.

Harm test

Both Acts contain exemptions, which are judged upon the harm that would be caused by the disclosure of information, as well as needing to have the PIT applied. In Scotland, there needs to be a substantial prejudice caused by disclosure for the exemption to apply. In the UK this is just a 'prejudice'.

Future publication

Under Section 22 of the UK Freedom of Information Act there are no specifications regarding the intended publication date for information when applying this exemption. In Scotland this is completely different. Authorities are not allowed to hide behind information that they may not even publish at an unknown future date. The Scottish legislation, at Section 27(1)(a), states that unless information is due to be published within 12 weeks of when the request is made, the exemption cannot apply.

Commissioner

The Commissioner in Scotland is appointed by the Queen, on the recommendation of Parliament, whereas in the UK the Queen appoints the Commissioner on the recommendation of the government (Brooke, 2006, p.23). This means that the UK's Commissioner could be appointed from a political viewpoint rather than that of a collected view of the government.

Scotland develops first

The current aim for Scotland in terms of FOI for Rosemary Agnew (2014), the Scottish Information Commissioner, is trying to make the overall process better now the major legal principles have been established.

> I think probably my biggest challenge is ensuring that FOI is part of a culture of openness and not just seen as a chore and an add-on of what you have to do. So it is very much coming from the perspective of trying to add value to both requesters and authorities to make sure the FOI regime works as well as it can and that it covers as many bodies as it should and I am not convinced that it does at the moment.

As Brooke (2006, p.22) says, because decisions are made by the more powerful Information Commissioner, it can be worth sending requests to public bodies in Scotland and then using a decision as a precedent in the rest of the UK.

USA

The Freedom of Information Act in the USA was the first modern Act to be introduced, on 4 July 1966 – if not for Sweden's, two hundred years earlier, it would have been the first. It came into force one year later (United States Department of Justice, 2011a). The Freedom of Information Act in the USA is only applicable to federal government agencies, while individual states apply their own FOI laws. The following sections only apply to the national Freedom of Information Act.

The United States Department of Justice (2011a) says the government's official position on the Freedom of Information Act is 'to apply a presumption of openness in responding to FOIA requests'. Federal agencies have a duty to respond to FOI requests within 20 business days, although the chance of getting a response to a request within this time frame is very low.

The Office of Government Information Services (2012) says that journalists making requests should follow up their requests as soon as the time limit is reached.

> If you haven't heard from an agency on day 21, a gentle inquiry to the agency's FOIA shop or the FOIA Public Liaison is a better option than threatening to sue. You may want to ask for the estimated date of completion or work out a strategy for regular updates if the delay is going to be lengthy.
>
> (OGIS, 2012)

The Department of Homeland Security, which receives more requests than any other agency, had a backlog of more than 50,000 Freedom of Information Act requests in 2014 (*Hill*, 2014). Security agencies such as the FBI, NSA and CIA, unlike UK security services, are covered by the Act. The security agencies are not covered by the same level of access as all of the government agencies, but it is possible to get information out of them.

Despite this, Congress is not covered by the Act. Fifteen Cabinet-level departments and more than 80 agencies, including the security ones, are covered by the Act but 'not the legislative or judicial branches of the Federal government' (OGIS, 2012, p.1).

Like the Act in the UK, a request has to be made in writing, and, in most instances, this can be done online, although this is a recent move. Historically, the Act, which was designed long before mass-internet connectivity, has relied on individuals using the postal system

> This is a written request in which you describe the information you want, and the format you want it in, in as much detail as possible. You should be aware that the FOIA does not require agencies to do research

for you, analyze data, answer written questions, or create records in response to your request.

(United States Department of Justice, 2010)

It is possible to apply for a request to be given special treatment and be dealt with as a priority, as an expedited request. If journalists are applying for an expedited response to the request they need to be able to show a 'compelling need'. Agencies will have ten calendar days to decide whether or not the request should be expedited (OGIS, 2012, p.1).

Exemptions and exclusions

There are just nine exemptions in the federal Freedom of Information Act in the USA, in addition to three exclusions that further stop information being released. It is clear that many of these cover similar areas to those of the UK Act, however the lower number instantly shows the greater levels of openness.

Exemptions

- Exemption 1: Information classified to protect national security. The withheld material must be classified under an Executive Order. This can include foreign government information (including relations), weapons of mass destruction, military plans and more.
- Exemption 2: Information that is related to the internal personnel rules and practices of an agency. Following a Supreme Court ruling the exemption was interpreted to only cover records that relate to issues of employee relations and human resources.
- Exemption 3: Information that is blocked from disclosure due to other federal laws. It can include certain census data, tax return information, wiretap requests and the contents of any information obtained from them and more.
- Exemption 4: Prohibits the disclosure of business trade secrets or other confidential commercial or financial information.
- Exemption 5: Information that concerns communications within or between agencies that are protected by legal privileges.
- Exemption 6: Any information that would invade an individual's personal privacy. These types of files will include medical and personnel ones.
- Exemption 7: This exemption blocks the publication of information that would cause harm to law enforcement purposes. It includes information that would infringe upon a fair trial, disclose

---

the identity of a confidential source, reveal techniques used for law enforcement and more.

- Exemption 8: Information that concerns the supervision of financial institutions.
- Exemption 9: Geological information on wells. This allows geological and geophysical information and data that concerns wells to be withheld.

(OGIS, 2014; United States Department for Justice, 2011b)

There are also three exclusions that are also used to justify withholding more information than is covered by the exemptions. These are:

- Information that relates to an ongoing criminal law investigation where the person who is being investigated does not know that they are, and disclosure would interfere with the proceedings.
- Protects the existence of an informant's records when the informant's status has not been officially confirmed.
- Relates specifically to the FBI and is made to keep the existence of foreign intelligence, counterintelligence, international terrorism records that are classified, a secret.

(United States Department for Justice, 2011b)

Advice

The following is first-hand advice from American journalists who have experience using the Act:

I treat FOIA officers in the same manner I treat my best journalistic sources – with patience and respect. Government employees who manage the FOIA process are inundated by requests. And they're often under scrutiny and pressure from above. By simply showing a modicum of respect, reporters can grease the wheels for faster, more effective FOIA yields.

(Scott MacFarlane, 2014, investigative reporter, NBC4)

I think the biggest advice is that FOIA requesters tend to 'file and forget', and aren't as persistent as they should be with federal agencies. FOIA officers tend to deal with lots of requests from the press and public, so staying on top of inquiries, as well as crafting requests that are as specific as possible, can go a long way in receiving relevant, timely government documents.

(Jack Gillum, 2014, reporter, *Associated Press*)

In my line of work, if you're planning to send a FOIA request to a particular department, read up on what documents are available, and call the department's compliance officer. A little bit of homework and phoning first will save a lot of time and frustration.

(Kevin Craver, 2014, reporter, *Northwest Herald*)

If necessary, be firm. Make clear that records belong to you, the tax-payer, not to the government employee. Always be willing to write a story about denials of records.

(Bill Dedman, 2014, senior writer, *Newsday*)

I also found it helpful throughout the process to stay in touch with not only the national FOIA department responsible for satisfying my request, but the regional office that would be providing them with the appropriate documents. Keeping the heat on both ends of the hierarchy likely expedited my request, even as it seemed to drag on, and hopefully kept them honest.

(Shea Johnson, 2014, staff writer, *Victorville Daily Press*)

Further information

Department of Justice FOIA website: www.foia.gov
List of agencies the Act applies to: www.foia.gov/report-makerequest.html

Australia

Australia, as with many of the other developed democracies in the world, implemented a Freedom of Information Act before the UK. It was first implemented in 1982 and has since been reformed. Most recently, the Australian government has announced plans that are set to abolish the Office of the Australian Information Commissioner (OAIC). The Office was only introduced in 2010 and a bill will mean the following changes happen:

- Complaint functions will move to the commonwealth ombudsman (which is being given no extra funds to deal with the additional work).
- Review functions moved to tribunals, which cost $800 to hear matters.
- The Attorney General's department would have the role of issuing guidelines.
- Moving the privacy commissioner into the country's human rights commission.

(*Guardian*, 2014b)

The closure of the Office will be a retrograde step for the country, as the OIAC has been working towards implementing standardised FOI performance from government bodies over the four years of its operation. Over the four-year period, the Office resolved more than 1,300 FOI reviews and closed more than 400 complaints (*Mandarin*, 2014). The Information Commissioner John McMillan says:

> I think we achieved a higher degree of consistency across government in terms of FOI practice, privacy practice [and] awareness of information policy issues ... One of the biggest complaints leading up to the creation of our office was that there was just inconsistency across government.
>
> (*Mandarin*, 2014)

Australian lawyer Peter Timmins (2014) says that although some aspects of the OAIC may have been inefficient, in some respects, there are better ways to resolve these than to abolish the entity.

> But there will be a lot of ways to accomplish that simplification rather than abolishing the Office of the Commissioner who had a wide range of other responsibilities apart from the review functions. The most important of which was leadership with regard to culture change and on that front that job is certainly not done and I think that's one of the major concerns of that initiative that leadership which was lacking for a long time after we adopted a FOI Act way back in 1982.

Using the Act

The 1982 Act applies to central government agencies. Individual states in the country have their own Acts, which can be overseen by local Information Commissioners and bodies. When making requests under the Australian Act, there is no need to say why the information is required but there are some hoops that need to be jumped through for requests to be accepted by the agencies.

A request must be made in writing, state that it is an FOI request, describe the information that is requested and provide an address for the authority to contact you, which may be by email (OAIC, 2014a, p.2). According to OAIC guidance, most authorities now have web-forms for requests. However, the country has been slow to shift the requesting onto digital platforms. Authorities have to respond to requests within 30 days of it being received (OAIC, 2014a, p.2).

As with other Acts, there are reasons for delaying a response. If an agency has to consult a third party (including another government agency) it is automatically granted an extra 30 days to answer the request. For requests that are complex or voluminous, agencies could apply to the Commissioner for extra time to answer the request, although it is not clear how this will be applied following the closing of the Office. Similarly, if the agency has run out of time but has almost finished compiling a response to the request, it could have applied to the Commissioner for extra time (OAIC, 2014b, p.2).

When receiving a rejected response, the agency or government minister has to give:

- the name and designation of the person making the decision;
- the reasons and facts that have led to the decision;
- the public interest factors that were taken into account for a 'conditionally exempt' document;
- information about the requester's rights to have the decision reviewed.

(OAIC, 2014a, p.3)

Charges

Australian agencies are able to charge fees for answering FOI requests. These fees have to be justified and it is possible to ask the authority not to charge a fee for a request. The OAIC (2010a, p.1) says: 'How the charge is calculated should be clearly explained to you. You can ask for the charge to be reduced or for the documents to be provided for free.' The fees that can be charged are:

- search and retrieval: $15 per hour;
- decision-making: $20 per hour;
- photocopy: 10c per page;
- transcript: $4.40 per page;
- supervised inspection: $6.25 per half hour;
- delivery costs.

(OAIC, 2010a, p.1)

The first five hours of decision-making time are free for all requests, and those for personal data are completely free. The authority must send out an estimate of the charge prior to undertaking the task and can require a deposit to be paid (OAIC, 2010a, p.2). The charge can be paid, disputed, asked to be waived or the request amended or withdrawn.

Exemptions

There are nine absolute exemptions and another eight that are conditional on a PIT (see Table 11.1).

Public Interest Test

For a conditional exemption to apply to a document, the public authority must conduct a PIT. This, as with other PITs, involves balancing the factors in favour of disclosure with those against disclosure.

Table 11.1 Australian Freedom of Information Act exemptions

Exemptions	Conditional exemptions
National security, defence or international relations	Commonwealth–State relations
Cabinet documents	Deliberative processes relating to agencies' or ministers' functions
Law enforcement and protection of public safety	Commonwealth's financial and property interests
Documents where secrecy provisions in other legislation apply	Certain operations of agencies, including audits, examinations and personnel management
Legal professional privilege	Personal privacy
Material obtained in confidence	Business affairs
Contempt of Parliament or court	Research
Trade secrets of commercially valuable information	The economy
Electoral roles and related documents	

Source: OAIC (2010b, p.1).

The FOI Act sets out some factors that favour giving access when applying the Public Interest Test. These factors include whether giving access would promote the objects of the Act, including scrutiny of government activity and promoting public participation in government decision-making.

(OAIC, 2010b, p.2)

The Commissioner goes on to say that the Act does not allow embarrassment, a loss of confidence in the government or misunderstanding to be reasons for non-disclosure.

Advice

Read every page of the FOI Act and understand it. Pursue stories with strong public interest to the end including through the appeal process.
(Michael Mckinnon, 2014, ABC)

Think hard about what you are asking for so it best marries with documents available. Do background research with people who might know precisely what documents you need. A lot of successful requests here come from sources telling you something about which they won't go on the record. In some cases, they'll tell you exactly what you need to ask for so you get the information but they don't get the sack.

(Anonymous reporter)

I guess it is just that one of the problems or challenges would be knowing what department or what to exactly FOI and I suppose doing the research and being very particular with the types of words that you use to phrase what you are actually requesting, any particular word or any particular variance on a word you might not be able to receive the documents you have actually requested, even though it is sort of written in a very similar way.

(Kara Irving, 2014, reporter, *Ballarat Courier*)

Ireland

The Freedom of Information Act in Ireland has been one of the most changeable Acts in the world. It has consistently caused issues for requesters and made it increasingly difficult for them to access information. A Freedom of Information Act was passed into law in 1997 and came into force the following year (McDonagh, 2003, p.3).

Unlike the UK Act, this Act includes a statement of purpose, which says that the Act is '[a]n Act to enable members of the public to obtain access ... to information in the possession of public bodies and to enable persons to have personal information relating to them in the possession of such bodies corrected' (Freedom of Information Act, 1997).

Since then it has undergone two major amendments, the first in 2003 and second in 2014. With the 2003 amendment, officials showed their disdain towards the Act. The changes 'represented a significant step back' from the original Act, as those in power tried to stop information being released (McDonagh, 2003, p.20).

Fees charged directly to requesters for making FOI requests were introduced. This led to a massive drop in the amount of requests that were made. The Office of the Information Commissioner (2004) says 5,846 fewer requests were made in the year after the fees were introduced, a 32 per cent decrease.

The House of Commons Justice Select Committee (2012), which was reviewing the UK's Act, heard evidence that the fees in Ireland had mostly affected the media, which made fewer requests than before. It had already been said that procedural changes, before the fees were introduced, were also driving down the amount of FOI requests that journalists were making. The publishing of all the details of FOI requests, as soon as they were received, was said by McDonagh (2003, p.14) to be one of the major reasons behind a drop in the proportion of requests being sent by journalists from 20 per cent in 2000 and 2001 to just 12 per cent in 2002. Journalist

Gavin Sheridan (2014) says: 'All the journalists I speak to tend to not do FOIs because of those administrative barriers.'

The charges that were introduced saw upfront fees being charged to make requests, as well as those to find and retrieve the information. The Freedom of Information Act 2014 repealed both the 2003 and 1997 Acts, and attempted to rebalance the failures of the earlier changes. As reported by RTE (2014), the new Act 'reverses many of the restrictions' that were imposed by the 2003 changes. This included reversing the upfront fees that were required when making a request. The Office of the Information Commissioner (2014a) welcomed the abolition of the €15 fee, particularly 'the decision to abolish the application fee, brings Ireland's FOI regime into line with its international counterparts'.

In addition to the removal of the restrictive fee, all public authorities were included in the Act's reach (Office of the Information Commissioner, 2014b). Although the changes are a step forward, there are still significant burdens for those who want to make requests. Fees still remain for most of the requesting process. Gavin Sheridan says, before the 2014 Act was implemented, that the fees will still remain due to the attitudes of officials in the country. 'There's an entire generation of civil servants who might have started working in the civil service in 2003 who now have over ten years of working in the system which says that fees are the right thing to do' (Sheridan, 2014).

Requests under the Act have to be made in writing, must state that it is a request under the Freedom of Information Act 2014, give details about the information and if it is required in a particular form or manner, as stated by Section 12.

Irish fees

There are no upfront fees anymore, but for an authority to search for documents and to appeal a decision against information being withheld there are still potentially large fees. They are as follows:

- Search and retrieval of records: €20 per hour.
- Photocopying: 4 cents per sheet.
- CD-ROM with documents: €10.
- Internal review: €30.
- Review by Information Commissioner: €50.

If it costs €100 or less, there will be no charge. However, above this the charge can be a maximum of €500. The Act, at Section 27, even goes as far to say that 'different maximum and minimum amounts

> may be prescribed under this subsection in respect of different public bodies'. For requests where the fees exceed an estimated €700, the authority does not have to comply with the request.
>
> (Citizen's Information, 2014)

Practically making a request

Authorities have to respond within four weeks of the request being received, in accordance with Section 12. In this they have to say if they are going to answer the request fully, in part or reject it. If they are going to give out information, the official must state how much any fee will be, and when and how the information will be given to the requester. If rejecting a request, the authority must, under Section 13, tell the requester why, and what exemptions have been used, and, where applicable, the reasons behind the PIT.

Section 14 allows the public body to extend the amount of time they have to deal with a request, if the request relates to 'such number of records' or there are other requests outstanding relating to the information that has been asked for and a decision on their disclosure has not yet been made. The public body can extend the period of time it has to deal with the request by four weeks (s.14).

Requests can also be rejected under Section 15 if the information is already in the public domain, it is due to be published, it is frivolous or vexatious, and more. Requesters are also given rights of assistance (s.11), internal reviews (s.21), reviews by the Commissioner (s.22) and the ability to further appeal to the courts (s.24).

Exemptions

There are 14 listed categories of exemptions for the Irish Act, covering everything from personal data to government meetings.

- Meetings of the government (s.28).
- Deliberations of FOI bodies (s.29).
- Functions and negotiations of FOI bodies (s.30).
- Parliamentary, court and certain other matters (s.30).
- Law enforcement and public safety (s.32).
- Security, defence and international relations (s.33).
- Conclusiveness of certain decisions pursuant to Sections 32 and 33 (s.34).
- Information obtained in confidence (s.35).
- Commercially sensitive information (s.36).

- Personal information (s.37).
- Procedure in relation to certain FOI requests to which Section 35, 36, or 37 applies (s.38).
- Research and natural resources (s.39).
- Financial and economic interests of the state (s.40).
- Enactments relating to non-disclosure of records (s.41).

Further reading:

The full 2014 Act can be found at: www.oireachtas.ie/documents/bills28/acts/2014/a3014.pdf

Office of the Information Commissioner: www.oic.gov.ie

Exemptions (Part 4 of the Act): www.irishstatutebook.ie/2014/en/act/pub/0030/sec0028.html#part4

Chapter 11 top tips

- There are at least 100 Freedom of Information Acts (or similar access schemes) around the world and the number is rising.
- Most countries allow requests from non-residents.
- Although two exceptions to this are Canada and New Zealand.
- However, the majority require the requests to be in the country's native language.
- Many countries have national and local/state/county FOI laws, which will allow differing levels of access.
- When making requests abroad, even through a familiar contact, beware that other regimes may impose fees upon requests.
- Broadly the exemptions for Acts around the world have many of the same classes of exemptions. These often relate to economic, political and national security issues.
- Although, in the USA the FBI, CIA and NSA are all covered by the Freedom of Information Act.

References

Agnew, R., 2014. *Interview.* Interviewed by Matt Burgess *[Telephone]* 20 June 2014.

Brooke, H., 2006. *Your Right to Know: A Citizen's Guide to the Freedom of Information Act.* London: Pluto Press.

Citizen's Information, 2014. *Freedom of Information.* Available at: www.citizensinformation.ie/en/government_in_ireland/national_government/standards_and_accountability/freedom_of_information.html [Accessed 16 November 2014].

Craver, K., 2014. *Interview*. Interviewed by Matt Burgess *[Email]* 4 November 2014.

Dedman, B., 2014. *Interview*. Interviewed by Matt Burgess *[Email]* 10 November 2014.

Dunion, K., 2014. *Interview*. Interviewed by Matt Burgess *[Telephone]* 23 May 2014.

Freedom of Information Act 1997, Number 13.

Freedom of Information Act 2000 (c.36). London: HMSO.

Freedom of Information (Fees for Required Disclosure) (Scotland) Regulations 2004 (SI 2004/0467).

Freedom of Information (Scotland) Act 2002 (asp 13). London: HMSO.

Gillum, J., 2014. *Interview*. Interviewed by Matt Burgess *[Email]* 9 November 2014.

Guardian, 2014a. Paraguay is 100th nation to pass FOI law, but struggle for openness goes on, 19 September. Available at: www.theguardian.com/public-leaders-network/2014/sep/19/paraguay-freedom-information-law-transparency [Accessed 27 October 2014].

Guardian, 2014b. Freedom of information may cost $800 as Coalition seeks to abolish regulator, 2 October. Available at: www.theguardian.com/australia-news/2014/oct/02/freedom-of-information-may-cost-800-as-coalition-seeks-to-abolish-regulator [Accessed 11 November 2014].

Hill, 2014. Homeland Security buried in FOIA requests, 21 October. Available at: http://thehill.com/policy/technology/221390-dhs-buried-in-foia-requests [Accessed 10 November 2014].

House of Commons Justice Select Committee, 2012. *Post-legislative Scrutiny of the Freedom of Information Act 2000: Three Costs and Fees*. Available at: www.publications.parliament.uk/pa/cm201213/cmselect/cmjust/96/9606.htm#n191 [Accessed 15 November 2014].

Irving, K., 2014. *Interview*. Interviewed by Matt Burgess *[Email]* 18 June 2014.

Johnson, S., 2014. *Interview*. Interviewed by Matt Burgess *[Email]* 10 November 2014.

Legal Leaks, 2014. *Legal Leaks Toolkit*. Available at: www.legalleaks.info/images/stories/legal%20leaks%20nov%202011_impresion.pdf [Accessed 17 November 2014].

Liddle, C., 2014. *Interview*. Interviewed by Matt Burgess *[Telephone]* 22 May 2014.

MacFarlane, S., 2014. *Interview*. Interviewed by Matt Burgess *[Email]* 3 November 2014.

Mandarin, 2014. Information Commissioner: Almost gone, but not forgotten, 13 October. Available at: www.themandarin.com.au/6651-australian-information-commissioner-almost-gone-but-not-forgotten [Accessed 11 November 2014].

McDonagh, M., 2003. *Freedom of Information in Ireland: Five Years On*. Available at: www.freedominfo.org/documents/ireland.pdf [Accessed 16 November 2014].

Mckinnnon, M., 2014. *Interview*. Interviewed by Matt Burgess *[Email]* 11 November 2014.

Office of Government Information Services, 2012. *Five Things Journalists Should Know About FOIA*. Available at: https://ogis.archives.gov/Assets/Requester+Best+Practices-+Five+Things+Journalists+Ought+to+Know+about+FOIA.pdf?method=1 [Accessed 11 November 2014].

Office of Government Information Services, 2014. *FOIA Exemptions* Available at: https://ogis.archives.gov/about-foia/foia/FOIA-Exemptions.htm [Accessed 11 November 2014].

Office of the Australian Information Commissioner, 2010a. *FOI Fact Sheet 7: Freedom of Information – Extensions of time.* Available at: www.oaic.gov. au/images/documents/freedom-of-information/foi-factsheets/FOI_fact_sheet7_ charges.pdf [Accessed 12 November 2014].

Office of the Australian Information Commissioner, 2010b. *FOI Fact Sheet 8: Freedom of Information – Exemptions.* Available at: www.oaic.gov.au/images/ documents/freedom-of-information/foi-factsheets/FOI_fact_sheet8_exemptions. pdf [Accessed 12 November 2014].

Office of the Australian Information Commissioner, 2014a. *FOI Fact Sheet 6: Freedom of Information – How to Apply.* Available at: www.oaic.gov.au/images/ documents/freedom-of-information/foi-resources/foi-fact-sheets/foi-fact-sheet-6. pdf [Accessed 12 November 2014].

Office of the Australian Information Commissioner, 2014b. *FOI Fact Sheet 16: Freedom of Information – Extensions of Time.* Available at: www.oaic.gov. au/images/documents/freedom-of-information/foi-factsheets/FOI-fact-sheet16_ extension_time.pdf [Accessed 12 November 2014].

Office of the Information Commissioner, 2004. *The Year in Review.* Available at: www. oic.gov.ie/en/Publications/Annual-Reports/Previous-Annual-Reports/2004- Annual-Report/The-Year-in-Review.html [Accessed 15 November 2014].

Office of the Information Commissioner, 2014a. *Information Commissioner Welcomes Proposal to Remove FOI Fee*, 1 July. Available at: www.oic.gov.ie/ en/News/Media-Releases/2014/removal-of-FOI-fee.html [Accessed 15 November 2014].

Office of the Information Commissioner, 2014b. *Information Commissioner Welcomes New Freedom of Information Law*, 3 October. Available at: www. oic.gov.ie/en/News/Media-Releases/2014/Information-Commissioner-welcomes- new-Freedom-of-Information-law.html [Accessed 15 November 2014].

RTE, 2014. President signs new FOI Act into law, 14 October. Available at: www. rte.ie/news/2014/1014/652358-foi [Accessed 9 March 2015].

Scottish Information Commissioner's Office, 2005. *Comparative Table: Freedom of Information Act 2000 and Freedom of Information (Scotland) Act 2002.* Available at: www.itspublicknowledge.info/Law/FOISA-EIRsLinks/FOISA_ FOIAComparative.aspx [Accessed 9 March 2015].

Sheridan, G., 2014. *Interview.* Interviewed by Matt Burgess *[Telephone]* 23 May 2014.

Timmins, P., 2014. *Interview.* Interviewed by Matt Burgess *[Telephone]* 30 May 2014.

United States Department of Justice, 2010. *How do I Make a FOIA Request?* Available at: www.foia.gov/how-to.html [Accessed 10 November 2014].

United States Department of Justice, 2011a. *What is FOIA?* Available at: www.foia. gov/about.html [Accessed 10 November 2014].

United States Department of Justice, 2011b. *Frequently Asked Questions* Available at: www.foia.gov/faq.html#exemptions [Accessed 10 November 2014].

The rise of open data

What can open data do?

The growth of open data has been one of the UK government's biggest drives – officials have pushed for proactive publishing of information since 2010 in a bid to increase the transparency and economy of the country. Open data schemes have been overseen and promoted from the highest ranks of British politics. UK Prime Minister David Cameron says that he wanted to make people 'armchair auditors', which marked the beginning of the UK's transparency agenda. In a podcast, Cameron also says that the information that would be revealed would not be perfect or necessarily in the most convenient format (Prime Minister's Office, 2010a). Despite everything not being perfect, the government went ahead with its plan to open up spending data. It announced, in some of the biggest changes to public sector openness, that the information in the following box has to be published by public authorities.

Central government

- New central government ICT contracts.
- Tender documents for contracts over £10,000.
- Spending over £25,000.
- All new central government contracts.
- Historic COINS spending data.

Local government

- Spending over £500 on a council-by-council basis.
- Contracts and tender documents for expenditure over £500.

Other data

- Crime data to show what is happening at street level.
- Names, grades, job titles and pay rates for most senior civil servants with salaries of more than £150,000.
- Organograms for central government departments and agencies that include all staff positions.

Cameron, when stating what authorities would have to publish, reiterated the government's thinking behind the publishing of more data. Since then there have been further requirements for authorities to publish information. Overall, the decisions behind making more data public come down to officials wanting it to be utilised by members of the public and developers. Cameron says the reasons were to

> enable the public to hold politicians and public bodies to account; to reduce the deficit and deliver better value for money in public spending; and to realise significant economic benefits by enabling businesses and non-profit organisations to build innovative applications and websites using public data.
>
> (Prime Minister's Office, 2010b)

At the time of writing, the UK government's data portal (data.gov.uk) hosts more than 15,000 datasets. These include everything from road safety data, which looks at personal injury road accidents from 1979 to the present day (Department for Transport, 2011), to codes that are needed to classify goods for import or export (BusinessLink, 2010). It is the hub of the UK's open data publications and allows for organisations to be able to upload their own data as well as acting as a repository for central government datasets (data.gov.uk, nd). The portal is overseen by the Public Sector Transparency Board, which was created to promote transparency and the publishing of data in a way that 'made sure that citizens have greater access to data from major public services' (Cabinet Office, 2013).

The Transparency board has also been responsible for promoting such schemes as the National Information Infrastructure, which lists datasets that would be important and benefit people if they were made freely available. Additionally, it has publicised the Release of Data Fund, and the Open Data Breakthrough Fund, created by government departments to encourage organisations to publish more data (Cabinet Office, 2013).

This type of information, if used in a 'more intensive and creative' way, can be used to add public value to the information that is created (Dawes, 2012, p.1). The use of open data can be focused on areas such as, but not limited to, 'education, public health, transportation, environmental stewardship, economic development' (Dawes, 2012, p.1).

This is backed up by the data.gov.uk website, which says people can use the data for applications and visualisations.

> This may be simply to analyse trends over time from one policy area, or to compare how different parts of government go about their work. Technical users will be able to create useful applications out of the raw data files, which can then be used by everyone.
>
> (data.gov.uk, nd)

Open data example

Walkonomics

The app combines data from the the data.gov.uk website along with crowdsourced information to rate how pedestrian-friendly the streets are for walking. It has ratings for every street in the UK and well as those in New York, San Francisco and Toronto. It combines open data on road safety, pavement quality, hilliness, fear of crime and more, into categories to produce a rating for the streets, which can then be refined by human users.

(Davies, 2011)

Dawes (2012, p.1) says that 'census, economic, and other formal statistical series are well understood and readily useable' as they apply to the standards of social research that are used in data collection and management. For the media, the challenge is to obtain datasets that are as trustworthy and accessible as those that are already established and published on a regular basis.

Chris Frost, head of the journalism department at Liverpool John Moore's University, says that the information that is published should matter. 'Whilst there are sort of some moves, the right to open data it's very easy to put data out there which actually doesn't mean very much and it doesn't matter if people see it or not' (Frost, 2014).

The BBC's FOI expert Martin Rosenbaum (2014) says that he believes open data is a 'very good thing' and that it has 'put a lot of information out into the open which otherwise wouldn't always be there'. However, he did qualify this:

It is not always done in the best way, it is not always done in the most accessible way, the most easy to use way, there are lots of ways you can complain about it but I think we are definitely heading in the right direction.

(Rosenbaum, 2014)

The idea of publishing as much data as possible has very noble roots and allows the data to be manipulated and combined into new services and information tools for members of the public, in addition to being used by journalists to back-up stories and provide context. However, it also poses challenges to FOI legislation, access to the data and cost issues that are associated with publishing.

Finding the benefits

As outlined above, the use cases for open data are almost unlimited. Information on all different sectors of public, and in some cases private, life (from businesses) can be used to enhance lives. The potential for open data and its publication was outlined in a *Guardian* article that stated that there are many possible gains from the initiative.

> Open data enables accountability: it is difficult to conceal something if the facts are there for all to see. Open data empowers communities: the truth about crime rates, educational achievement, social services and so on is laid bare. Open data even drives economic growth.
>
> (*Guardian*, 2012)

The Guardian (2012) article concluded that open data may be able to lead to better decisions being made, based upon accurate conclusions, while also allowing a wider variety of interested parties to examine all the facts.

Australian lawyer Peter Timmins (2014) says that open data and pro-active publishing is being increased significantly by advancing technology and there is 'an enormous opportunity to take big steps in that direction'. It is possible to combine regular publications of spending data to compare how an authority's spending changes over time, and if there are any major changes to the services that individual contractors are providing.

The sheer amount of data that has been published is a vast increase on what was previously published. Local authorities' and central government bodies' commitment to publishing regular spending data allows for an increased level of scrutiny by both journalists and members of the public.

A report by Deloitte (2012, p.1) says that at first the government's open data initiative gave the ability to 'uncover poor performance or behavior', but has now has shifted to hold different benefits. These include an 'important role to play in the economy', which can also be aided by some private companies' publishing data. The Deloitte report says the UK's scheme is more popular than larger schemes in different countries.

> Although the UK does not have the same quantity of data as open data sites in the US or France, in the period studied, data.gov.uk received more daily visits than either of these, and also benefits from a similar number of external links pointing to the site.
>
> (Deloitte, 2012, p.9)

It has also created a new type of licence, which allows for information to be reused by people without the fear of breaching copyright.

Open government licence

The reuse of public information has often been a thorny issue, with advocates of openness arguing that public data should be free to reuse. The Open Government Licence was created to help with the reuse rights of information it is applied to. The licence states: 'You are encouraged to use and reuse the information that is available under this licence freely and flexibly, with only a few conditions' (National Archives, nd).

Specifically, it gives the right to people to copy, publish, distribute, transmit, adapt and use the information either commercially or non-commercially by combining it with other information (National Archives, nd). The only direct requirement the licence provides is that when reusing the information you acknowledge the source by including or linking to a statement by its providers and, where possible, provide a link back to the licence (National Archives, nd). The full licence can be found at: www.nationalarchives.gov.uk/doc/open-government-licence/version/3.

Problems with open data

Tony Roberts (2012) says, in *Computer Weekly*, that releasing data alone does not mean that it is open, or has any value to the wider public. 'It is only open to a small elite of technical specialists who know how to interpret and use it, as well as to those that can afford to employ them.' To put the data to its best use, there needs to training available for those that want it, Roberts (2012) says.

This view was echoed by the government, which says, in response to a House of Commons Public Administration Select Committee, that the ability to access data being published is crucial. These accessibility issues are important ones in the larger picture of open data. What is being published needs to be able to be used by those accessing it.

This has since been recognised by the government, which says 'there is more work to be done to increase engagement and participation' (House of Commons, 2014, p.5). However, the Commons (2014, p.5) argued that the level of engagement does not 'fall solely on the shoulders of the Government. We are keen to use our networks and mobilise existing communities to bring the power of open data to a wider audience.'

During the early years of the open data scheme being pushed by the government, it appeared that those in charge had not fully comprehended many of the challenging issues. The Public Accounts Committee (2012) produced a critical report of the open data scheme, which touched upon deep issues and raised questions about the strategy behind publishing a large amount of data in a short time. Its conclusions say:

- The data that is being released in some cases is not comprehensive enough to allow accountability, service improvements and economic growth.
- The presentation of the government's data is poor.
- Different types of providers are releasing different information that cannot be compared.
- The government does not know the costs and benefits of its transparency agenda.
- There is not a clear, evidence-based policy on whether or not to charge for data.
- There are concerns that 'commercial confidentiality' may be used inappropriately to not disclose information.
- Departments do not make it easy for users to understand the range of information that is available to them.
- There is a risk that those without internet access will not be able to benefit from public data.

The statistics published by the government cannot always be trusted, as demonstrated by *The Guardian*'s reporting of inaccurate hospital statistics and the way they are collected. The story showed that operations were recorded inaccurately. This led to one leading expert calling for the way data is collected to be changed. He went on to say that this has been a problem since 1982 (*Guardian*, 2010).

Although there has been criticism, and the admission from Cameron, of the data occasionally being inaccurate or published in an inaccessible manner, there is still work to be done to fix these issues. Deloitte (2012, p.1) says that 'like any other raw material, it needs investment to locate, extract and refine it before it yields true value'.

Relationship with FOI

Open data can also be a threat to the Freedom of Information Act and the right to ask for specific information. Cabinet Minister Francis Maude has said that he wants the government to publish so much data that people do not need to request it. In a speech, reported by Information Age (2012), Maude says: 'I'd like to make Freedom of Information redundant, by pushing out so much [open] data that people won't have to ask for it.'

The problem with this attitude is that it only gives people the information that the government wants to publish. It is unlikely that the government would be willing to automatically publish information that has been uncovered by FOI and could be embarrassing out of its own free will. The Information Commissioner Christopher Graham (2014) agrees with the view that open data should not be a way for the government to weaken, or diminish, the scope of Freedom of Information. Although, he says that open data is not just for journalists and they should not consider it to be so, as it can have a multitude of other uses by those with different skills.

> We must make sure that open data isn't seen as a substitute for Freedom of Information. Open data mustn't just be what the public authorities would like us to see and not the bits that are sometimes less convenient but I have no patience with journalists that say all this stuff which is being served up to us raw we can't possibly analyse it.
>
> (Graham, 2014)

Former Scottish Information Commissioner Kevin Dunion (2014) says that the attitude expressed by politicians is 'highly suspect':

> Things like policy-making decisions and the political procedure, these are not open data, these are the kind of things that will be requested and will be requested in the way which sometimes is uncomfortable for governments. Certainly governments are not going to put some of these documents out in real time whilst it is deliberating options that it may discard as being politically unattractive, which is exactly what journalists will be asking for.

If it was not possible to ask for information, it is highly unlikely that details of the 3,000 lost and stolen guns in the UK (*BBC News*, 2012) or that border agency staff were protecting illegal immigrants (*Daily Mail*, 2012) would be revealed by the government willingly. However, this is not to say that FOI and open data cannot exist side by side – it is not the case that without one the other cannot exist.

Jon Stone (2014) says it is in the authorities' interests to publish more information.

> They should probably want to get stuff online without requests because it is less of a story if it is not a scoop. So I think maybe it is sort of a

presumption of putting stuff online would be a good way of adapting to a newer media landscape where everything tends to be more online based.

Heather Brooke (2014) says that senior managers have to take transparency seriously as it can benefit their organizations.

> I always think that transparency is very much an early warning system, it is across everything. It flags up things when they are really tiny or small and then you can deal with them when they are very small. If you have a culture of secrecy all it means is, if you've got a bad surgeon for example, in a more transparent system his practices would be flagged up early on and he could be dealt with.

Academic Ben Worthy (2014) says that the two regimes can work together to complement each other.

> I think the first thing to say is that open data and Freedom of Information can work together very well. Francis Maude probably put it too highly when he said that open data will make Freedom of Information redundant and I think there is also a danger that there is some political angle to this – the publication of spending data at local government level is probably in part designed to make local authorities look frivolous and wasters.

Reliability

A government Select Committee also found, in 2014, that police-recorded crime statistics could not be trusted, after a police whistleblower PC James Patrick approached the Committee about the validity of crime statistics. The damning report entitled 'Caught red-handed: Why we can't count on Police Recorded Crime statistics' says that misreporting of crime figures had become 'ingrained' in England and Wales (Public Administration Select Committee, 2014, p.3).

Incidents of this nature highlight the importance of data and how its accuracy can influence the lives of members of the public. *Trinity Mirror* data journalist Claire Miller (2014) says that she believes that in some cases requesting specific information from the public authorities via FOI will appear to be less accurate than what is published proactively.

> But, I think that is the thing with FOI, is that you feel like they are more incomplete than the data that is published or to do with specifics or open data, even though in some cases they probably aren't.

As previously stated by Deloitte (2012), work needs to be done by the government to improve the accuracy and reliability of open data that is published by the government.

Cost of transparency

The Brookings Institute (2014) warned that, when it comes to open data, 'transparency can be costly'. This is something that the UK government has been wary of with the implementation of open data schemes, and the cost of publishing data is one of the potential limiting factors to increasing the amount that is published.

As demonstrated in Chapter 2, councils regularly complain about the amount that it costs them to answer FOI requests, but they do not appear to put this argument forward against the information that they are required to publish under the government's transparency programme.

The Brookings Institute (2014) went on to say that there has been little research into whether proactive publishing has actually increased 'transparency, collaboration, or participation'. In fact, councils can actually be paid to publish certain types of open data. The Local Government Association (LGA) runs an open data incentive scheme, which tries to get more authorities to publish datasets and provides them with money for doing so.

The LGA (2014) pays authorities up to £7,000 if they publish three extra datasets, which are not required by central government. Between June 2014 and March 2015, authorities are being encouraged to publish planning applications, premises licences and public toilet data, and are paid £2,000 for doing each, with an extra £1,000 if they do all three. The LGA says the documents must be provided in Comma Separated Value (CSV) format and provide a schema, with a list of the fields of the data provided. However, this data can be put to good use by those with the skills to transform it into an application that the public can use.

Case study: the Great British Public Toilet Map

'What frustrates me is that public toilets are a public service for a public need', yet finding information out about them, and their location, was not the easiest thing to do, says Gail Ramster (2014) who helped create the Great British Public Toilet Map.

The map was created using open data and FOI requests to collect locations of public toilets which were then combined and put onto OpenStreetMap for anyone to access. At present, there are more than 8,000 toilets mapped that are run by public authorities and even some private businesses. The straightforward idea, which in reality is harder to execute, shows how useful publishing open data can be.

Ramster (2014) says that making a case for more open data to be published was aided as there was a need for this information to be made public.

> I think it helps to have a use for the data, so in our case it was problem led and then open data happened to be part of the solution. So then it is easier to make the case for why you need, but even then it can still be a lot of work because this one person wants this dataset.
>
> (The toilet map: http://greatbritishpublictoiletmap.rca.ac.uk)

Who's looking after the future of open data?

Since the government's push on open data began in 2010, the schemes have come a long way. To reinfroce the commitment to open data, and partly down to the passion of the individuals involved, a number of groups have been set up to promote open data's use and its benefits. These groups are at the forefront of shaping how open data is perceived and how it can be accessed by a wider group of people.

Further reading

Open Data User Group: www.gov.uk/government/groups/open-data-user-group
Open Government Partnership: http://opengovpartnership.org
Open Data Institute: http://theodi.org
G8 Open Data Charter: www.gov.uk/government/publications/open-data-charter

Chapter 12 top tips

- The government's open data website data.gov.uk has more than 15,000 datasets online.
- On data.gov.uk it is possible to make recommendations for datasets that you would like to see published.
- The Open Government Licence allows information covered by it to be reused without any copyright issues.

References

BBC News, 2012. Almost 3,000 guns lost or stolen in UK, figures reveal, 29 August. Available at: www.bbc.co.uk/news/uk-19416579 [Accessed 13 September 2014].

Brooke, H., 2014. *Interview*. Interviewed by Matt Burgess *[In person]* London: 23 May 2014.

Brookings Institute, 2014. Measuring the value of open data. Available at: www.brookings.edu/blogs/techtank/posts/2014/10/29-value-open-data [Accessed 27 October 2014].

BusinessLink, 2010. UK tariff codes. Available at: http://data.gov.uk/dataset/uk-tariff-codes-2009-2010 [Accessed 27 October 2014].

Cabinet Office, 2013. Improving the transparency and accountability of government and its services. Available at: www.gov.uk/government/policies/improving-the-transparency-and-accountability-of-government-and-its-services [Accessed 27 October 2014].

Daily Mail, 2012. Ten Border Agency staff caught harbouring illegal immigrants, shocking Home Office figures reveal, 1 February. Available at: www.dailymail.co.uk/news/article-2094846/Ten-Border-Agency-staff-caught-harbouring-illegal-immigrants-shocking-Home-Office-figures-reveal.html [Accessed 4 October 2014].

data.gov.uk, nd. About. Available at: http://data.gov.uk/about [Accessed 27 October 2014].

Davies, A., 2011. Walkonomics: How walkable is your street? Available at: http://data.gov.uk/apps/walkonomics-how-walkable-your-street [Accessed 25 October 2014].

Dawes, S., 2012. A realistic look at open data. Center for Technology in Government at University at Albany. Available at: www.w3.org/2012/06/pmod/pmod2012_submission_38.pdf [Accessed 26 October 2014].

Deloitte, 2012. Open growth: Stimulating demand for open data in the UK. Available at: www2.deloitte.com/content/dam/Deloitte/uk/Documents/deloitte-analytics/open-growth.pdf [Accessed 9 March 2015].

Department for Transport, 2011. Road safety data. Available at: http://data.gov.uk/dataset/road-accidents-safety-data [Accessed 27 October 2014].

Dunion, K., 2014. *Interview*. Interviewed by Matt Burgess *[Telephone]* 23 May 2014.

Frost, C., 2014. *Interview*. Interviewed by Matt Burgess *[Telephone]* 21 May 2014.

Graham, C., 2014. *Interview*. Interviewed by Matt Burgess *[In person]* Wilmslow: 20 May 2014.

Guardian, 2010. Flaws in hospital episode statistics revealed by FoI requests, 13 June. Available at: www.theguardian.com/society/2010/jun/13/nhs-statistics-flawed [Accessed 15 September 2014].

Guardian, 2012. Open data is a force for good, but not without risks, 10 July. Available at: www.theguardian.com/society/2012/jul/10/open-data-force-for-good-risks [Accessed 20 October 2014].

House of Commons, 2014. Statistics and open data: Government response to the Committee's tenth report of session 2013–14. London: HMSO. Available at: www.publications.parliament.uk/pa/cm201415/cmselect/cmpubadm/620/620.pdf [Accessed 27 October 2014].

Information Age, 2012. Flaws in hospital episode statistics revealed by FoI requests, 4 July. Available at: www.information-age.com/technology/information-management/2111138/francis-maude%3A-%22id-like-to-make-foi-redundant%22 [Accessed 13 September 2014].

Local Government Association, 2014. Local government open data incentive scheme. Available at: http://incentive.opendata.esd.org.uk/documents/LocalOpenDataIncentiveSchemeOverview.pdf [Accessed 27 October 2014].

Miller, C., 2014. *Interview*. Interviewed by Matt Burgess *[Telephone]* 22 May 2014.

National Archives, nd. Open government licence for public sector information. Available at: www.nationalarchives.gov.uk/doc/open-government-licence/version/3 [Accessed 27 October 2014].

Prime Minister's Office, 2010a. PM's podcast on transparency. Available at: www.gov.uk/government/news/pms-podcast-on-transparency [Accessed 8 August 2014].

Prime Minister's Office, 2010b. Letter to government departments on opening up data. Available at: www.gov.uk/government/news/letter-to-government-departments-on-opening-up-data [Accessed 10 August 2014].

Public Accounts Committee, 2012. PM's podcast on transparency. Available at: www.publications.parliament.uk/pa/cm201213/cmselect/cmpubacc/102/10204.htm [Accessed 13 September 2014].

Public Administration Select Committee, 2014. Caught red-handed: Why we can't count on police recorded crime statistics. London: HMSO. Available at: www.publications.parliament.uk/pa/cm201314/cmselect/cmpubadm/760/760.pdf [Accessed 15 September 2014].

Ramster, G., 2014. *Interview*. Interviewed by Matt Burgess [*Telephone*] 6 November 2014.

Roberts, T., 2012. The problem with open data. ComputerWeekly.com, February. Available at: www.guardian.co.uk/science/blog/2009/jun/18/conservation-extinction-open-ground [Accessed 23 June 2009].

Rosenbaum, M., 2014. *Interview*. Interviewed by Matt Burgess *[In person]* London: 30 May 2014.

Stone, J., 2014. *Interview*. Interviewed by Matt Burgess *[Telephone]* 13 June 2014.

Timmins, P., 2014. *Interview*. Interviewed by Matt Burgess *[Telephone]* 30 May 2014.

Worthy, B., 2014. *Interview*. Interviewed by Matt Burgess *[In person]* London: 21 May 2014.

Appendix
Request templates

Freedom of Information Act request

When authorities reply to requests, they often use a template section in their answers. Requesters, to an extent, can do the same when asking for information. Making it as easy as possible for an authority to identify an FOI request will reduce the potential for initial delays. The following template for a request may be a useful starting point. All requests should be tailored to the authority and the particular information.

Dear [*Authority name*]

I am writing to you under the Freedom of Information Act 2000 to request the following information from [*authority name/department*]:

[*Insert what is being asked for*]

Please provide the information in the form [*insert form to be received in*].

If it is not possible to provide the information requested due to the information exceeding the cost of compliance limits identified in Section 12, please provide advice and assistance, under your Section 16 obligations, as to how I can refine my request to be included in the scope of the Act.

In any case, if you can identify ways that my request could be refined please provide further advice and assistance to indicate this.

I look forward to your response within 20 working days, as stipulated by the Act.

If you have any queries please don't hesitate to contact me via email or phone and I will be happy to clarify what I am asking for. My details are outlined below.

Best wishes,

[*Name*]

Environmental Information Regulations (EIR) request

If you ask for environmental information it should be treated it as an EIR request, not FOI. It does not have to be specifically outlined as an EIR request.

Dear [*Authority name*]

I am writing to you under the Environmental Information Regulations 2004 to request the following from [*authority name/department*]:

[*Insert what is being asked for*]

Please provide the information in the form [*insert form to be received in*].

In accordance with Regulation 9 please can you provide any advice and assistance that may help my request to be more effective? In any case if my request is too general please provide advice and assistance as to how it can be refined.

I look forward to receiving your response within 20 working days, as stipulated by Regulation 5.

If you have any queries please don't hesitate to contact me via email or phone and I will be happy to clarify what I am asking for. My details are outlined below.

Best wishes,

[*Name*]

Internal review

Almost all public authorities allow for an internal review to be completed before a complaint with the Information Commissioner's Office and the Commissioner, in almost all circumstances, requires one to be completed before he will review a complaint, which has been made to the office. The following template can be used to make a request for an Internal Review.

Dear [*Authority name*]

I write in reference to my previous FOI request [*insert reference number given by the authority here*].

Please may you conduct an internal review of the decision to withhold information in the request referenced above.

I am asking for an internal review because of the following reasons:

[*Insert reasons why you are complaining, relating to misuse of the exemptions, etc.*]

I am aware that guidance from the Information Commissioner, in 'The Guide to Freedom of Information', says that internal reviews should (in most cases) be completed within 20 working days.

I look forward to receiving your response in line with the Commissioner's guidance.

Best regards,

[*Name*]

Index

emissions, and EIR exceptions 34
enforcement notices 169; ICO's
    responsibilities 5
environmental information, European
    Council's Directive on access to 31
Environmental Information Regulations
    (EIR): challenging non-disclosure
    under 32; classes of exception
    33; confidentiality of proceedings
    exemptions 34; differences from
    FOI 32–5; environmental protection
    exemptions 34; incomplete data
    exemptions 33; intellectual property
    rights exemptions 34; justice and
    inquiries exemption 34; justifying
    non-disclosure under 32; manifestly
    unreasonable requests exemptions
    33; the nature of environmental
    information 31; overview 30;
    permissible response time 30;
    personal interest exemptions 34;
    Public Interest Test 32; public safety
    exemptions 34; scope of request
    formulation exemptions 33
European Convention of Human Rights
    (ECHR) 43
Evans, R. 3, 15, 114, 141
Evans v Information Commissioner 81,
    84
exemptions 50–88; absolute
    exemptions, listed 50; audit
    functions 72; Australian perspective
    200; case law 53 (see also case
    law on exemptions); commercial
    interests 87; confidential
    information 34, 83–4, 130; cost
    compliance exceeds appropriate
    limit 54–6; court records 71–2; Data
    Protection Act 36; defence of the
    nation 63–4; the economy 67–8;
    environmental information 30, 80
    (see also Environmental Information
    Regulations (EIR)); future
    publication 59–60; government
    policy formulation 74–6; health
    and safety 79–80; information
    accessible by other means 57–9
    (see also access regimes other
    than FOI); INSPIRE directive 39;
    internal relations 66–7; international
    relations 64–5; investigations and
    proceedings 68–9; Irish perspective

204; law enforcement 70–1; legal
    privilege 84; national security
    61–3; neither confirm nor deny
    responses 54; obligations on refusal
    53; parliamentary privilege 73;
    personal information 83; prejudice-
    and class-based exemptions 52–3;
    prejudicial to conduct of public
    affairs 76–8; private providers 161;
    prohibitions on disclosure 87; public
    authority's duties 58; qualified and
    absolute exemptions 51, 53 (see
    also qualified exemptions); Royal
    7, 22, 79; security matters 60–1;
    Subject Access Requests 38; under
    EIR 33–5; US perspective 196–7;
    vexatious request exemptions 56–7
expense claims by MPs, FOI request 8
    (see also MPs' expenses scandal)
Express and Star 20

fair dealing 183
Falconer, Lord 21
fees 161; Australian perspective 200;
    Irish perspective 203
Fees Regulations 33, 54–5, 156
financial information, environmental
    classifiability 31
Financial Times 14–15, 101, 103, 142,
    150, 159–60
FOI officers: attitudes of 103; attitudes
    towards 102; contacting 98, 102,
    104; pay and responsibility levels
    102
FOI requests: 'business as usual'
    handling 10; estimating and
    calculating costs 54–6; financial
    burden for local authorities 20;
    making 9–10 (see also writing
    a request); by social media 10;
    stipulations 9
France, Elizabeth 4
Frankel, Maurice 115
Freedom of Information Act Scotland 3
frequently asked for requests 118
Fukushima Daiichi nuclear plant 126
future publication exemptions 59–60

Galloway, George 43
Ganesh Sittampalam v Information
    Commissioner and Crown
    Prosecution Service 72